Accounting for Ministers

Accounting for Ministers uses the tools of modern political science to analyse the factors which determine the fortunes of cabinet ministers. Utilizing agency theory, it describes cabinet government as a system of incentives for prime ministerial and parliamentary rule. The authors use a unique dataset of ministers from 1945 to 2007 to examine the structural and individual characteristics that lead to the selection and durability of ministers. Sensitive to historical context, the book describes the unique features of different prime ministers and the sorts of issues and scandals that lead to the forced exit of ministers. The authors identify the structural factors that determine ministerial performance and tenure, seeing resignation calls as performance indicators. Probing the nature of individual and collective responsibility within Westminster forms of government, their rigorous analysis provides powerful new insights into the nature of cabinet government.

SAMUEL BERLINSKI is Lead Research Economist in the Research Department of the Inter-American Development Bank.

TORUN DEWAN is Professor of Political Science in the Department of Government at the London School of Economics and Political Science.

KEITH DOWDING is Professor of Political Science in the School of Politics and International Relations, Research School of Social Sciences, and Director of Research at the College of Arts and Social Sciences at the Australian National University.

Accounting for Ministers

Scandal and Survival in
British Government 1945–2007

SAMUEL BERLINSKI
TORUN DEWAN
KEITH DOWDING

CAMBRIDGE
UNIVERSITY PRESS

CAMBRIDGE UNIVERSITY PRESS
Cambridge, New York, Melbourne, Madrid, Cape Town,
Singapore, São Paulo, Delhi, Mexico City

Cambridge University Press
The Edinburgh Building, Cambridge CB2 8RU, UK

Published in the United States of America by Cambridge University Press, New York

www.cambridge.org
Information on this title: www.cambridge.org/9780521519724

First published 2012

Printed in the United Kingdom at the University Press, Cambridge

A catalogue record for this publication is available from the British Library

Library of Congress Cataloguing in Publication data
Berlinski, Samuel, 1970–
Accounting for ministers : scandal and survival in British government, 1945–2007 /
Samuel Berlinski, Torun Dewan, Keith Dowding.
    p.   cm.
Includes bibliographical references and index.
ISBN 978-0-521-51972-4
1. Cabinet officers – Great Britain.   2. Cabinet system – Great Britain.   I. Dewan,
Torun A. (Torun Andreas), 1967–   II. Dowding, Keith M.   III. Title.
JN405.B47   2012
352.2'930941 – dc23   2011045292

ISBN 978-0-521-51972-4 Hardback

Contents

List of figures	page	vii
List of tables		viii
Preface and acknowledgements		ix
1	Introduction	1
2	Managing the cabinet: principal–agent relations in government	6
	Principals and their agents	7
	Agency models of elections	8
	Parliamentary democracy	13
	The prime minister and cabinet	14
	Applying the agency model in parliamentary democracies	15
	Our data and questions	19
3	The structure of British government	21
	Constitutional situation	21
	The cabinet	26
	Ministers	30
	The jobs of ministers	33
	Choosing ministers	37
	Ministerial responsibility	42
	Government changes	46
4	Who serves in government and how long do they last?	54
	Who serves	55
	How long do ministers last?	65
	Political effects	76
	Separating the effect of individual characteristics	76
	The determinants of ministerial hazard rates	78
	Conclusion	83

5   The prime minister and cabinet   87
    Prime ministerial styles   89
    Survivor functions for different prime ministers   109
    Conclusion   115

6   Performance measures and forced exits   117
    Introduction   117
    Resignations and non-resignations   119
    Differences between prime ministers and parties in power   127
    Proximate causes of forced exits   132
    Conclusions   148

7   Ministerial performance and tenure   150
    Our assumptions   152
    Performance and tenure   154
    Descriptive analysis   157
    Empirical strategy   160
    Hazard rate estimates   165
    Conclusions   170

8   Conclusion   173

References   179

Index   190

Figures

4.1 Ministerial survivor function and education   *page* 73
4.2 Ministerial survivor function and gender   74
4.3 Ministerial survivor function and ministerial experience   75
4.4 Ministerial survivor function and parties   77
5.1 Ministerial survivor function and prime ministerial terms   109
5.2 Ministerial survivor function: Churchill versus Major
    government   110
5.3 Ministerial survivor function: Thatcher's three governments   111
5.4 Ministerial survivor function: Wilson's three governments   112
5.5 Ministerial survivor function: first versus second terms   113
6.1 Forced exits and resignations by year   123
6.2 Forced exits and non-resignations by year   124
6.3 Forced exits smoothed   125
6.4 Forced exits and non-resignations by parliament   128
6.5 Forced exits and non-resignations by prime minister   128
6.6 Forced exits by party   130
6.7 Resignation issues by category   134
7.1 Survivor function for ministerial duration by individual
    resignation calls   158
7.2 Survivor function for ministerial duration by individual
    resignation calls for minister with at least one resignation
    call   158
7.3 Survivor function for ministerial duration by cumulative
    number of government resignation calls below or above
    the median   159

Tables

3.1 Size of government at the start of prime ministerial term:
1945–2007   *page* 28
3.2 Comparing cabinet posts   48
3.3 Categories of departments   51
4.1 Definition of variable and descriptive statistics   60
4.2 Average characteristics of ministers by government   62
4.3 Average tenure and characteristics of ministers by
ministerial rank   66
4.4 The determinants of ministerial durations   80
4.5 The determinants of ministerial durations for selected
sub-samples   84
6.1 Forced exits and non-resignations by prime minister   126
6.2 Annual resignation issues by prime minister   126
6.3 Honour ratio   129
6.4 Proximate reasons for resignation issue by party   134
7.1 The impact of individual and government calls for
resignation on ministerial tenure   165
7.2 The impact of individual and government calls for
resignation on ministerial tenure   168
7.3 The total impact of an individual call for resignation on
ministerial tenure at different levels of cumulative
government resignation calls   170
7.4 The impact of individual and government calls for
resignation, and their interaction, on ministerial tenure
by number of months in office and two eras (1945–1970,
1970–1997)   171

Preface and acknowledgements

This book is the culmination of a research project that was initiated a long time ago. Keith Dowding started collecting data on ministers in the British cabinet as far back as the early 1990s. The collaboration of the three authors began in the early 2000s and has been enabled through funding by the Leverhulme Trust in 1991, a small Nuffield Foundation grant (SOC 100/302) in 1992, and the LSE STICERD in 1996–7. Collecting the data was extremely time-consuming, though it became considerably easier when newspapers and other sources of information went online. We should begin by thanking our coders over the years including Helen Cannon, Norman Cooke, Won-Taek Kang and Gita Subrahmanyam.

Our collaboration has resulted in earlier publications from which we have drawn for this book, though in all cases the chapters are original, not least in that our data in this book reach the end of the Blair government; previously we had not gone beyond Major. Those articles include:

Keith Dowding and Won-Taek Kang, 'Ministerial Resignations 1945–97', *Public Administration*, 76(3), 1998, pp. 411–29;

Torun Dewan and Keith Dowding, 'The Corrective Effect of Ministerial Resignations on Government Popularity', *American Journal of Political Science*, 49(1), 2005, pp. 46–56;

Samuel Berlinski, Torun Dewan and Keith Dowding, 'The Length of Ministerial Tenure in the UK, 1945–1997', *British Journal of Political Science*, 37(2), 2007, pp. 245–62;

Samuel Berlinski, Torun Dewan and Keith Dowding, 'The Impact of Individual and Collective Performance on Ministerial Tenure', *Journal of Politics* 72(1), 2010, pp. 1–13.

We have accumulated many debts over the years and would like to thank the following people for comments on earlier versions of the ideas and for commenting on the manuscript itself: Gian Luigi Albano,

Jim Alt, Tim Besley, Phil Cowley, Patrick Dunleavy, Anne Gelling, Simon Hix, George Jones, André Kaiser, Valentino Larcinese, Mik Laver, Simon 'Sokbae' Lee, David Myatt, Ken Shepsle and Jim Snyder. Samuel Berlinski's contribution to the book occurred while he was working as a lecturer in economics at the Department of Economics of University College London. He gratefully acknowledges the support from the European Research Council research grant (ERC-2009-St G-240910-ROMETA).

We thank John Haslam for commissioning the book and being an understanding publisher, as well as Josephine Lane and Gillian Dadd at Cambridge University Press for their help in production. Pat Harper was a skilful copy-editor who pointed out several errors as well as cleaning up some of the prose. We also thank Mark Nesbitt (Luke Warm) for his superb cartoon and his patience as we decided what we wanted him to draw. This book is the culmination of many years of work and could not have been completed without the love and support of our families.

1 | Introduction

Who serves in government and how long they serve for are important determinants of political performance. Whilst this much is understood, at least since Max Weber (1978), there are few data available that allow us to explore in more depth how political careers are formed and what determines the career trajectories of members of the ruling executive. This book looks at the careers of ministers who served in British government between 1945 and 2007. Using a unique dataset on the personal characteristics of ministers it analyses when they entered government, what happened to them during their spell in government, and the timing of their exit from government. One of the key variables of interest in our analysis is how long these ministers serve. We ask: to what extent does the length of their spell depend upon characteristics that are fixed at the time of their entry? What effect do political events, such as calls for a minister to resign perhaps connected to performance-related issues or other scandals, have upon their tenure? And what do the data on ministerial careers tell us about the nature of accountability in British politics?

The book is the first to offer micro-level data on British political careers that allow us to understand the career trajectories of different ministers in British government: some ministers rise whilst others fall, but what determines these patterns? This aspect of our book provides a much-needed addition to the study of parliamentary democracies. Whilst we know a lot about why governments survive – or, in the jargon of the government-termination literature, what makes some governments more *durable* than others – we know much less about the constituent units of these governments. Our unit of analysis is the individual minister; we provide analysis based on the background of these individuals; we ask whether the characteristics of certain ministers make them more durable than others; and we explore how ministers' expected tenure reflects strategic considerations between the prime minister and her government.

Of course there is a large literature on British government that adopts a historical-cum-descriptive style, concerned with the idiosyncratic elements of the relationships between the prime minister and cabinet colleagues, charting the ever-advancing dominance of the prime minister (Hennessy, 1986a; Heffernan, 2003; Blick and Jones, 2010). Useful histories have charted the differing styles of prime ministers (Thomas, 1998; Hennessy, 2001; Leonard, 2005). Studies in constitutional law have examined the changing role of collective and individual ministerial responsibility (Scott, 1996; Woodhouse, 2002).

Much of this literature highlights the strategic tension that lies at the heart of British government. Whilst the prime minister is, in principle, *primus inter pares* with her cabinet colleagues, she is in fact the head of a government that consists of individuals whose policy goals and private ambitions do not always coincide with her own. What is lacking in these analyses is a systematic account of how the prime minister uses the tools that are available to her to align the actions of ministers with those she would like. We provide a coherent framework based on principal–agent analysis for assessing these relations.[1] Our particular focus is on a particular instrument that the prime minister has at her disposal. In the British system of government the prime minister has the power to appoint Members of Parliament to specific government roles but also to take away such responsibilities. In short, the prime minister has the power to hire and fire her ministers. As a consequence, the length of a ministerial spell in office is directly under the control of the prime minister. Few would argue against the view that the prime minister seeks to wield this instrument with strategic effect, but even the British prime minister, who in contrast to prime ministers elsewhere has few constraints upon her hiring and firing power, is not as free in this regard as she might wish. The question we then ask is whether the data we gather on ministerial careers are consistent with basic hypotheses about how the prime minister will wield her power.

We develop our analysis in several chapters. In Chapter 2 we discuss the principal–agent approach for evaluating accountability in liberal democracies and, in particular, for analysing relations in parliamentary democracies. We also develop a framework that will subsequently

---

[1] In this book the prime minister is generally treated as the principal and the ministers as agents; following standard practice in the literature, we refer to the prime minister (principal) as 'she' and the ministers (agents) as 'he'.

prove useful for analysis of our data. Our basic argument is that the prime minister uses her powers of appointment and dismissal to align the incentives of her ministers so they act in accordance with her own wishes. Our main focus is on how the prime minister uses the information that becomes available to her about a minister's skills and performance, unavailable at the time of the appointment, to determine how long ministers serve under her. In Chapter 3 we then set the scene by providing a full account of the details of the core of the British system of government, and how the powers of the prime minister with regard to the hiring and firing of ministers have evolved over time.

The major drawback in studying ministers systematically, certainly in the UK, has been the lack of data. Indeed James Alt begins his essay on continuity and turnover in the British cabinet in the mid 1970s with the words 'It is perhaps more difficult to place this study in the context of the academic literature than to show that it covers a topic of some importance' (Alt, 1975, p. 23). This lacuna is beginning to be addressed and whilst it is no longer true that the 'study of ministers and ministerial careers is in its infancy' (Blondel, 1985, p. 8) it has surely not yet reached maturity. In Chapter 4 we present data that record the employment spells for all ministers in the UK from 1945 to 2007, their rank (full cabinet minister, minister of cabinet rank, junior minister or whip), the government and prime minister under which they served as well as various personal characteristics (education, gender, date of birth, and whether they were an elected MP or an non-elected member of the House of Lords). We use these data to ask some preliminary but pertinent questions about British politics. In particular, we ask whether the characteristics of ministers that are fixed at the time of the minister's appointment to government – such as gender, education, and experience – play a role in determining how long the minister will survive.

Our analysis in Chapter 4 shows, perhaps surprisingly, that knowing the background characteristics of a minister at the time of his appointment provides an indicator of how long that minister will survive in office. This holds true even when we take account of the characteristics of the government in which the minister serves. Our central question is, however, whether we can improve upon such benchmark analysis. Does unpacking the black box of relations between the prime minister and her ministers provide additional insights into ministerial tenure over and above what can be gleaned from analysis of the effects of the individual characteristics of ministers alone? Much has been written about how different prime ministers have run their cabinets, though much of it is based on the specific 'style' of particular prime ministers and so does not allow us to make broader inferences about British politics or other parliamentary democracies. Nevertheless in Chapter 5 we evaluate whether there is any evidence to suggest that the expected tenure of ministers does indeed reflect differences in a prime minister's style.

In Chapter 6 we begin to assess the relationship between the prime minister and her ministers more systematically. The key element of our analysis is that during the course of a ministerial career, new information, not available to a prime minister at the time of making the appointment, will become available. Here we consider, in particular, interventions that are made from the back benches, more serious elements of the media, or elsewhere, that call into question a minister's performance, and which suggest that the minister in question should resign from his post. We provide and apply a method for developing a systematic analysis of such events and how the prime minister responds to such calls. The analysis codes newspaper reports from the period of investigation, counting the number of resignation calls by government and according to the nature of the issues that led to the resignation call.

In Chapter 7 we bring this analysis together. There we show that the length of time a minister serves is related to his background characteristics; also that it is affected by the resignation calls that he receives and those received by other members of the administration in which he serves. In particular we show that, whereas a minister's chances of survival are diminished upon receiving a resignation call, a second resignation call effectively signals the death of his (immediate) ministerial career. Perhaps more surprisingly, we show that a minister's prospects for survival in government are inversely related to the aggregate performance of those around him. Put simply, when his colleagues are doing well, so that few have had their performance called into question via a call for their resignation, then the probability that a minister's term will end early is higher. When more ministers are involved in resignation calls then this risk recedes: a minister is safer in his position when surrounded by other ministers tainted by scandal or other accusations of wrongdoing. Although this result may appear surprising, we show that it is consistent with what we would expect from principal–agent analysis. In particular these empirical results are consistent with what we would expect when the prime minister is using all of the information at her disposal to evaluate whether a minister has been involved in wrongdoing when called upon to resign, and may therefore not be up to the job, or whether he has just been the victim of circumstance. When few ministers are involved in resignation calls, then a resignation call sends a strong signal to the prime minister that the former conditions apply.

In the concluding chapter we consider the implications from our analysis for understanding the relations between the prime minister and her ministers and broader issues of responsibility and accountability of ministers in the UK central government. Unlike most other books on cabinet or ministers, ours is not simply descriptive nor does it draw normative conclusions from sets of examples. Rather, it uses the tools of modern political science to model the relationships between the prime minister and her ministers, and among the ministers as a collective organ of government. Using these tools, we try to provide a greater analytical grasp of those relationships. We produce hypotheses about how we expect the channels of accountability to work and utilize unique data on ministerial movements: from being appointed, through promotions, demotions, sideways moves and finally removal from office; as well as systematic data on the criticisms levelled at individual ministers as they do their jobs. We can thus see how far the accountability mechanisms available to Parliament through the prime minister – the effects on ministerial career – are sensitive to how Parliament, and the public as reported through the media, views individual ministers. To be sure, our data are not a comprehensive measure of either the mechanisms or the full judgements of individual ministerial worth, but they do allow systematic analysis to back up or challenge more intuitive judgements. We hope that our systematic analyses will shed new light upon previous reflections on ministerial accountability, helping to confirm some of the arguments of earlier writers, but also suggesting new avenues for research. Our data are drawn from the end of the Second World War, or more precisely from the beginning of Clement Attlee's post-war Labour government (26 July 1945), until the end of Tony Blair's third administration when he resigned to let Gordon Brown take the reins as prime minister (28 June 2007).

2 | Managing the cabinet: principal–agent relations in government

In a now-famous book, the late William Riker offered a critical assessment of the ability of liberal democracies to craft policies that reflected the will of the public. Using the insights of social choice theory, Riker argued that politics was inherently susceptible to the whims and strategic calculations of agenda-setters, and challenged what he called the 'populist' view of government that policy outcomes reflect the desires of citizens (Riker, 1982). Riker offered an alternative, liberal view of democracy, in which democracy is effective because it provides the institutional means by which citizens can hold to account those elected to power.

Riker's definition of liberal democracy draws on the writings of some of the great liberal philosophers of the Enlightenment whose interest was in understanding the proper function of government. Hume (1742/1978), for example, believed that government would be effective only when power was kept in check. It was not enough to rely on the good intentions of those who stood for office and better to set up a system of governance based on an assumption that those holding public office were knaves.

Of course, we need not take such a dim view of the motives of politicians to hold the liberal view of democracy. Suppose that one took an arguably more realistic view that although some politicians enter the profession for the noblest of reasons, some do not. Moreover, even public-spirited servants may succumb to temptation and take actions in the service of narrow private interests. Exactly how can government be used to keep in check the inherent self-interest of politicians?

One view is that democratic procedures provide *incentives* for politicians to take account of the public good. This was expressed famously by Tocqueville (1835, ch. 8) and Madison in *The Federalist Papers* (Hamilton, Madison and Jay, 1787–8/1982, p. LVII). In more recent years, Barro (1973) and Ferejohn (1986) have demonstrated that the desire for re-election provides incentives for politicians that curb their knavish desires. We return to this point below where we discuss more fully the motivations of politicians.

A related view to that already described is that liberal democracies provide for better governance because they allow citizens to choose for office those best able to serve. Here democracy is not about providing incentives to govern properly once in power, but about selecting those best able to govern in the first place: to choose knights rather than knaves. Tim Besley (2006), a modern proponent of this view, traces this view to V. O. Key who argues:

The nature of the workings of government depends ultimately on the men who run it. The men we elect to office and the circumstances we create that affect their work determine the nature of popular government. (Key, 1956, p. 10)

So there are two methods by which liberal democracy can provide better governance. Facing the electorate gives politicians incentives to govern as the majority wishes. And it provides a mechanism through which better candidates for public office are chosen.

Principals and their agents

The idea that politics is about both selecting those best able to govern, on the one hand, and providing incentives, on the other, is related to the principal–agent view of democratic elections. The basic agency problem is that a principal hires an agent to carry out certain activities on her behalf, but the agent may not carry out those activities efficiently or effectively. The problem can emerge because of asymmetric information. For example, the agent knows more about his abilities and proclivities at the time of being hired than does his principal. If such information were common knowledge then the principal might not have hired the agent at all. Moreover, after being hired, the agent can observe more closely what he is doing than can his principal.

The former problem is related to the notion of adverse selection. In these situations Gresham's Law that bad money drives out good is the classic expression of adverse selection. When money was composed of real silver, holders of coins might shave a sliver before exchanging the coin for some goods. Given the positive probability that any coin that one receives might have been shaved, one would not exchange as much in return for it as for a fully unshaved silver coin. Holders of unshaved coins would then not spend them or would shave them before using them. Bad money drives out good.

In modern literature Akerlof (1970) reintroduces adverse selection in his analysis based on used car markets. In his model a car owner knows if his car is good or bad, but the buyer cannot tell. Good cars are worth a high price to both buyer and seller, but buyers do not know if used cars are good or bad so will only pay low prices. Good cars will thus not come on to the market.[1]

In agency terms adverse selection generally occurs because those least qualified for a job are those most keen to attain it. For any job at whatever level of remuneration those least qualified are likely to gain the most comparative advantage over their current position and so be keener to attain the position. Adverse selection occurs where there is heterogeneity in the population of qualified candidates and those with some characteristics that the principal does not want are most likely to be those who come forward.

Asymmetric information that arises due to the actions taken by agents is related to the concept of moral hazard. This is a term first used in banking and insurance in the eighteenth century and reintroduced into the economics of risk by Kenneth Arrow in the 1960s (Arrow, 1963). In Arrow's sense, moral hazard can occur where the population is homogenous, but the act of making a contract or agreement itself creates perverse incentives. The very act of taking out insurance suggests that the insured will not act as carefully as hitherto with regard to his property or his health since he is insured against damage to either. Thus if one is insured against personal injury one might take greater risks. If one is insured against household burglary one will spend less on door and window locks, and so on.

Agency models of elections

It is easy to see how the agency perspective can be related to politics. At a basic level, the electors can be viewed as the principals whilst the elected politicians are their agents. At the time of election voters do not know all of the relevant characteristics of those who stand for office:

---

[1] Weakening the assumption that buyers have no information about cars on the market to one that they have less information than sellers might bring good cars on to the market; however, the used car market will still be swamped by bad cars.

they must make their selection upon the basis of imperfect information about the candidates' attributes as well as any other inferences they may draw from the electoral environment. Moreover, once politicians are elected, and although their actions are scrutinized by the media, lobby groups, and other intermediaries, the actions they take are (in part) hidden.

The earliest models that sought to understand elections as problems of agency are due to Barro (1973) and to Ferejohn (1986). Their work focused mainly on the moral hazard aspects of elections. Just as in the classic moral hazard problem, where insurance provided incentives for bad or risky behaviour for those insured, these authors asked whether the basic institutions of representative democracy provided incentives for better (or worse) performance by politicians. We have seen that the liberal philosophers Madison and Tocqueville both believed that the control that electors have over the tenure of their officeholders leads to better outcomes and they used this to justify their support for democratic institutions. This theme has provided a central core to modern political economy.

In his seminal contribution, Ferejohn (1986) analysed a model in which in each period an incumbent chooses an unobserved level of effort and voters use retrospective voting strategies to evaluate her performance. Voters receive utility that depends positively on the effort the incumbent devotes to her political task. The signal is, however, imperfect in that unobserved shocks may push up or down voters' utility irrespective of the effort the elected official devotes to the job. To induce incentives the principal (a representative voter) re-elects the incumbent only if his performance is above a threshold. From the principal's perspective, she chooses one of two effort levels. If the threshold is too high, so that he is elected only at a personal cost that is prohibitive, then he puts zero effort into being re-elected. Otherwise he chooses an effort level that, given the threshold chosen by the principal, leaves him strictly indifferent between putting in the required effort and maintaining his job and losing it. The problem the voter faces is in choosing the threshold: set it too high and an incumbent will deliver zero performance; set it too low and the incumbent will put in less performance than is optimal from the voters' standpoint – that is, the agent would have delivered more if the threshold had been higher.

In Ferejohn's model, as in that of Barro, incumbents and their replacements are of the same type: they share the same preferences and are of the same (*ex ante*) quality. The model thus captures, in a very pure form, the *sanctioning* aspect of elections – voters use their votes to sanction moral hazard – and Ferejohn is able to show the conditions under which such electoral control are effective.

An alternative approach, already discussed, is that voters use their votes to select between different politicians. Of course, for selection to have beneficial effects it must be that, in contrast to the models of Barro and Ferejohn discussed above, the agents between which the principal selects are heterogenous in their type. An important question then arises: can voters simultaneously use their votes to select their preferred agents and to sanction performance? In an important contribution to this literature Fearon (1999) illustrated a logical inconsistency in this view. The ability of voters to sanction performance implies that, conditional upon performance, they must be strictly indifferent between re-electing the incumbent or a challenger. As Fearon argues, once this indifference is broken, then voters cannot credibly commit to sanctioning (or rewarding) the incumbent.

To see why, consider a situation where a voter is faced with the choice between electing either agent A or B but has a preference for B. Now suppose the voter offers A a deal by which she is re-elected if her performance exceeds a threshold (optimally chosen). Under this contract A might, upon putting in the required effort, expect to be re-elected. But of course once she has done so then, since her actions are in the past, the principal would prefer to elect B. Anticipating that she will not be retained, then A will choose zero effort. Of course, it is possible that the principal has a preference for A. Does the principal's incentive scheme now work? The answer is no. Whatever A's effort level the voter prefers to retain her. In sum, since the incumbent's prospects of election are not conditional on past performance, the voter's incentive scheme will unravel.

Since, according to Fearon's argument, elections serve as incentive mechanisms only in the limiting case where agents are identical, elections might then best be seen as selection mechanisms. They allow electors to select higher-quality politicians. A necessary condition for this to be so is that the talented are willing to stand and that, when they do, they are elected. This need not be so, as adverse selection can occur. Besley and Coate (1995), in developing the citizen-candidate framework, provide analysis of situations where, even when voters are informed as to who the most competent politicians are, they are unable to coordinate their votes to ensure that such politicians are in fact elected. In their model, citizen-candidates decide (a) whether to stand for office and thus act as candidates and (b) if not, then which of the candidates to vote for. Unlike in the classic spatial model of politics developed by Duncan Black (1958) and Anthony Downs (1957), where the set of candidates who stand is fixed exogenously and voters choose between them, the Besley and Coate model breaks down the arbitrary distinction between citizens and those voted into office. Focusing on the entry decision of candidates (the policies they stand on are fixed exogenously) thus allows for a close examination of the characteristics of those elected to office. More generally, in a world where voters choose between agents who are distinguished by their policy preferences and by their ability, and where there is correlation between these elements – so that, for example, politicians who are more representative on policy are less competent at performing their tasks – then a majority may vote into office politicians whose policy preferences are more aligned with their own but who are of inferior quality to their opponents.

A stark case of adverse selection is considered by Caselli and Morelli (2004) who assess a world where citizen-candidates are of heterogenous talent. They stand for office if and only if the rents that accrue to them, conditional upon being elected, exceed the benefits they receive when pursuing an alternative career. The key insight of Caselli and Morelli is that, in politics, 'rewards do not adjust to elicit an increase in the supply of the scarce resource'. In particular, it is not the case that society generally sets the benefits of officeholders to elicit a sufficient supply of talented or competent officeholders. Rather these rewards are directly controlled by current political elites. For example, the salaries of politicians are set by sitting members of parliament. Caselli and Morelli have in mind, however, a more general notion of reward. In particular they use the concept of an 'ego-rent' that consists of both material and non-material elements that go together with office holding. Non-material elements are hard-to-measure factors such as the esteem in which politicians are held by the general public. Within their set-up, the authors show the existence of an equilibrium in which only 'bad', by which they mean incompetent, politicians stand for office. The logic is compelling: when the current elite consists of bad politicians who set the level of reward (via the actions they take or the pay that they award themselves) then there is nothing to attract a better class of politician to stand for office. Caselli and Morelli's analysis is thus a stark example of adverse selection in politics. An important consideration raised by their work is that effective governance is not just about the selection mechanism for politicians (that is, in their world, elections) but about creating the incentives for talented politicians to stand.

Empirical evidence

To what extent elections serve to resolve issues of moral hazard, by providing incentives, or issues of selection, and to what extent political pay affects performance, is an empirical point. Luckily, politics is sometimes structured in a way that allows political scientists to make evidence-based distinctions between different hypotheses.

Gagliarducci and Nannicini (2009) exploit a nice feature of Italian local politics to get at these questions. In Italy the salary of the mayor depends upon population size. The mayoral salary increases at discrete population levels. By comparing towns that fall either side of these thresholds, and looking at the quality of mayoral candidates in each, they are thus able to identify the effect of the difference in salary. Such towns are, in expectation, and save for the marginal difference in population, identical in all of the demographic and other local features that determine entry into political life. The key difference is that just above the population threshold politicians are paid more relative to those who fall just below the threshold. Gagliarducci and Nannicini show that higher salaries are causally related to the entry of better-educated politicians.

Moreover these higher-quality politicians also put in a better performance (at least they turn up more often). This latter effect may be due to selection (higher-quality types are more apt to turn up) or to incentives. Following the efficiency wages argument, since they are paid more and so have more to lose they put in the extra effort to ensure re-election. Once again, Italian local politics is designed in such a way as to distinguish between these hypotheses. Local mayors can serve at most two terms. Thus second-term mayors face no re-election incentive. If second-term mayors who earn higher salaries are more likely to turn up than their second-term colleagues who are lower paid, then this can only be due to their being of higher quality – their incentives are the same. And in fact this is what the authors found.

Parliamentary democracy

The agency literature on elections can then shed light on whether and how electors can hold the elected accountable for their actions and how electoral features affect the selection of politicians. The insights of agency models, and in particular those that emphasize moral hazard, are particularly valid where, as in Italian mayoral elections or the US gubernatorial elections, those elected have a direct influence on policy outcomes. In parliamentary democracy, however, the relationship between the election of constituency MPs and policy outcomes is more nuanced.

In his analysis of British political development, Gary Cox (1987) presents evidence that supports his argument that, over the course of the nineteenth century, British politics evolved from a system whereby voters cast votes for individuals who would represent them in parliament to one where individuals cast votes for one or other prospective executive teams. The efficient secret of British government was, Cox argued, that the work of parliament came under increasing control by the executive. A dual party system emerged in which different parties – first the Tories and Whigs, then, following the Peelite split, the Tories and the Liberals – vied for control of executive power. Upon gaining power the executive was then formed from members of the majority party, and the government was supported by the backbenchers.

Using the agency model to assess the structure of parliamentary democracy is, then, more complicated than when assessing the direct link between a voter and her representative. For how can a voter hold her locally elected MP to account for actions taken by an executive several steps removed from her? At the very best a voter might hold a party accountable for its actions when in government. This form of representation drives a wedge between the individuals who take executive decisions and the votes of local constituents who are affected by these decisions. In a system of parliamentary governance voters elect representatives to parliament and the governing executive must enjoy the confidence of that chamber.

To analyse accountability in parliamentary democracies, Strom (2000, 2003) develops a useful metaphor of parliamentary democracy as a 'chain of delegation' linking electors to the executors of government policy. The first link in this chain is that running from voters, who are the principals, to the MPs who serve as their agents. The constituents delegate to their MPs the task of forming and maintaining a government. Once a government is formed, the backbenchers in turn act as principals, delegating the task of policy initiative and proposal to the cabinet whose ministers act as the agents of their party backers. The prime minister, whilst the principal of her ministers, is also an agent of her backbenchers and must maintain the confidence of her cabinet and party. The final link in the chain is that between the governing principals who delegate the task of administering policy to their bureaucratic agents.

The prime minister and cabinet

Our focus in this book is on the relation between the prime minister and her cabinet, though we will also consider some of the broader agency relationships described above. In particular, our concern is to unpack the specific relationship between a prime minister and the members of her government that lies at the heart of the parliamentary model of governance. As a starting point, and in order to run her government effectively, a prime minister must delegate tasks to her ministers. The themes we have discussed above with regard to the agency literature applied to elections are pertinent here: a division of labour is a necessary prerequisite of government organization, and this can lead to an agency loss, due perhaps to adverse selection or to a misalignment of incentives that gives rise to moral hazard. Our focus is on the prime minister's role with regard to the selection of ministers and in creating the correct incentives to align ministerial ambitions with her own. These twin elements are, as we will show, critical for understanding cabinet relations. On the one hand we can think of the cabinet as a system of incentives: a prime minister seeks to align the actions of her ministers with those that she finds most desirable. But the performance of the cabinet is also about selection: the government will perform well when the most able are in post, though, of course, the prime minister may have other reasons for appointing a particular minister and problems of adverse selection can occur. As discussed earlier with regard to elections, part of the problem of selection is in providing incentives for the most able (or those aligned with the prime minister in some way) to be willing to accept higher office. In the following section we expand upon these themes and assess how they have been developed in the literature.

Applying the agency model in parliamentary democracies

Although Strom developed his metaphor some time ago, work on analysing complex agency relations in parliamentary democracies has been piecemeal. Very little empirical work has fleshed out the implications of principal–agent analysis for understanding parliamentary democracies. Our motivation is to look at the structure of the cabinet and how the prime minister exploits the tools that are available to her to minimize agency loss. In order to make sense of the extensive data we gather on ministerial careers in the UK, which we describe in more detail below, we make use of some simplifying assumptions.

Our first assumption, which provides the starting point for our analysis, refers to the nature of the relationship between a prime minister and her ministers. In the following chapter we provide a full account of how these relations are described in the British constitution and how they have evolved historically in the United Kingdom. For now, however, we point out that, although the prime minister and her minister form part of a governing team, and as members of the governing team receive credit when the administration runs well, their incentives are not perfectly aligned. There are two major and underlying causes of such misalignment. First, the cabinet may consist of ministers with different viewpoints over policy. This is most likely when the cabinet is formed by different parties, but of course such divisions can arise under single-party governments also. The second source of misalignment relates to the career concerns of ministers. Although ministers might rise through the ranks through hard work and performance, there are also other resources that they can utilize. For example, politicians with a strong network of influential supporters are less dispensable than those without. This means that a minister who wishes to remain at the forefront of political life must balance different objectives and allocate time to different activities. A misalignment of incentives occurs when the prime minister wishes the minister to spend more time performing his government tasks than the minister is willing to allocate to such tasks.

Our second assumption concerns the motivations of ministers. We assume that ministers are career politicians. They seek high office and once they have attained high office they wish to stay there. A contrasting view is offered by Mattozzi and Merlo (2008). In their world, whilst some politicians are interested only in a political career, others use politics as a means of showcasing their talents. The idea is that talented individuals will be paid a market wage that accords with their abilities but the private sector offers few opportunities for individuals to display their abilities to the market. This might not be true of the highest executives whose actions are scrutinized by the financial press, but is certainly true for most employees. Public service, so the argument goes, then provides a showground that allows individuals to distinguish themselves from their competitors and so increase their market wage. Our assumption of ministers as career politicians abstracts from the financial concerns of politicians: we view ministers as intrinsically motivated by the desire for public office.

Our third assumption concerns information. Our view of cabinet government stems from the standard model of delegation: we assume that the prime minister cannot formulate and implement policy on her own; rather she must delegate many of the essential tasks of government to her ministers. Our concern is with several potential sources of informational asymmetry that may prohibit the effective running of government under a system in which separate tasks are delegated to the ministers who head the departments. In particular, upon appointing a minister, we suppose that the prime minister does not have all the relevant information as to whether that individual is in fact up to the task of playing a role in the running of government. For example, she (the prime minister) may have a notion that some MPs are more able than others, and may have some notion of the distribution of talent amongst her backbenchers, but there must be some uncertainty as to how such raw talent translates into ministerial competence. In short, the prime minister is uncertain as to the minister's *type*.

A further informational asymmetry relates to the fact that the prime minister does not directly observe the actions taken by her ministers. Rather she observes some indicators that are correlated with ministerial actions and that serve as imperfect measures of ministerial actions and performance. Here the career concerns of ministers may lead to less-than-optimal effort being expended on the tasks of government. Although the prime minister would like ministers to devote their efforts to their government tasks she does not have sufficient resources to ensure they do so. Instead she relies on the use of imperfect measures of performance that are imperfectly correlated with the actions taken by her ministers.

The distinction we draw here is similar to that already adopted in the bureaucratic agency literature. In a series of papers that in aggregate offer a seminal contribution to that literature, the team of writers known as McNollGast distinguished between types of tools that a legislative principal (an oversight committee) could use to control her bureaucratic agents. On the one hand the principal could make use of police patrol procedures (McCubbins, Noll, and Weingast, 1987, 1989; McCubbins and Schwartz, 1984). This boils down to an intensive investigation and monitoring of each and every ministerial action. On the other hand a more efficient mechanism is reliance on the use of 'fire-alarms'. When things go drastically wrong in the agency, then consumer complaints and pressure will alert the principal to this fact. In our analysis, which we develop below, the prime minister can be alerted to shortcomings in the running of a department by the arrival of scandals which implicate a minister. These shocks can act as effective fire alarms.

Building upon these assumptions, we ask how the prime minister organizes her cabinet in order to achieve her goals. There are different tools that the prime minister has at her disposal in order to align the incentives of ministers with her own, and we shall discuss these more fully in the following chapter. Here, however, we highlight perhaps the main tool that the prime minister has that allows her to do her job effectively. The central role that the prime minister plays concerns the hiring and firing of government ministers. This power, more than any other, helps define a government and its performance. In short, the prime minister has the power to decide who will serve in government and how long they will stay there. This fact, combined with our assumption that ministers are intrinsically motivated to serve in office, provides the leeway for a prime minister to determine the direction of government policy and its performance.

The cabinet as a system of incentives

A minister may wish to allocate less effort to his government task than his principal finds optimal. And the minister may have personal policy preferences on some issues that are at odds with those of the prime minister. We assume that the prime minister uses the tools that are available to her to align the incentives of her cabinet ministers with her own. We use some simple insights from the agency literature and we use a large sample of observations from British government to explore whether the data are consistent with what we should expect from an application of these models. As we shall discuss throughout, even when starting with these limited ambitions the obstacles we face are large.

The prime minister has at her disposal a large number of tools. At the government formation stage the two main tools are the appointment of her ministers to government and the allocation of their ministerial portfolios. Once the government is formed, the prime minister may periodically revisit the decisions she made when forming her government. She may choose to shuffle ministers between portfolios or to remove a minister from office and return him to the back benches. Nevertheless, and although it might appear that the prime minister is thus in a powerful position, when compared with executive chiefs in other domains the tools available to a prime minister are somewhat blunt. In particular, executive pay is not directly controlled by the prime minister. Directly paying ministers for higher performance or, conversely, penalizing them for any aspect of their performance that casts the government in a bad light is not possible as executive salaries are (usually) determined by the legislature.

This does not mean, of course, that the prime minister cannot align the incentives of her ministers with her own. In particular, and precisely because the prime minister determines whether a minister will serve in government at all, and if so for how long, she directly controls a variable that is of utmost importance to a minister (or prospective minister). The desire for public service is an important source of intrinsic motivation for politicians: serving your country by attaining and maintaining ministerial office is high on the list of politicians' objectives. A number of studies have exploited this fact to explore the interrelationship between the prime minister and her ministers. The basic idea that connects these papers is simple: by pursuing rents rather than performing their tasks as their principal would have them do, ministers increase the risk that the prime minister will cut short their tenure. Thus ministers face a trade-off; by pursuing their private objectives they increase the risk that they lose their jobs. This means the loss of the current value of their ministerial career which includes the reward they receive from serving the public as well as the opportunity to extract rents in the future.

Cabinet selection

A second source of informational asymmetry occurs because the prime minister may not fully observe whether a minister is up to the task that the prime minister has allocated to him. This may appear a strange assumption to make: after all, prior to his appointment the prime minister and her advisors will have observed the performance of the prospective minister as a backbench MP both in electoral campaigns and in the House. Nevertheless, the prime minister may be unsure to what extent the observed talents of a backbencher translate into executive competence. There are a number of aspects of the job of a minister such as running a large department, dealing with civil servants, working with colleagues through complex committee systems, speaking on television and radio for which being an effective election campaigner or backbench MP do not necessarily demonstrate suitability. Furthermore, ministers are subject to much closer media scrutiny of their private lives and working habits. Thus we can assume that the prime minister makes appointments under conditions of some uncertainty.

Our data and questions

Our evidence does not cover every aspect of ministerial accountability. It largely utilizes the crudest, but also most effective, form of holding ministers to account: sacking and the threat of sacking (or demotion), the curtailing of a career. We note from the outset that whilst a forced exit at the time of some scandal is the most obvious form of retributive accountability for a minister, being moved or removed under the cover of a larger set of ministerial movements (a major cabinet reshuffle) months after he has been criticized is equally a part of a retributive accountability mechanism. Ministers know that their jobs are on the line every time a prime minister takes the opportunity to shift the chairs in the cabinet and show some colleagues the way back to the back benches. Most commentators on British politics will note that the threat to a minister's career is an important part of the structure of ministerial accountability, but will add that ministerial responsibility, constitutionally and practically, involves a much wider set of issues and behaviours. We discuss these other aspects in Chapter 3 and reflect back on them in our final chapter. We shall argue that the central concerns of this book constitute the heart of accountability, and without it all the rest would be just cheap talk about how the world ought to be.

3 | The structure of British government

As stated in the previous chapter, the principal–agent approach offers a rich theoretical approach for investigating relations in parliamentary democracy. In this book we use data from the British case to illustrate how selection and incentives operate under the cabinet system in the United Kingdom. Our choice of the system of government in the UK as the source of our investigation is deliberate, and is prompted by the comparatively unconstrained nature of the prime minister's powers over her ministers. The task of this chapter is then to introduce the nature of cabinet government in the UK. We begin by describing the constitutional requirements of forming a government in the UK. We briefly discuss the history of cabinet government in the UK and introduce the notions of individual and collective responsibility. We define the different levels of ministers we discuss in the book and what their responsibilities are and discuss the job, or rather jobs, of each. We end with a discussion of what sort of ministers and cabinet a prime minister would ideally like, and briefly consider some of the constraints upon that choice. We discuss the ideas of individual and collective ministerial responsibility. These two forms of accountability lie at the heart of ministerial accountability and whilst they are, in some ways, mutually supportive notions, they also work, so we shall demonstrate in this book, in contradictory fashions. The tensions inherent in these twin notions are a major source of political problems within British government.

Constitutional situation

The UK is a constitutional monarchy which can be traced back to at least the ninth century. The crown is the symbol of all executive authority, though some authority now proceeds from outside the borders of the nation. In Anglo-Saxon and Norman times the monarch ruled with a court of advisors; power was not absolute and the King was expected to consult with leading men, both secular and clerical, to discover the

law. The Magna Carta of 1215 reaffirmed and expressed those relationships as understood at that time. Parliament developed to support
the monarch; the Civil War and interregnum of the mid seventeenth
century occurred because of the King's arbitrary rule, ignoring acts of
parliament and abrogating property rights. Following the restoration
of the crown, and notably under William and Mary, parliament gained
further powers. The 1689 Bill of Rights embodied in statute the ille-
gality of suspending laws or levying taxation without the approval of
parliament. This established the dependence of the monarch on parliament (Mackintosh, 1977; North and Weingast, 1989; Jones, Gray,
Kavanagh, Moran, Norton, and Seldon, 1994).

   The monarch still retained governing powers, largely through his
prerogative of appointing the Privy Council of advisors; when that
proved too unwieldy the King drew on a smaller set of advisors who,
as early as the 1660s, became known as the cabinet, council or junto
(Mackintosh, 1977, p. 27). The cabinet became important, not simply
as advisors to the monarch but as a channel to parliament. It also provided a bulwark that ensured accountability through parliament and
protected the monarch during governance difficulties, since it could
take the flak, deflecting a direct threat to the monarch, and its members were ultimately expendable. The monarch could largely ensure
that the cabinet was supported in parliament through his control of
the Commons. This control was enabled by royal patronage: the ability to raise Commoners to the Lords and to create MPs for the rotten
boroughs was effectively within the royal gift. The cabinet grew in
strength throughout the late eighteenth and nineteenth centuries, the
role of prime minister being clearly recognized by the 1740s. Representative democracy emerged in its present form through the nineteenth
and early twentieth centuries, the Great Reform Act of 1832 introducing a more uniform electoral system and subsequent acts extending
the franchise to all British subjects born in the realm. The monarch still
formally appoints ministers, and signs legislation, though no monarch
since Queen Victoria has considered vetoing any law (Queen Anne in
1707 was the last actually to withhold royal assent, from the Scottish
Militia Bill) or successfully pushed for particular legislation (Hardie,
1970, p. 67).

   There are two houses of parliament at Westminster, the House
of Commons and the House of Lords. Since the seventeenth century the government has primarily depended upon its support in the
Commons, but the Lords were never explicitly subordinate. Until 1832

the connections between the two houses were intimate; based largely on shared landowning interests, their outlook was very similar (Mackintosh, 1977; North and Weingast, 1989, pp. 112–13). From 1832 the importance of the Lords diminished rapidly, and throughout the twentieth century (certainly since 1911 when powers were formally transferred) the Commons has been completely dominant. Not since Lord Salisbury (who resigned in July 1902) has there been any prime minister sitting in the Lords. Lord Home (Sir Alec Douglas-Home) on becoming prime minister on 19 October 1963 renounced his peerage and entered the House of Commons on 7 November after winning a by-election in Kinross and West Perthshire. Though full cabinet ministers are still drawn from the Lords, and both houses must have government spokespeople on all issues, the major officers of state sit in the Commons. The appointment of Lord Carrington as Foreign Secretary in 1979 was the last time one of the four major offices went to the Lords. The Commons is now elected from around 650 constituencies in England, Scotland, Wales and Northern Ireland.[1] From the time of the 1911 Parliament Act the House of Lords has provided oversight of legislation, able to amend and reject legislation but without the ability to block money bills or to delay other public bills beyond a maximum of two parliamentary sessions (one session since the 1949 Parliament Act). Non-controversial public bills and private bills can also be initiated there.[2] It is constituted of hereditary peers and, since the 1958 Life Peerages Act, peers ennobled by the Queen on the advice of the prime minister. The hereditary nature of the Lords gave the Conservatives an inbuilt majority. The 1999 House of Lords Act removed the right of hereditary peers to sit and vote in the Lords with the exception of 92 of them (elected by their fellows from the 759 hereditary peers) as an interim measure to full reform. From 1999 the total membership of the Lords was reduced from 1,295 to 695.[3]

---

[1] The precise number has varied. The lowest number in the post-war period was 625 in the elections of 1950 and 1951, the highest 659 in 1997 and 2001. There were 646 MPs elected in May 2005.

[2] A public bill is one which is in the general interest, and usually introduced into parliament by a minister, though backbenchers can introduce public bills. Private bills refer to some specific individual or organization. Some bills are hybrid.

[3] Further reform has never taken place; see Judge (2005, pp. 64–77); Shell (2000); McLean, Spirling and Russell (2003) for an account of the 1999 reform and the failure to take this interim reform further. For a more complete account of the duties and abilities of the Lords consult Walters (2003).

Following an election, the outgoing prime minister will have an audience with the monarch. If the prime minister has lost her majority in parliament she will resign and the monarch will ask another member of parliament whether she can secure enough support in parliament to form a government. Where once the monarch might have had to ask several people before one was successful, the development of the party system through the nineteenth century ensures that the process is much easier now. The monarch will ask the leader of the party with an overall majority to form a government. Failing that she will ask the leader of the party with the most MPs. However, as with much else in the British Constitution, this happens by convention, rather than constitutional provision. Outside of some parliamentary rules governing payments for expenses, there is no mention of political parties in the British Constitution. However, throughout the twentieth century there has been a strong party system and, de facto, the structures and rules of the political parties have determined whom the monarch should ask to form a government on the resignation or death of the prime minister.

Very rarely in the UK has there been an occasion where there is not a majority party. At the election of 28 February 1974 there was no party commanding a majority of seats in the Commons. Edward Heath's Conservatives gained more votes but fewer seats than Labour. After the Unionists from Northern Ireland refused to support Heath and following failed negotiations with the Liberal Party, Heath resigned as prime minister on 4 March. Harold Wilson was asked to form a government though he could not command a majority in parliament. It was understood by all that this government would be of a temporary or interim nature and no major legislative programme was attempted. New elections were called in October 1974.

When a prime minister resigns without an election the choice of successor might be more problematic. During the period analysed in this book there have been two occasions of some difficulty. When Eden resigned in January 1957 the Queen's Secretaries sounded out feeling amongst senior Conservatives as to who should replace him. Following consultation with Lord Salisbury (grandson of the PM at the beginning of the century), Churchill, the Chief Whip, and the cabinet, Harold Macmillan was then chosen rather than R. A. Butler (Mackintosh, 1977; Leonard, 2005, pp. 423, 219). More controversial still was Macmillan's successor, Lord Home (Alec Douglas-Home), chosen over Lord Hailsham and Butler on Macmillan's recommendation (Leonard, 2005, pp. 234–6). However, usually the succession is clear and since Douglas-Home's appointment the major parties have elected their leaders (though under varying electoral rules). When Harold Wilson announced he was stepping down whilst in office, James Callaghan was elected leader in a ballot of the Parliamentary Labour Party. He was also Wilson's chosen heir, having been confidentially informed three months earlier of Wilson's intention. Margaret Thatcher was deposed after Michael Heseltine announced he was standing against her for the leadership, though in the complicated ballot procedure that followed, John Major, who did not stand until Thatcher withdrew after the first ballot, became leader and prime minister.

During the Second World War the King asked Churchill to name a Deputy Prime Minister, in case he should be killed, and he named Anthony Eden. When he named Eden again in 1951 as Deputy Prime Minister and Foreign Secretary the King deleted the first title. Macmillan refused to name a deputy as the position was not constitutional, though four months later it was announced that Butler would act as deputy and would be given the name First Secretary of State (Heasman, 1962). There were no more Deputy Prime Ministers until Major made Michael Heseltine Deputy Prime Minister and First Secretary of State in July 1995 following Heseltine's support of Major's re-election as party leader (see Chapter 5). Blair made the Deputy Leader of the Labour Party, John Prescott, Deputy Prime Minister and First Secretary of State on assuming office in 1997. However, in neither of these latter cases would the Deputy have been likely to become prime minister other than as a placeholder; when Blair resigned, with Prescott also stepping down, Gordon Brown assumed the premiership as unchallenged leader of the Labour Party, with an election held for Deputy Leader of the party. Brown did not create a Deputy Prime Minister in his cabinet. Eden and Butler were both favourites to replace their prime minister should he step down; Eden did so, Butler did not (see Chapter 5). In 2010, for the first time since the wartime national coalition, a coalition government was formed and the leader of the minority Liberal Party Nick Clegg took on the position of Deputy Prime Minister. We do not theoretically consider the complications of coalition government and our data end in 2007.

In the British system there is no formal investiture of ministers or government and no confidence vote in new ministers or a new government. Governments can face a motion of no confidence tabled by the opposition, or a prime minister can let it be known that a vote on a given bill is a vote of confidence: if it is lost she will resign. However, it is known that to lose a vote on some aspects of legislation, such as a budget, would in practical terms be equivalent to a vote of no confidence. James Callaghan was forced to ask the Queen for a dissolution of parliament and a general election after losing a vote of no confidence tabled by the opposition on 28 March 1979 after the defeat on the referendum on devolution for Scotland and following the notorious 'winter of discontent' marked by major public sector strikes over the pay restraint policies of the government.

The cabinet

Constitutionally the executive in Britain is cabinet government. We saw above that it resulted from the need for the monarch to take advice and to control parliament, and it became the governing machine in the representative democracy that has evolved. Of course, as the reach of the state has increased, the cabinet as a committee that meets and discusses all the business of the state has dissolved. The departments and ministries themselves consider policy initiatives and oversee policy implementation; they liaise with cabinet informally through their network channels or more formally through bilateral meetings or the cabinet committee system. Most major decisions that in the inter-war years would have been taken in cabinet are now taken in cabinet committees, and those committees have proliferated and grown in importance in the past fifty years (Hennessy, 1986b, 2005). The number of political advisors has grown both around the prime minister and more recently around other ministers too (Lee, Jones and Burnham, 1998; Blick and Jones, 2010). Successive prime ministers have been concerned with policy coordination across the government machine as a whole. Churchill in 1951 introduced 'overlords' who oversaw departments, something which had been successful in his wartime cabinet but signally failed in peacetime. Heath created and desired to create 'super-departments' combining responsibilities, Thatcher strengthened the Cabinet Office. Blair, renowned for 'sofa government' where he tried to do more business with ministers on a one-to-one basis, talked about 'joined-up government', strengthening his policy unit not only for policy initiatives but also to try to ensure implementation of service promises. Even so, more decisions about the detail of policy, and far more about policy implementation, are taken by civil servants all the way down to street level than are taken by ministers and, for all the resources at the centre, for efficiency that must remain so.[4] The UK still has cabinet government and any prime minister that loses the support of her cabinet, as Margaret Thatcher discovered, will not remain in power (Smith, 1999, pp. 97–100); the government executive remains the full machinery of government including those carrying out policy who are not public servants.

These facts about 'the core executive' (Dunleavy and Rhodes, 1990) together with the growing importance to state policy of international organizations, notably the European Union, have fuelled much debate amongst British political scientists about the nature of power and network governance, the 'hollowing out of the state' and what this means for the 'Westminster model' (Rhodes, 1997; Smith, 1999; Richards and Smith, 2002). In essence they mean nothing. It has always been the case that ministers are advised by civil servants and their own policy friends, and cabinet oversees policy and policy change, with greater or lesser parliamentary oversight. Greater complexity is greater complexity and nothing more.

The full cabinet constitutes what has been described as the 'core of the core executive' (Smith, 1999), with the rest of the core being made up not only of other ministers but also of the civil servants and others who work in agencies and quasi-governmental agencies. Changes within the 'core of the core executive' may lead to a strengthening of prime ministerial power vis-à-vis other ministers or may simply be shifting sands (King, 1985; Hennessy, 1986a; Madgwick, 1991; Rhodes and Dunleavy, 1995; Burch and Holiday, 1996; Smith, 1999).

The size of the full cabinet has not varied much over the sixty or so years from 1945 to 2007, ranging from 15 to 23 members. However, full cabinet members form only the very central executive of the government, which includes ministers who do not attend cabinet (or attend only when called for specific issues). We describe these in more detail in the following section. The size of the government

---

[4] Blair's policy unit did go right down to street level for implementing his policy initiatives, but only for short periods, until his attention went elsewhere.

Table 3.1. *Size of government at the start of prime ministerial term:*
1945–2007

Prime Minister (term)	Cabinet ministers	Ministers of cabinet rank	Junior ministers	Whips and members of HM Household*	Total
Attlee (1945–50)	21	26	52	18	117
Attlee (1950–51)	17	25	38	12	92
Churchill (1951–5)	17	31	42	16	106
Eden (1955)	15	27	32	8	82
Eden (1955–7)	17	29	42	11	99
Macmillan (1957–9)	15	28	41	14	98
Macmillan (1959–63)	16	33	60	23	132
Douglas-Home (1963–4)	17	35	34	9	95
Wilson (1964–6)	22	40	38	16	116
Wilson (1966–70)	23	39	58	30	150
Heath (1970–4)	20	37	35	31	123
Wilson (1974)	20	35	32	15	102
Wilson (1974–6)	21	39	34	23	117
Callaghan (1976–9)	19	38	38	28	123
Thatcher (1979–83)	20	43	41	29	133
Thatcher (1983–7)	20	36	44	34	134
Thatcher (1987–90)	18	41	43	39	141
Major (1990–2)	21	40	31	17	109
Major (1992–7)	17	45	56	42	160
Blair (1997–2001)	21	43	60	32	156
Blair (2001–5)	18	38	48	36	140
Blair (2005–7)	19	31	45	27	122

*Whips in the House of Lords (see page 33).

as a whole has leapt from 82 in 1955 to 160 in 1997 (see Table 3.1).[5]
Governments have grown as state business has increased, but slight
variations in cabinet size are due partly to the personality of the
PM and partly to political exigencies. Attlee's cabinet was large,

[5] Table 3.1 gives the size of government at the beginning of each government. 23
is the largest full cabinet listed there, but this figure has been exceeded on several
dates by our count.

following the overblown size of the wartime cabinets. Heath wanted a small cabinet, and created larger departments, toying with the idea of super-ministries for efficiency. In fact he had a cabinet larger than he would have ideally desired, feeling obliged to give posts to certain influential people. Prime ministers have continually tinkered with departments in responding to circumstances. Some reorganizations are purely political: John Prescott was made Deputy Prime Minister in 1997 and given an enormous department in his role as Minister and First Secretary of State for Environment, Transport and the Regions. Blair bowed to Prescott's demands here, given Prescott's vital role within the Labour Party before the election (Seldon, 2005). The size of the government payroll overall has increased by about 25 per cent comparing Attlee's 1945 government with Blair's government of 1997 (see Table 3.1.)

The payroll does not include all those who are covered by collective responsibility: neither whips nor Parliamentary Private Secretaries are on the payroll but certainly neither will keep their jobs unless they strictly follow the government line. Our concern here is specifically with the tensions that exist between the government as a single agent (constitutionally defined as collective responsibility) and with ministers as agents in themselves (constitutionally individual responsibility).

Constraints on government action have increased with the strengthening of the European Union and globalization, but these are changes in constraints, not changes at the heart of how government works. We are not much concerned about these global changes in this book. Our concern is directed at ministers themselves rather than their relative importance vis-à-vis the prime minister, civil servants or other advisors, or their power overall in the general scheme of running people's lives. Cabinet, indeed the government, can be viewed as a single agent bound by the doctrine of collective cabinet responsibility (which is discussed below) and unified by single interests (for example, running the country smoothly, getting re-elected). But of course ministers are themselves single agents, and are constitutionally seen as such, with individual ministerial responsibility (see below) in themselves and for what they formally oversee. And as single agents ministers have interests conflicting with those of their colleagues and of the government as a collective agent (such as getting their legislative programme through, enhancing their careers). Indeed, it is the working through of these two doctrines, and the interrelationship of the government as a single agent and ministers as multiple agents, that is one of the central themes of this book.

Ministers

Blondel (1985, p. 8) defines a minister as someone in 'the top echelon of the government, directly under or alongside the leaders. Either they are in full charge of a sector of government or their role is to assist these leaders.' Officially a civil service department is defined in terms of the minister who is held accountable to parliament for that department's activities (Dowding, 1995, pp. 17–18). Large departments will be headed by a cabinet minister, smaller and less important departments by ministers of cabinet rank (these terms are defined below). Large departments will also have ministers of state taking on specific responsibilities (and these days ministers of state are usually named in terms of the responsibilities they hold). Large departments also have junior ministers usually with specific responsibilities; they are sometimes drawn from the Lords in order to give that House a spokesperson for that departmental brief. They will report to their cabinet minister or minister of state. Ministers are generally defined by their departmental responsibilities, though some carry specific historical titles. For each part of a departmental remit there will be a spokesperson in each house of parliament; in the Lords these are usually ministers of cabinet rank or junior ministers (though some full cabinet ministers sit in the Lords). Junior ministers also usually have defined responsibilities within the department and answer questions on their specific responsibilities in the Commons or Lords as appropriate. Legal officers have the status of ministers of state (see below) and may sit in either house, though increasingly they are drawn from the Lords. The opposition parties also appoint shadow spokespeople (a shadow cabinet) to cover all areas of responsibility. All ministers receive state salaries, but of those not on the government payroll only the leaders of the opposition in both houses and the Chief Whips receive state funding (beyond their parliamentary salaries). In much of our analysis we include whips though they do not receive state funding (some whips in the Lords do speak on behalf of the departments at times).

In some of our empirical analysis we define ministers in five categories (though in many models we only use four of them), and strictly speaking, by Blondel's definition and constitutionally, only three of the categories are ministers. Our categories also do not correspond directly to constitutionally defined ministerial roles, but rather to functions of government positions. The top rank we define is 'full cabinet ministers'. In addition to the prime minister, this includes the Chancellor of the Exchequer and in general the heads of the major departments or ministries. Most full cabinet ministers carry the title Secretary of State. Those who do not carry such titles include the Lord President of the Council, the Lord Privy Seal, the Chancellor of the Duchy of Lancaster, the Paymaster General, the Chief Secretary to the Treasury (who answers to the Chancellor). Ministers carrying these titles are often full members of the cabinet (though not all of them during all periods of our study). Some of these, such as the Lord President and the Duchy of Lancaster are sinecure posts (with some privileges – fancy offices and apartments) without departmental responsibilities. Important members of the party might be awarded them along with the chair of several cabinet committees, making them more powerful and influential than ministers with full departmental responsibilities. Similarly, the Lord President of the Council is the government Leader in the House of Lords; the Lord Privy Seal is the Leader in the House of Commons. They can often be considered as ministers without portfolio, allowing a prime minister to include in cabinet a few individuals valued for their talent (or personal or policy proximity to the prime minister) who can chair cabinet committees. The Paymaster General has generally had a job in the Department of Employment or functionally similar department similar to a Minister of State; or has spoken in the Commons on behalf of a Secretary of State in the Lords. We even consider some ministers of state as full cabinet ministers if they regularly attend cabinet. By the 1975 Ministerial and Other Salaries Act there can only be 22 ministers in addition to the prime minister, so government overcomes that problem by terming some full cabinet ministers 'ministers who also attend cabinet meetings'. For our analyses we make no distinction between these ministers if they regularly attend cabinet.

The second level we define as 'ministers of cabinet rank' who are generally ministers of state. Such ministers often have specific responsibilities within a department, such as minister of state for higher education, and are answerable to their department head; they may attend cabinet if an area within the remit of their particular responsibility is being discussed (they attend for that item only). Some ministers of state are not answerable to any other minister than the prime minister and attend cabinet only when their portfolio is discussed.

The third level we code is 'junior ministers' who are parliamentary undersecretaries of state or parliamentary secretaries (not to be confused with Parliamentary Private Secretaries). Junior ministers might attend cabinet for a specific item; they might also attend cabinet committees, and those who sit in the Lords might answer all questions there concerning their department.

These three categories constitute ministers under Blondel's definition. Our fourth category is Parliamentary Private Secretaries (PPSs). These posts are attached to full cabinet ministers and their holders often act as a conduit from parliament to the minister (the minister's 'ear in parliament'). Whilst all ministers are crown appointments decided by the prime minister, most cabinet ministers will choose or at least have a strong influence on the choice of their PPS.[6] For that reason, in some analyses, notably those concerned with prime ministerial hiring and firing rules and decisions, we exclude the PPSs from our analysis.

Our fifth category is whips. In the strong party system of the British parliament the whips' job is threefold. It is to ensure party discipline and, almost literally, whip the members in to the correct voting lobby. (Actually whips will say that persuasion and handholding are more usual these days.) Second, they help organize 'pairing' arrangements so that MPs who cannot attend a voting division are paired with a member of an opposition party who also wishes to avoid attending. Third, they report back, through the Chief Whip, the feelings of the party to the prime minister.

In fact, the Chief Whip (officially the Parliamentary Secretary to the Treasury) in recent years has attended cabinet as a full cabinet minister; previously he would attend cabinet on occasion for the purpose of advising the likely view of the party on policy issues. In the

---

[6] This is true for the period we study. In the nineteenth century some junior ministers were appointed by ministers with apparently only the barest oversight from the prime minister and were not thought to be bound by collective responsibility. In 1880 Gladstone refused the resignation of Lord Lansdowne as Under-Secretary of State for India, over the Government's Irish policy, suggesting that an undersecretary was not responsible for government policy and could express his own opinions on the matter publicly (Milne, 1950, pp. 439–40).

whips category, we include both whips (officially called Lords of the Treasury) and assistant whips in the House of Commons. We also code as whips those who perform that role in the Lords including the Captain of the Honourable Corps of Gentlemen-at-Arms, and the Captain of the Queen's Bodyguard of the Yeoman of the Guard, even though at times these people also perform greater roles, including speaking on behalf of the government in the Lords in areas where there is no appropriate minister of state or junior minister.[7] We also include the Lords in Waiting who can be considered as equivalent to assistant whips in the Commons (though again they may take on more duties). We classify all these people as whips since they hold no departmental responsibilities (other than speaking on behalf of a department) and generally would be no better known to the public than other whips.

We include whips in many of our analyses since their involvement in scandal and forced resignation can prove embarrassing for government and they are certainly bound by collective responsibility. Furthermore, a job as a whip, especially in the House of Commons, can be a stepping stone on the way to a ministerial career. Hence for some aspects of our analysis the inclusion of whips makes sense.

The jobs of ministers

Since we have discussed whips and PPSs above, neither of whom are, by Blondel, or ordinarily thought of as ministers, this section concerns only our first three categories of what we term 'minister' for our quantitative analyses. Even so, we still operate with a broader conception of ministers than appears in many research monographs and textbooks. Blondel (1985), Rose (1987, p. 18) and Madgwick (1991, pp. 22–3) define ministers in terms of departmental responsibilities, thus excluding ministers without portfolio. Yet sometimes the most powerful ministers, at least in terms of the policy domain they influence as chairs of cabinet committees (Dunleavy, 1995), have few departmental responsibilities.

Even under narrower definition, the job of a minister varies enormously. Some departments have fairly constrained roles: the Department of Health, despite having a large budget, is a constrained

---

[7] Some also have more esoteric responsibilities: the Vice-Chamberlain of Her Majesty's Household has to write daily to the Queen, reporting on the day's activities in parliament.

department with a policy role relatively easily defined. To be sure, it involves rather different aspects of health, from oversight of the management of large hospitals to smaller General Practitioner (GP) surgeries and small-scale health schemes, the ambulance service and so on. And at times Social Welfare has also been part of the Health and Social Security remit. But its policy concerns are more easily defined than those of some other departments. The Home Office, until its recent break-up into ministries of Justice and of Home Affairs, looked after a wide variety of policy issues – justice broadly, the police, the prison service, immigration, home security (secret services), and so on. It was thus broken down into component parts with ministers of state and junior ministers given responsibilities for one or more of those component parts. Ministers take on responsibility for oversight of the efficient running of those programmes though of course most implementation decisions will be taken by civil servants at various levels in the hierarchy. For example, prison break-outs often lead to calls for the resignation of the Home Secretary (though those calls are rarely taken seriously: see Chapter 6), but operational decisions – about relative spending on closed-circuit TV sets versus high-security fences – will be taken by senior officials in the prison service together with the prison governors. The Foreign Office too has a wide remit that, after Britain entered the European Union, increased, so that it became involved in such domestic policy as that concerning EU rules (Dowding, 1995, ch. 7).

There are numerous articles and books by former ministers suggesting what the role of a minister is (for example, Jenkins, 1975; Kaufman, 1997), and a major work examines ministers largely through interview-based analysis (Headey, 1974a). Emerging from these insider accounts is how unprepared most ministers are on being first appointed. Being an MP provides no training for the administrative tasks of ministers. New ministers face a wealth of material they must review and master. From the outset they are asked to make decisions based on civil service advice, and the tasks involved leave little room for long-term strategic planning. Most ministers agree they act as 'intelligent laymen', and except for the legal officers few come to office with any expertise in their departmental field.

Headey (1974a) identifies five types of ministers: policy initiators, policy selectors, executive ministers (just concerned with managing departments), ambassadors (mostly concerned with public relations) and minimalists (who only wish to retain office and credibility), but also admits that most ministers perform some aspects of each role. Circumstances as much as personality might determine what 'type' of role a particular minister adopts (Rose, 1971). Headey (1974b) details eight functions of ministers: (1) formally each minister is responsible in several senses of that term; he is expected (2) to speak on areas of responsibility in parliament, to announce, explain and defend; (3) to represent his department in interdepartmental negotiations and in cabinet: not only over administrative details but also over competition for scarce resources – both money (especially these days to defend his department against detailed Treasury scrutiny, though a great deal is also done by his civil servants) and parliamentary time for his departmental bills; (4) to negotiate with pressure groups (though the bulk of this is done by his civil servants with the minister usually only involved in the final stages) (Jordan, 1991); (5) to present and publicize the department and its plans in the media; (6) to contribute to cabinet decisions over major issues. These are six roles specific to ministers, but ministers drawn from the Commons are also still elected members of parliament and career politicians; so they also (7) represent their constituents and (8) are concerned with future advancement. In Rose's (1971) list of three ministerial types the roles of interdepartmental representative and negotiator have become ever more complex over the period we discuss; the role of pressure groups has grown, though conversely the importance of the minister in this process may have diminished overall (Jordan and Richardson, 1987; Jordan, 1991). The role of ministers in the media has probably waxed and waned over the period. Certainly the interest of the press, radio and especially television in reporting what ministers do grew enormously from 1945 to the present. From the 1970s, ministers' media performance was vitally important to their reputation and advancement, though from 1997 the Labour government managed a media machine that reduced individual ministerial exposure, especially on radio and television. Senior ministers do contribute to cabinet decisions over the major issues, though one of the vibrant debates is how much this has changed over the period we study. Some argue that the prime minister is now so dominant that we have 'presidential government' (e.g. Foley, 1993, 2000). Nevertheless, Rose's list provides a nice summary of the major roles of ministers.

Headey (1974a) reports that most ministers see their major function as providing input into key issues – both those that emerge and in terms of future legislation. He also points out that reality does not quite fit with ministerial perceptions; a far more important role is as departmental representative both within the executive and to parliament. When it comes to judging how well a minister performs, his parliamentary role is vital. In 1964 Frank Cousins was brought in as Minister of Technology by Harold Wilson. Never having held a parliamentary seat previously he became MP for Nuneaton in January 1965, three months after his appointment to the cabinet. He lasted only two years in the job, finding parliament too difficult to handle, something noted by the Opposition who promoted a number of debates on issues within his remit; in addition, the Select Committee on Estimates issued a critical report on his Department (Headey, 1974a, p. 89).[8]

Ministers take on responsibilities for policies and programmes set by their predecessors and accumulated over decades or even centuries. Rose (1987, p. 17) suggests that the multiplication of such responsibilities gives a private-sector analogy not with a single-product company but with a conglomerate company with many products, factories and markets. Ministers of state and junior ministers might be considered as the managers of certain product lines or factory outlets. Ministers of course rely upon their civil servants for their oversight. Full cabinet ministers remain, on average, in their jobs for 28.7 months, ministers of cabinet rank for 28.3 months and junior ministers for 27.6 months; often they cannot be expected to learn much detail about many areas of their responsibility.[9] What many ministers would be more interested in is the development of policy, though even here detailed policy initiatives come from civil servants working, at best, to a plan they understand to be in the minister's mind. And his mind might have been set by directions from the prime minister or Cabinet Office. Rarely does a minister initiate a policy, see it through parliament, and then take on oversight of its implementation. Given the time frame of these three stages, each is likely to be overseen by a different minister. This has an important effect on accountability. Ministers rarely take the rap for a failed policy, since they have gone long before the policy failure is noted, and it is difficult to judge whether a policy fails because it is intrinsically bad or because of implementation failures that are the responsibility of the minister's successor.

[8] The proximate cause of his resignation was policy disagreement; see Chapter 6.
[9] Whips remain for 26.8 months.

Choosing ministers

Ministers, by convention, are also appointed by the monarch, but of course these days they are chosen by the prime minister. In recent years prime ministers have announced the appointment of ministers through the press office without consulting the monarch. There are no rules governing whom a prime minister can choose as a minister, though as they are accountable to parliament they should be drawn from it. In 1964 Wilson named Patrick Gordon Walker as his Foreign Secretary despite Gordon Walker having lost his seat at the election. Two Labour MPs stood down so that Gordon Walker and the trade union leader Frank Cousins could enter the House of Commons. However, Gordon Walker lost his by-election in January 1965 and had to stand down as Foreign Secretary. Otherwise, a prime minister might ennoble someone in order to give them a government post. For example, following the 2005 general election Andrew Adonis, special advisor to Tony Blair, was ennobled, allowing him to become Minister of State for Higher Education. Both houses of parliament are set up with the government benches facing the opposition benches, and in principle anyone sitting on the government side could be chosen as a minister. In practice, however, the prime minister will normally only draw ministers from her own party except in coalition or national governments (where ministers might be drawn from any side of parliament) of which there are no examples in the data we analyse in this book.

As we have already noted, the prime minister is responsible for all ministerial appointments. She might consult her cabinet colleagues about minor appointments in their department or ministry, though not necessarily (and she will generally allow ministers to choose their own PPS). There has been a strong convention in the Labour Party (and a weaker one in the Conservative Party) for an incoming prime minister to appoint her pre-election shadow ministers – that is, spokespeople for the Opposition – to the relevant ministerial roles, though for example Tony Blair moved several people around when he formed his cabinet in 1997. The whips on both sides of the house are also appointed by the leader of their party, and here the prime minister will be strongly advised by the Chief Whip as to whom to appoint.

Prime ministers move ministers around for a number of reasons. Some of these changes are forced upon them. Deaths and ill health cause vacancies, occasionally a minister will resign for other reasons:

for example, peers especially (if not exclusively) may leave to concentrate upon their business interests or a minister might move to a post in an international organization. Some resignations are forced exits where ministers feel they have to resign under the terms of individual responsibility. Generally speaking, such forced exits occur when a minister offers to resign following parliamentary and media pressure as a result of scandal or specific political or personal errors, and the prime minister accepts the resignation. Far more frequent are cases when ministers offer to resign but the prime minister asks them to stay and weather the storm. Occasionally a prime minister forces a reluctant minister to resign. Such resignations are the subject of Chapter 6.

In all these cases a prime minister has to reshape her cabinet. This may not have been her wish or design. A single minister resigning might entail several more changes as individuals are promoted, with perhaps one full cabinet minster being moved to another similar or more important position, a promotion into the cabinet and then some movement amongst junior posts with new people entering the government lower down. Some of these movements might be necessary to ensure that latent conflicts do not come into the open in inter-departmental conflict, or to accommodate the junior minister the full cabinet minister prefers, or simply to provide a balance within a department. At times a prime minister might choose to utilize the opportunity to reshuffle the cabinet more than necessary, to redirect priorities sooner than she had intended. Other reshuffles are more explicitly strategic from the start. The 'mid-term' reshuffle is something of a tradition, at least in the eyes of the media, as prime ministers remodel their cabinet halfway through the planned life of the government (that is, between two and three years into a term of office) to look towards the upcoming election. Ministers who have performed disappointingly might be moved on, those that have done well promoted, and some new blood from the backbenches brought into the government team. These strategic reshuffles are an important aspect of government as the prime minister attempts to set the tone and direction of her government.

Reshuffles do not always go as the prime minister wishes. Ministers will be called to Number 10 and the prime minister will thank them and ask them to stand down or to serve in another position. Sometimes these offers, when considered a demotion, are turned down, or the particular post will not appeal. Some posts are considered difficult.

Traditionally the Minister of Defence was considered problematic for Labour ministers in a party that once had a large pacifist component. The most spectacular failure of a reshuffle was Macmillan's 'night of the long knives' in July 1962 when he sacked seven full cabinet ministers, including his Chancellor of the Exchequer, and sixteen members of the government altogether in a major reshuffle that was meant to revitalize a flagging government. However, the reshuffle was portrayed as a desperate move by a failing prime minister who himself resigned over a health issue fifteen months later.

We can view the relationship between a prime minister and her minister in terms of agency or principal–agent models. The prime minister can be viewed as the principal who sets tasks for her agents, the ministers. The prime minister and her minister share many aims, but their interests are not identical. Here we introduce some strategic constraints on prime ministers' choice of ministers.

Many factors come into play when the prime minister chooses her ministers. Some of these factors form constraints upon the shape of her cabinet; others are more strategic factors about the type of personnel she wants and how these fit into the specific jobs available. How much autonomy is given to ministers and how far they are directed by the prime minister will depend in part upon her policy interests and the personalities of all the actors. Some prime ministers are more ideologically or policy-driven than others and want to get involved in the policy detail, becoming occupied and associated with specific policies. Some may want to take the lead in certain policy areas if they expect that to be rewarding in terms of personal popularity and votes. Others still prefer to delegate, either because they are less policy-driven or simply because they believe that governing involves consensus and teamwork. Prime ministers' leadership type may be to a large extent determined by whether they occupy the median position in their cabinet or whether they are cabinet or party outliers needing to force others into their way of thinking. It is notable that two prime ministers often proclaimed as 'strong leaders', Margaret Thatcher and Tony Blair, were policy outliers in their cabinets, and at times were forced to push policies against the median views of their own party (Dowding, 2008). We discuss the individual style of prime ministers in Chapter 5; here we ask, what would a prime minister, as chief executive, want from her ministers?

It is a mistake perhaps to think in terms of the ideal minister rather than the ideal cabinet. To be sure, those on the inside assert that a good minister must be able to make decisions; handle his civil servants and manage his department; read briefs quickly and take advice (Kaufman, 1997). Loyalty to the party is important, and voting against the party line is strongly correlated with MPs who have either left office, have had office pass them by, or have no desire for office (Bennedetto and Hix, 2007). A minister must be able to deal with questions in parliament, and politicians generally, and with the media, coming across well on television – this latter aspect especially in the most important posts. Should the minister be full of policy ideas? No government can push all the buttons simultaneously. The highest number of bills entered by a government in the post-war period was 98 in 1964, the lowest 24 in 2005 (though these gross figures do not take into account the complexity of bills).[10] Thus ministers must be aware that whilst they develop policies, they need to wait their turn in the legislative queue. What a prime minister wants in some portfolios is a safe pair of hands who can answer questions, manage the department, and oversee small bills for small problems produced by relatively junior civil servants (Page, 2001). However, the prime minister will also want some dynamic ministers who can develop big policy ideas, especially in problem areas or areas designated for initiatives, such as health or education. Thus the ideal cabinet will have a mix of safe hands and dynamic policy leaders.

The ideal minister would do well to have a stable and supportive family, and keep well away from financial, social and sexual scandals – though it might be the case that the dynamic personality types right for the policy entrepreneur roles are also those more prone to scandals. This is an issue we explore a little in chapters 5 and 6. The prime minister would also like a cabinet of like-minded people (most like-minded to herself), who are efficient and who get on well together. But we are considering the real world of ambitious politicians; let us not move too far into fantasy.

So these constitute some of the desiderata for a prime minister. What about the constraints? There will be politicians to whom the prime minister, no matter how much she distrusts, fears or loathes them, simply cannot avoid offering (usually senior) cabinet positions. Political parties are coalitions of people and factions. Some of those people and factions have helped push the leader to the top, others she has crawled over and defeated along the way. As Don Corleone advised his son

---

[10] Note that both years were election years.

Michael in *The Godfather*, 'keep your friends close, but your enemies closer'; a prime minister cannot afford to offend some of those she defeated along the way to the top.

Harold Wilson presided over a cabinet of political heavyweights, many of whom he feared were after the top job, and who were supported by relatively well-organized sections of the Parliamentary Labour Party who might have withdrawn support – at least from many important bills if not the government as a whole – had their factional leaders not kept places in the cabinet. Margaret Thatcher's first (1979) cabinet was certainly not one in her own image. Although she cleverly ensured that most of the major economic positions were filled by those who shared her monetarist views, she had little choice but to employ the heavyweights largely drawn from her party predecessor's administration of 1974. In July 1993 John Major was overheard describing three of his Eurosceptic ministers as 'bastards' within minutes of a confidence vote that kept him in office. Certainly he would have liked to have expelled those three from his cabinet (they were almost certainly Michael Howard, Michael Portillo and Peter Lilley), but his government could not have survived without such Eurosceptics in cabinet given that his party was so completely divided along pro- and anti-European Union lines. Indeed, the entirety of Major's seven years as Prime Minister was overshadowed by this major split within his Conservative Party. Similarly, it was unthinkable in 1997 for Tony Blair not to have had Gordon Brown in his cabinet whether he wanted to or not. To be sure, in 1997 he did want to have Brown, though their rivalry in private and public defined his government from the start; it is also clear, however, that whilst Blair was able to remove several Brown supporters from his cabinet over his years in office, it is inconceivable that he could have shifted Brown from the Treasury, let alone the cabinet. King (1994) describes ministers that cannot be kept out of the cabinet as 'big beasts of the jungle'. We consider them further in Chapter 4.

It might be thought that a chief executive would want a cabinet whose members work together well as team players, supporting each other. However, some prime ministers – Wilson is an example – seem to thrive on playing off factions against each other. Nor do they always support their ministers; sometimes the prime minister might be happy to see a minister's pet policy fail. Certainly, Wilson second-guessed some of his ministers. He used George Brown as a counterweight against the Treasury, and he kept Tony Benn in his cabinet as a man too dangerous to leave outside, while constraining him within portfolios where he judged Benn could do little damage. In other words, whilst the agency models we employ capture important elements of the hiring and firing of ministers and elements of accountability, some aspects of cabinet formation are more like coalition formation, albeit of non-equal bargainers. Some of these complex strategic considerations suggest the role of the prime minister is more that of the central figure in a kaleidoscopic series of policy coalitions.

Ministerial responsibility

Ministerial responsibility has been divided into two forms: individual ministerial responsibility and collective cabinet responsibility. The first concerns the conduct of the minister himself and his responsibilities given the role or job that his ministry involves. Collective responsibility is the doctrine that all ministers are collectively responsible for the policies and conduct of the government.

Individual ministerial responsibility

What ministers are responsible for differs a great deal. Most whips (not considered ministers in most texts), for example, have few responsibilities other than to persuade MPs to vote the right way, help ensure pairing arrangements work, and report on problems to those higher up. PPSs have responsibilities to liaise with their minister and parliament. Junior ministers will be responsible for specific tasks as will ministers of cabinet rank, whilst full cabinet ministers generally have broader responsibilities. But what do these mean in accountability terms? This has been widely studied in legal-constitutional, normative and regulatory literatures which cover the three aspects of accountability dubbed by Diana Woodhouse (1994) 'informative', 'explanatory', and 'amendatory'. The first two are concerned with informing and explaining policy and policy failures within the area for which the minister is held responsible, the last with rectifying errors. Ministers can inform parliament about the activities of their department and they can explain and justify why those activities take place. They are also expected to rectify errors, or at least to ensure, and assure parliament, that errors are being rectified. These include errors that ministers themselves bring to the attention of parliament and those brought to their attention by other monitors of government policy. These departmental errors may have nothing whatsoever to do with the minister himself, perhaps being the result of decisions taken by low-level civil servants, or problems caused by organizational or policy changes initiated by his predecessor. However, the minister in place has amendatory responsibility to try to rectify the problems and to carry the can if he fails. In terms of the pragmatics of ministerial accountability, however, none of the three aspects could be expected to take place without the fourth aspect, what Woodhouse calls 'sacrificial' responsibility. Sacrificial responsibility is the sanctioning of ministers up to and including their sacking. Sacrificial responsibility usually refers to the individual resignations resulting from scandals or problems that beset a minister – we call the set of such cases 'resignation issues' (see Chapter 6). They often, though not always, follow calls for a resignation in parliament or by parliamentarians or other important commentators in the media. They are a subset of what we call forced exits.

An exit is 'forced' if the resignation is forced on the prime minister by events of the day, though in the case of sacrificial responsibility they are also forced on the minister himself. We also include as forced exits those resignations where the minister cites personal or family reasons for resigning, as such resignations are not in the control of the prime minister (even if she welcomes them). Furthermore, such 'official' reasons for resigning can also hide other tensions or problems within the government. Deaths also constitute forced exits, as again they force the prime minister to reshuffle where otherwise she would not have. Resignations due to policy disagreement, or even personality clashes within government, are also forced exits, as they are forced on the prime minister by the resigning minister, again even if she welcomes them. However, resignations over policy do not form part of individual ministerial responsibility. Rather they come under the heading of collective responsibility; the minister resigns because he is not prepared to support some aspect of government policy, or finds it impossible to work within the government.

It is a mistake, however, to consider sacrificial responsibility as defined here as the only check upon the other aspects of ministerial responsibility. Ministers can be embarrassed through questioning and debate and there are other sanctions that affect their career. Problems can affect their future career advancement to more important ministerial posts, and they might exit sooner than otherwise through a planned reshuffle. Ministers might depart through planned exits some time after they are involved in resignation issues. Being involved in resignation issues may increase the *hazard* of a minister, that is, reduce his *durability*, even if it does not lead to an immediate forced exit. Both unforced and forced exits might be due to the activities of the minister himself and thus form part of the accountability mechanism. Whilst 'sacrificial responsibility' as a term rightly only applies to forced exits, unforced exits caused by the individual activities of ministers still form part of the accountability mechanism; that is, they can be considered part of *individual* ministerial responsibility. And ministers are well aware that even if they survive a given set of criticisms at the time, those problems are on their record and might well affect their future career. This knowledge should affect their behaviour in office.

One of the earliest statements of individual ministerial responsibility was laid out by Earl Grey in 1858:

It is a distinguishing characteristic of Parliamentary Government that it requires the powers belonging to the Crown to be exercised through Ministers, who are held responsible for the manner in which they are used ... and who are considered entitled to hold their office only while they possess the confidence of Parliament, and more especially the House of Commons. (Grey, 1969, cited in Woodhouse, 2003, p. 281)

As a doctrine, Earl Grey's statement makes absolutely clear the relationship between those issues for which the minister must account to parliament and the sacrificial aspect of individual responsibility. However, it is well recognized around Westminster that prime ministers do remove ministers who have been criticized long after the event; it is an important check upon ministerial behaviour that ministers recognize that the immediate sacrificial sanction is not the only sanction that the prime minister might demand for errors they commit.

Collective cabinet responsibility

Collective cabinet responsibility, on the other hand, says that each minister takes responsibility for the policies of the government as a whole and is expected to defend the policies of their colleagues. The beginnings of collective responsibility can be found in the eighteenth century through the practice of collusion between ministers in the advice they gave to the sovereign (Gay and Powell, 2004). Such collusive practices acted as a check on the sovereign, allowing the prime minister and the cabinet to develop and pursue specific policy agendas. Moreover, this collusion also provided protection for individual ministers, limiting the monarch's ability to single out individual ministers for blame. The convention that government ministers support government policy or resign appears as early as 1792 and was generally followed during the early part of the nineteenth century (Cox, 1994). The convention that anything a minister proposed to parliament was government policy developed during the nineteenth century and with the coming of Peel's ministry in 1841 became established practice. It was thus that Dicey identified a convention of collective ministerial responsibility that evolved in the nineteenth century which involved unanimity in the advice given to the crown (Turpin, 1993). The current practice on joint or collective responsibility was set out in a speech to parliament by Lord Salisbury during his second ministry in 1878:

For all that passes in cabinet every member of it who does not resign is absolutely and irretrievably responsible and has no right to say afterwards that he agreed in one case to a compromise, while in another he was persuaded by his colleagues . . . It is only on the principle that absolute responsibility is undertaken by every member of the cabinet, who, after a decision is arrived at, remains a member of it, that the joint responsibility of Ministers to Parliament can be upheld and one of the most essential principles of Parliamentary responsibility is established. (Ellis, 1980, p. 387)

Salisbury laid out these principles so that his ministers would not, in the language of today, brief against each other in the political clubs and at dinner parties. We can also see the principle of collective responsibility emerging through the growing strength of the party system: parliamentary coalitions are not floated so easily, the party lines are more clearly drawn, and the factions within parties recognize that they need to present a united front to the outside world. Such collective responsibility also implies solidarity with one's fellow ministers, and thus acts as a form of protection for individual ministers. Because each minister takes responsibility for the policies of the government as a whole, and so is expected to defend colleagues, all receive at least some protection should a policy within their remit be deemed to have failed. As Turpin (1993, p. 58) argues, 'Collective responsibility provides a shield for the individual minister, only rarely so emphatically withdrawn as to leave the minister no alternative but resignation.'

In this way collective responsibility means that ministers share the blame when a policy goes wrong. It also enables ministers to take difficult decisions within their own policy domain without having to take the entire risk of any public disapproval or policy failure upon themselves. This factor is very important to governments generally. Whilst the doctrine of collective responsibility is noted and most thoroughly discussed in Westminster systems,[11] it is observed in some shape or form in all parliamentary democracies:

On balance and with a few notable exceptions, the constitutional principle of collective cabinet responsibility is diligently observed as a matter of political practice... This is because collective cabinet responsibility and confidentiality are usually in the interest of all ministers – despite short-term incentives individual ministers might on occasion have to defect from them. Cabinets often have to take politically unpopular decisions, and there is comfort for ministers in the knowledge they can shelter from the fallout of these decisions under the cloak of collective responsibility. (Gallagher, Laver and Mair, 2006, p. 41)

Government changes

Although the focus of our analysis is the relationship between the prime minister and her ministers and in particular how this relationship determines the length of a minister's career, it it important to realize that hiring and firing are not the only ways in which the prime minister can influence a minister's career. Most obviously, and as discussed above, the prime minister is responsible for allocating different jobs of government to ministers. But the prime minister also has leeway to decide which policy tasks are associated with which role. Indeed the organization of policy functions is a core element of a prime minister's responsibilities and below we provide an overview of several critical changes in departmental responsibilities in the UK in the post-1945 era. Reorganization of the policy responsibilities and functions of British government falls under the Royal Prerogative which is exercised by

---

[11] For Australia see, for example, Weller (1999, 2004, 2007); for Canada Sutherland (1991); for New Zealand McLeay (1995, 2006), Palmer (2006), Palmer and Palmer (2004).

the prime minister.[12] No primary legislation is required and changes are made in the absence of an objection from either House. Indeed, in response to the question put on 6 February 2006 by Lord Stoddart of Swindon, who asked Her Majesty's Government 'whether they will issue a Green Paper on the proposed reorganisation and splitting of the Home Office, and allow for a period of public debate and consultation and the issuing of a White Paper before any Bill to implement such reorganization is presented to parliament', the Minister of State for the Home Office, Baroness Scotland of Asthal, replied unequivocally: 'questions of changes to the machinery of government are decided by the prime minister'. Note that, by contrast, it was Congress and not the US President that set up the Homeland Security Department in response to the 11 September 2001 terrorist attacks. Indeed a recent report of the House of Commons Public Administration Select Committee stated that 'it is anomalous that it is so procedurally straightforward for the prime minister to reorganize the Civil Service by amending the functions of the ministers it serves, when reorganizing other public services may often involve statutory consultation, parliamentary approval, or even primary legislation'.[13]

However, this being said, the basic structure of government has changed little in the sixty-two years we analyse. The three major departments are still recognizable – the Treasury, the Home Office, the Foreign Office – as are other departments, but some departments have disappeared and others have come into being. To give a flavour of the departmental changes over time, in Table 3.2 we list 24 cabinet posts included during Attlee's first government together with 24 posts included in Blair's final administration; these constituted the major ministries and departments of government. Table 3.2 is only illustrative, not a precise historical record.

We see several wartime posts disappearing over the period, as well as the formation of several new major departments – major at least in expenditure terms, such as Social Security. Including the prime minister, we list 24 members of the cabinet in each case, though neither man had 24 full cabinet ministers at any one time. Rather we

[12] Relatedly, in the German Federal Republic the reassignment of policy competencies ultimately falls under the *Richtlinienkompetenz* of the Chancellor according to Article 65 of the Basic Law.

[13] Seventh Report of Sessions 2006–2007 of the House of Commons Public Administration Select Committee: Machinery of Government Changes.

Table 3.2. *Comparing cabinet posts*

Attlee (1945–50)	Blair (2005–7)
Prime minister	Prime minister
Chancellor of the Exchequer	Chancellor of the Exchequer
Foreign Secretary	Foreign Secretary
Home Secretary	Home Secretary
Lord President	Lord President
Lord Chancellor	Lord Chancellor
Privy Seal	Privy Seal
Duchy of Lancaster (from 1948)	Duchy of Lancaster
Defence	Defence
Health	Health
Scotland	Scotland
Minister w/o Portfolio (short periods)	Minister w/o Portfolio
Education	Education and Employment
Agriculture and Fisheries	Agriculture, Fisheries and Food
Board of Trade	Trade
Admiralty	Chief Secretary to the Treasury
Air	Deputy Prime Minister (also Regions at this time)
Civil Aviation	Northern Ireland
Commonwealth Relations (from 1948)	Social Services
Economic Affairs	International Development
Fuel and Power	Transport
India and Burma	Wales
Labour and National Statistics	PS to Treasury (Chief Whip)
War	Minister of State for Europe

Note: These are lists of 24 posts within each cabinet that were filled during Attlee's first administration and during Blair's final administration; in neither case were they all filled.

choose these posts simply to illustrate what has remained and what has changed over time. Blair had a minister of state in cabinet all of the time, the Minister of State for Europe attached to the Foreign Office. The Chief Secretary to the Treasury was also a full cabinet minister, and Blair continued the recent tradition of having the Chief Whip in the cabinet. Apart from that, we can see eleven posts have not altered, or rather, there are eleven posts whose titles have not changed. These are the familiar big four – Prime Minister, Chancellor, Foreign and Home Secretaries – plus the sinecure titles – Privy Seal and Duchy of Lancaster – the Leaders of the two Houses, plus Defence, Health and Scotland; both prime ministers also, at least at times, had ministers without portfolio. So half the cabinet posts in the respective time periods (five and three years respectively) were the same, and two other posts seem very similar. Education took on a broader portfolio adding employment under Blair, while under Attlee it included Labour and National Statistics. This change signals that employment was not seen as such a major issue under Blair, whereas in post-war Britain getting the returning soldiers back to work was key. Agriculture and Fisheries has taken on the added title of 'Food', demonstrating that in the modern era, shifting food on to tables from farms via big food manufacturers and supermarkets is seen as a major aspect of that issue area. The Board of Trade morphed into the Department of Trade and Industry, Edward Heath amalgamating it with the Ministry of Technology in 1970 (the Ministry of Technology was a Wilson creation in 1964). The functions of the Trade Department and the Board of Trade are roughly equivalent, given the changing nature of regulatory practices over the period.

The rest of the posts largely concern different issue areas that have either become of medium- to long-term importance or signal a change in the times. Economic Affairs was used for longer-term planning and its role has been taken over by the Treasury, but the Chief Secretary to the Treasury has become a full cabinet minister, signalling the longer reach of the Treasury into all areas of policy now. India and Burma indicate the retreat from Empire and the specific goal of independence in the sub-Asian continent. We might pair that with the role of the Minister of State for Europe and how important the EU has become to the UK. International Development has also become, at times, a full cabinet post, at others subordinate to the Foreign Office. Wales has joined Scotland in having its own post, whilst, of course, Northern Ireland has been a major cabinet position since 1971 because of the Troubles and the suspension of the Stormont Government (reinstated in a new form by the Northern Ireland Act 1998). The presence of Admiralty, Air and War ministers signals the importance of the navy and air force in post-war Britain's defence of the Empire – by the end of Blair, British troops were once more engaged in foreign action in Afghanistan and Iraq. The Civil Aviation post marks the new dawn of passenger air transport, and the growing importance of air for imports; whilst Fuel and Power reflects a key issue in a post-war Britain struggling to revamp its natural resources and stoke industry on to a peacetime footing.

Social Services is a long-term department, created following the growth of the welfare state. It has been part of the Department of Health (the Department of Health and Social Security) at times, and at others a stand-alone department. Of the final two posts, the Deputy Prime Minister was a creation to reward John Prescott for securing Blair's position as Leader of the Labour Party prior to Labour coming to power. (He also presided over the Regions portfolio, a pared-down responsibility from his initial enormous Department of Environment, Transport and the Regions.) The Chief Whip has been a cabinet post for the past twenty years.

The comparison between the two prime ministers' cabinets in Table 3.2 does not show the constant tinkering at the margins over the sixty-two years, nor the departments that came and went. It does not show the various couplings and separations which often reflect passing fads or phases. For example, when it was believed that future economic growth would rely upon Britain being at the forefront of new technology, education was paired with technology and innovation. Industry pressure arguing that the educational system did not suit the needs of employers caused a union between education and employment. Nor does Table 3.2 show the departments or full cabinet responsibilities that came and went such as Prices and Consumer Protection; or minor shifts of responsibility for specific issues. Shifting responsibilities across portfolios is a tool that a prime minister might use to control ministers. A prime minister might be forced to put a particular person in her cabinet, but can shift some responsibilities around at the margins, or set up new responsibilities for a minister to create checks upon another.

It is difficult to track changing responsibilities through time in a flowchart as there have been so many and the chart soon becomes too messy to read.[14] Instead in Table 3.3 we list sixteen 'virtual' departments where responsibilities have been carried out in various different

---

[14] The changing architecture of the central government from 1964 to 1992 can be viewed at 'The Organization of Central Government Departments, 1964–1992' at www.nuffield.ox.ac.uk/politics/whitehall.

Table 3.3. *Categories of departments*

Department	Including
Prime minister	
Home	Civil Service
Foreign	Empire, Colonies, Commonwealth, EU, Overseas Development and International Development
Treasury	Chief Secretary
Paymaster	Pensions*
Other economic	Economic Affairs, Trade, Industry, Employment, Energy, Consumer Affairs, Technology, Transport, and Aviation
Environment	Works, Housing, Local Government Construction, Labour, and Regions
Agriculture	Food and Fisheries
Defence	War, Admiralty, Army, Air, and Procurement
Education	Science
Health and Welfare	Social Security, Women and Children
Scotland/Wales	
Northern Ireland	
Legal	Lord Chancellor and Attorney General
Without Portfolio**	Lord President, Privy Seal, Overlords and Duchy of Lancaster
Other minor	Arts and National Heritage
Whips	Lords of Treasury and HM Household

Notes: *Could be bundled with Treasury or 'other economic' but has taken on important other roles.

**Some of these sinecure positions are not strictly 'without portfolio', as the posts do come with specific (minor) functions. And people in those positions have often been given specific tasks by the prime minister. The Overlords also were given specific responsibilities (though they were not always sure what these were). However, it seems best to bundle these together, even though there are many cabinets with full cabinet members as Lord President, Privy Seal and Duchy of Lancaster.

guises over the years. Some of the titles on the left correspond to actual departments that have existed at some point during the sixty-two years, others suggest similar types of portfolio. And vastly different numbers of people have filled the positions within the titles on the left. As well as ministers filling some of the posts listed on the left (for example, Home Secretary, Secretary of State for Defence) we have listed actual titles of full cabinet ministers in cabinets over the period on the right-hand side of the table. We have also included some non-full-cabinet ministers under these categories (this list includes ministers of cabinet rank and junior ministers), though even in our broad categories some non-cabinet ministers might have served under senior ministers listed in a different category on the left-hand side. Table 3.3 does not, in any sense, track cabinet changes – we have placed the sinecure posts all together even though these posts are generally filled at cabinet level – rather it shows the functional nature of responsibilities which might be thought to track strategic responsibilities and have some effect upon accountability issues. What we can see in Table 3.3 is the vast range of departmental responsibilities that have been filled over the years.

With regard to the institutional apparatus that supports the chief of the executive, the role of the prime minister has not altered much although the prime minister has much greater institutional support at the end of the period than at the beginning. Attlee entered with a permanent cabinet secretariat not that different from when it was created in 1916, though it had been increased in size and depth during the Second World War (back to its First World War size). The Cabinet Office continued to grow, though it should be noted that it served the government as a whole and not just the prime minister, providing some kind of central coordinating device. The secretariat was extended and consolidated under the Conservative governments of the 1950s and 1960s, and under Macmillan we saw the beginning of what became the political section (Burch and Holiday, 1996, p. 21). Edward Heath doubled the number of senior Cabinet Office staff and set up specific units, and importantly the 24-person Central Policy Review Staff as part of his attempt to remodel Whitehall and provide greater strategic direction to government. Housed within the central complex around Downing Street, this unit provided strategic advice to the prime minister, but its staffing levels remained low (Blackstone and Plowden, 1988).

The Cabinet Office has grown since the 1970s from around 600 to over 2,000 by the 1990s, and to 2,500 by the end of Blair's government. Furthermore, under Blair the Cabinet Office tended to service the prime minister rather than the cabinet as a whole, as had been previous practice (Rentoul, 2001, p. 540), partly as Blair cut back on formal cabinet meetings (see below).

Staff numbers within the Prime Minister's Office (PMO) have also increased. From under 30 in Attlee's day to around 70 under Heath, to just over 100 under Major, numbers grew to over 200 under Blair. Special advisors, earlier numbered in ones or twos, increased under Thatcher, going up to 8 under John Major, and to 27 under Blair (Burch and Holiday, 1996; Blick, 2004; Blick and Jones, 2010).

Thatcher undid most of the structural changes introduced by Heath for long-term strategic planning, preferring that it be run through the PMO. Most controversies in recent years relating to the PMO have concerned the political offices. Prime ministers have always had political advisors around them, though the *Civil Service Yearbook* did not recognize the political office as a distinctive element in the PMO until 1983. Political advisors, and the blurring between civil servants and political appointees, are important in considering the accountability of ministers, especially if advisors take on what has traditionally been the ministerial role of directing civil servants, but without accountability for their actions reflecting back on to ministers (King, 2003; Tiernan, 2007). Whilst this mix has caused some problems in the UK, responsibility, or so we will argue, has generally reflected back onto the relevant ministers, including the prime minister, though not always as directly or critically as some might have wished.

4 | *Who serves in government and how long do they last?*

The units of analysis in this book are ministers, in particular British ministers and the length of time that they serve in their posts. Why should we think of the length of time that British ministers serve in their posts as an important political variable? The starting point of our analysis is that British ministers are essentially career politicians. Becoming a minister represents the pinnacle of political careers that may have begun several decades earlier. Once ministers attain such high position they are in general reluctant to return to the back benches. Our analysis of political careers in the UK complements similar studies carried out on the careers of US Congressmen. Amongst these studies, Groseclose and Krehbiel (1994) look at the decisions of politicians in the 102nd Congress to retire when faced with a one-off 'golden parachute', and Diermeier, Keane and Merlo (2005) provide a more general framework within which to study how pecuniary and non-pecuniary incentives affect the career choices of US politicians. Recently, the financial post-career rewards of British politicians have been studied by Eggers and Hainmueller (2009), and Merlo, Galasso, Landi and Mattozzi (2010) provide detailed evidence of the career choices of Italian legislators from 1945–2008.

Our focus is on a particular variable of interest: conditional upon the length of government in which they serve we ask whether the background characteristics of ministers affect their length of service. Later in the book, we build upon these estimates to explore whether and how the length of time that ministers serve reflects the strategic incentives of prime ministers, the way in which they manage their cabinets, and how they utilize information about their ministers that may not have been available at the time of the ministers' appointment.

Here we present some of the main data that we will use to explore our hypothesis that personal characteristics affect ministerial longevity. These consist of a detailed account of who serves in British government and how long they last. Analysing these raw data, as we will argue in this chapter, allows us not only to assess the validity of our key hypothesis, which we do later in the book, but also to address important questions about power in British politics. Specifically, we ask whether background characteristics of ministers, fixed at the time they enter government, influence how long they serve.

The question is simple: if we know the fixed characteristics of ministers at the time at which they take office, can we predict how long they will in fact remain in office? As we will show in this chapter, gender, education, and age play strong roles in determining how long a minister will last upon being appointed to office; as we will show, this result holds even when conditioning on aspects of the governments that these ministers serve.

Who serves

In this chapter we analyse data gathered on all ministers who served in British government between 1945 and 2007. In our data each minister is coded according to rank and the government and prime minister under which he serves.[1] For each minister in our data we obtained a large number of individual characteristics. These are the individual traits of ministers that are fixed at the time of their entry into the government. For example, we code each minister according to their date of birth, thus allowing us to assess the effect on the length of their tenure of their age when entering government. It is clear that age may be an important determinant of how long a minister serves as it may be correlated with experience and also perhaps arguably less observable traits (such as wisdom). But age may also be an important conditioning variable when assessing performance and tenure. Those who enter the government relatively late in their careers may behave differently from those who enter government relatively early. Losing a position early on in a ministerial career, when one might be expected to bounce back quickly, is not the same as losing one's job when in the twilight of a political career. But age is not the only individual characteristic that can have both a direct and an indirect effect. To

---

[1] If they appear in Butler and Butler (2000, 2006, 2011), then virtually all ministers as we define them are included in our sample. Reasons for exclusion include lack of information on age or inconsistencies in Butler and Butler that we were not able to rectify from other sources.

account for gender-specific career choices and types of performance we code for gender too; we also consider whether a minister is a peer of the realm or not as this allows us to control, in a very crude form, how wealth (in this case inherited wealth) can determine the length of time that a minister serves.

Power relations in British government

Utilizing this data allows us to answer pertinent questions about power relations in parliamentary democracies. Do exogenous characteristics of individuals who serve in parliament affect the likelihood that they will eventually serve in government and, upon doing so, how long they then serve? Such questions go to the heart of key issues concerning how representative a democracy is. Elite theory, developed by economists, political scientists and sociologists writing in the nineteenth century, claims democracy to be a facade: established elites maintain power whatever the political systems; rule by the many is impossible.

The elite theorists differed in their views as to the mechanism by which elites maintained control. Pareto studied the statistical distribution of property and wealth and claimed that in all societies across ages the concentration of these factors amongst an elite was a 'social law' (Pareto, 1935). Michels (1915/1958), on the other hand, was more interested in the concentration of political power. He believed that elites controlled the vital organs of parliamentary democracy, namely the party organizations, and that popular control of these organizations was a myth. His analysis was based mainly on a single case, that of the German Socialist Party. Like other socialist and social democratic parties, the German Socialists claimed that decision-making authority lay with the party conference which was, ostensibly, the delegate of the broader party membership. Michels claimed, however, that the sovereignty of conference was a facade, as key decisions were made not by the party congress, to which the party's constitution granted decision-making authority, but rather within the party caucus (or *Fraktion*) in the Reichstag.

A different mechanism was explored by Mosca (1896/1939). He believed that all power was hereditary. Mosca wrote that 'every class displays the tendency to become hereditary, in fact if not in law'. Thus, although constitutionally all citizens are equal and may stand for public office, in practice power is wielded by a few. In particular, Mosca highlighted the disproportional distribution of wealth as a source of wider political and social power wielded by an elite.

Does the evidence support the contentions of the elite theorists? Michels, Mosca, and especially Pareto did provide evidence that supported their theories, but the techniques available for identifying the social and political laws that they claimed existed were fairly rudimentary by today's standards. In contrast to the elaborate models of strategic interaction used by political analysts today, Michels' theory boiled down to a simple claim: the mass did not have the abilities to understand complex decision-making and would gladly delegate to experts: they had what Michels described as 'a psychological need for leadership'.

Recent work has explored this claim. Dewan and Myatt (2007) develop a model of strategic interaction between rational agents. Underlying their analysis is a coordination game played by a mass of party activists each of whom advocates one of two policies. Party success hinges upon one or other of these policies attaining the support of a critical mass of activists. If this does not occur then the party is seen to split and fail. Such a coordination problem has a simple resolution if one or other policy allows activists to attain higher payoffs. For added realism, however, the authors allow for uncertainty in the (party-wide) payoffs associated with these policies. Within this context Dewan and Myatt contrast two different institutional environments. In one, activists gather at a party conference to discuss the merits of policy, with each receiving a (private) signal of the party mood. Within that context they consider that such a 'conference' might be guided by an elite perhaps represented by an individual or an oligarchy. Under certain conditions the views of an elite could provide a focal point around which the party can coalesce. Although the policy prescriptions of the elite do not accurately reflect the party's needs, Dewan and Myatt were able to show precise conditions under which the sovereignty of conference would then be transferred to such an elite.

Mosca's work and its implications for the study of political power have also been revisited. Dal Bo, Dal Bo and Snyder (2009) analyse data for the US Congress from 1789 to 1996 and ask whether there is a hereditary basis in Democratic politics. Using this data they examine whether having a relative serve in Congress increases the chance of being elected, and so address the question of whether power really does beget power. They present a wealth of descriptive data that supports the hunch that this is in fact the case, exploring the dynastic nature of many congressional careers. However, to some extent, it is unsurprising that the sons and daughters of congressmen are also likely to serve; just as the sons and daughters of doctors and butchers are more likely than the average citizen to pursue these careers so also the sons and daughters of the political class are more likely than the average citizen to enter politics. Dal Bo et al. then compare a 'dynastic bias', measured as the proportion of the population in the same profession as their father, weighted by the size of the profession, across different occupations. They show that the dynastic bias is considerably higher amongst the political class than elsewhere. Moreover, and what is perhaps particularly surprising about this fact, is that congressmen, unlike doctors and butchers, are elected. So it is not just that the offspring of politicians are more likely to choose a political career, the data also suggest that citizens are more likely to select such offspring to be representative of their concerns.

Does power beget power? And if so why? Dal Bo et al. push further to explore the question: 'do political dynasties exist because some families are somehow more politically able or talented than others or is political power self-perpetuating?' The problem faced when trying to explore dynastic relations is that factors that may relate the political career of a descendant to that of his or her parents may be common to other would-be politicians. For example, it is possible, even likely, that voters elect to Congress members from the same family because they share a set of skills that voters deem desirable. If this were so, then the observed correlation between the election of the parent and that of her offspring would be spurious: the son or daughter would likely have been able to make her own political career without the springboard of having had a previous relative serve in Congress. It is thus difficult to identify the parameter of interest – namely the increase in the likelihood of serving in Congress *that is due to* a member of the same family having previously served – as we do not observe the relevant counterfactual: what would have happened if the said congressman had no ancestors or relatives who previously were elected to the same institution. To get at the relevant counterfactual, Dal Bo et al. use a regression discontinuity design (RDD): they look at the relative likelihood of descendants entering Congress from amongst a sample of candidates involved in close congressional races. Some of these contestants won their congressional race, albeit marginally, whereas others narrowly missed out. On all observable factors that affect their election these contestants can be seen as almost identical. Using the parlance of the experimental literature, some (the winners) received the treatment (and so went to Congress) whereas others did not: within the narrow band that distinguishes victory from defeat, the assignment can be seen as random. Using this quasi-experimental design Dal Bo et al. find that, evaluated at the narrow threshold that distinguishes winners from losers, the offspring of those who served in Congress had a 5 per cent higher chance of entering Congress. The analysis thus suggests that the presence of political dynasties does not merely reflect differences in ability across families.

In contrast to that study, our analysis focuses specifically on executive politics, namely the tenure of those who serve at the highest levels of British politics. Might we also find evidence that exogenous characteristics of individuals, fixed at the time they enter government, have an effect on how long they serve? A recent study by Gagliarducci and Paserman (2008) suggests that this may in fact be so. They analysed the tenure of directly elected mayors in Italian municipalities. Under the system of local government in Italy the mayor, although directly elected, can survive in office only so long as s/he maintains the confidence of the elected assembly: s/he can be forced out of office by a vote of no confidence supported by the assembly. The authors ask whether female mayors are more likely to face early termination of their spell than their male counterparts. They find that this is indeed so: the probability of early termination of the legislature is between 3 and 5 per cent higher when the head of the executive is female than when it is run by a male. This result is robust to the inclusion of a wide range of controls; and the estimated effects are larger, moreover, when performing an RDD similar to that utilized by Dal Bo et al. as described above.

Our aim here is to introduce our data and to ask similar explorative questions that allow us to assess whether background characteristics – including gender – of those who serve in office affect how long they serve. As in the studies mentioned already, identifying these effects is not straightforward. There are many variables that may confound the relationship between the background characteristics of those who serve and the length of their tenure. Here there is an additional concern. Because ministers serve in government as part of a governing team it is hard to unpick the individual effect of a characteristic be it age, sex, or experience assigned to an individual from the effect of the same

Table 4.1. *Definition of variable and descriptive statistics*

Variable	Definition	Mean (Std. Dev.)
Tenure	Ministerial tenure in months by government. Failure is defined as leaving government at least two weeks before the end of government. There are no left-censored variables. Right-censoring occurs when someone is still in post two weeks before the end of a government term. Ministers who fail during the first two weeks of government are dropped.	27.81 (16.15)
Public school	Dummy variable equal to 1 if attended public school and 0 otherwise.	0.56
Oxbridge	Dummy variable equal to 1 if attended university at Oxford or Cambridge and 0 otherwise.	0.46
Age	Age in years at the start of ministerial spell.	49.40 (8.63)
Female	Dummy variable equal to 1 if female and 0 otherwise.	0.08
Some experience	Dummy variable equal to 1 if a minister has served under previous governments and 0 otherwise.	0.58
Experience in years	Years of experience in previous governments at the start of ministerial spell.	2.55 (3.30)
Noble	Dummy variable equal to 1 if unelected peer and 0 otherwise.	0.21
Cabinet ministers	Dummy variable equal to 1 if cabinet minister and 0 otherwise.	0.16
Ministers of cabinet rank	Dummy variable equal to 1 if minister of cabinet rank and 0 otherwise.	0.29
Junior ministers	Dummy variable equal to 1 if junior minister and 0 otherwise.	0.36
Whips and members of HM Household	Dummy variable equal to 1 if Whip and member of HM Household and 0 otherwise.	0.19
Majority	Majority is defined as the share of the house commanded by the governing party in percentages.	55.36 (4.58)
Labour	Dummy variable equal to 1 if prime minister belongs to the Labour Party and 0 otherwise.	0.47
Term	Term currently being served by the prime minister. When we condition on this variable in the regression analysis we use two dummies.	
Prime minister	Twelve prime minister identifiers. When we condition on this variable in the regression analysis we use eleven dummies.	

Notes: The source of information is Butler and Butler (2000). There are 2,647 spells in total.

characteristics evaluated at the group level. Put simply, whilst a minister's tenure may reflect gender or experience there may be fixed characteristics of the government that he serves that can have an independent effect on the likelihood that he remains in post. One such factor, the preferences and managerial style of the prime minister, is discussed more fully and analysed in subsequent chapters. But in general the characteristics of those who serve alongside a minister can indirectly determine the length of time that he serves in post and this is the effect which we explore. Of course, and as mentioned above, were we to find that certain characteristics are associated with longer tenure then this might be because the same characteristics are associated with political ability or talent. Later on we will attempt to distinguish between these connections, but for now we merely seek to evaluate the relationship between the characteristics of individuals that are fixed at the time of their entry into the government and the length of time that they remain in office.

Ministerial characteristics

Table 4.1 provides a basic definition of each of the variables concerning our individual characteristics that we will use in our analysis and provides basic descriptive statistics for the whole sample of ministers who have served in British government since 1945.

Over the period of our analysis some 1,145 people have been ministers (548 Conservatives and 605 Labour, with 8 people holding positions under both party labels). Of these only 108 have been women. Over that time there have been 414 full cabinet ministers, 779 ministers of state, 944 junior ministers and 510 whips making 2,647 ministerial spells.[2]

Until the Blair government, the number of female ministers ranged from 2 per cent of the government during the premiership of Macmillan to 8 per cent under the Major government. There was a relatively low number of female ministers even under the Thatcher administration. During her first administration in 1979 only 3 per cent of ministers were female; the figure rose to 6 per cent in her subsequent administrations. A big change occurred under Blair. In his first

---

[2] The numbers in the latter four categories of observations of ministers is larger than the number of people since many people have had positions at various levels and during several administrations. Thus we have 2,647 ministerial spells whilst only 1,145 people have been ministers.

Table 4.2. *Average characteristics of ministers by government*

Variables	Attlee 1945–50		Attlee 1950–1		Churchill 1951–5		Eden 1955		Eden 1955–7	
	Mean	Std.D.	Mean	Std.D.	Mean	Std.D.	Mean	Std.D.	Mean	Std
Observed tenure in months	38.53	17.59	17.72	5.36	32.33	13.15	1.55	0.09	16.28	5
Public school	0.32		0.35		0.91		0.93		0.91	
Oxbridge	0.25		0.30		0.64		0.66		0.68	
Age	51.21	10.82	51.92	10.93	48.92	9.41	49.89	8.46	48.74	8
Female	0.03		0.02		0.02		0.01		0.02	
Some experience	0.23		0.77		0.25		0.95		0.84	
Experience in years	1.03	2.11	3.72	3.23	1.42	2.97	3.96	3.48	3.23	3.
Noble	0.16		0.21		0.23		0.27		0.22	
Labour	Yes		Yes		No		No		No	
Observations	117		92		106		82		99	

Variables	Wilson 1974		Wilson 1974–6		Callaghan 1976–9		Thatcher 1979–83		Thatcher 1983–7	
	Mean	Std.D.	Mean	Std.D.	Mean	Std.D.	Mean	Std.D.	Mean	Std
Observed tenure in months	6.86	0.91	16.36	4.15	32.34	10.73	38.54	14.71	38.46	14
Public school	0.25		0.24		0.24		0.79		0.79	
Oxbridge	0.33		0.34		0.34		0.58		0.58	
Age	50.59	9.06	49.74	9.17	49.63	9.60	48.31	7.64	48.27	7
Female	0.06		0.08		0.07		0.03		0.03	
Some experience	0.50		0.83		0.83		0.38		0.38	
Experience in years	2.17	2.55	2.39	2.60	2.89	2.63	1.33	2.46	1.31	2
Noble	0.16		0.19		0.18		0.19		0.20	
Labour	Yes		Yes		Yes		No		No	
Observations	102		117		123		134		133	

Note: See Table 4.1 for the definition of variables.

	Macmillan 1957–9		Macmillan 1959–63		Douglas-Home 1963–4		Wilson 1964–6		Wilson 1966–70		Heath 1970–4	
	an	Std.D.	Mean	Std.D.	Mean	Std.D.	Mean	Std.D.	Mean	Std.D.	Mean	Std.D
	)8	9.55	31.51	14.93	11.56	2.01	16.42	3.38	36.77	16.74	32.28	15.46
	)0		0.84		0.84		0.33		0.31		0.85	
	58		0.65		0.66		0.30		0.31		0.65	
	36	7.46	47.39	7.17	48.36	7.33	52.90	8.70	50.38	9.66	47.07	7.51
	)2		0.03		0.02		0.07		0.07		0.02	
	73		0.59		0.89		0.17		0.67		0.33	
	)6	3.45	2.90	3.44	4.67	4.56	0.70	1.73	1.29	1.55	1.49	3.01
	26		0.23		0.25		0.17		0.15		0.24	
	No		No		No		Yes		Yes		No	
	98		132		95		116		151		123	

	Thatcher 1987–90		Major 1990–2		Major 1992–7		Blair 1997–2001		Blair 2001–5		Blair 2005–7	
	an	Std.D.	Mean	Std.D.	Mean	Std.D.	Mean	Std.D.	Mean	Std.D.	Mean	Std.D.
	33	13.351	16.24	1.73	40.24	18.52	35.53	14.18	37.82	12.92	22.94	5.74
	75		0.76		0.69		0.31		0.25		0.17	
	55		0.53		0.48		0.27		0.26		0.22	
	45	8.07	48.52	8.08	48.62	8.30	5 0.58	7.04	50.03	7.86	51.11	8.58
	)6		0.08		0.08		0.24		0.31		0.30	
	67		0.94		0.62		0.03		0.63		0.74	
	71	3.83	5.47	4.32	3.88	4.44	0.00	0.00	2.06	1.82	3.68	2.93
	22		0.21		0.19		0.21		0.21		0.20	
	No		No		No		Yes		Yes		Yes	
	141		109		160		156		140		122	

administration, one quarter of the government posts were allocated to women, and the allocation rose to just over 30 per cent in the second Blair administration.

Of all the ministerial spells 552 have been filled by unelected peers. The average age of those on the payroll has remained about the same at around fifty, or just below, over the period. Blair, although the youngest serving prime minister, and more liberal in his appointment of women, did not alter the average age of government members.

In all, our analysis spans 22 terms from the first Attlee administration until the end of Tony Blair's third term.[3] These include 10 Labour governments and 12 Conservative governments. Table 4.2 provides some summary statistics of the attributes of ministers in our sample by the government in which they served. We observe, for example, that one quarter of Attlee's first administration in 1945 had been to either Oxford or Cambridge whereas nearly 70 per cent of those serving in Macmillan's government of 1957 had attended one or other of these universities. In the same government 90 per cent of ministers had attended public school[4] whereas in the Callaghan government of 1976–79 and the Blair government of 2001 the equivalent figure is around 25 per cent.

A good way of summarizing the information in Table 4.2 is to focus on the differences between Labour and Conservative governments. The mean observed tenure for Conservative ministers is 28 months, whereas for Labour ministers the corresponding figure is 27 months. There is quite a large variation in education between Conservative and Labour administrations. On average 81 per cent of Conservative ministers have attended public school and 60 per cent of Conservative ministers have been to Oxbridge. This compares with an average of 28 per cent of Labour ministers with a public school education, with 31 per cent of Labour ministers having been to Oxbridge.[5] Another

---

[3] From now on, prime ministers are excluded from the sample.

[4] Non-British readers should note that in the UK a 'public school' is a private school; publicly funded schools are called 'state schools'.

[5] It is also worth noting that the distinctions are maintained at full cabinet level. Whereas only half of Attlee's initial twenty ministers had attended university (five going to Oxbridge), twenty of Major's initial twenty-two went to university (seventeen to Oxbridge). It is also worth noting that it was not unusual in some of the early Conservative administrations for all the cabinet ministers to have been to public schools. Indeed ten of Eden's eighteen-member cabinet had been to Eton, as had six of Thatcher's first cabinet (and two of Attlee's had also been to Eton). See Butler and Butler, 2000, p. 71.

interesting difference in the partisan composition of governments is that 23 per cent of Conservative ministers are nobles, which compares with only 18 per cent of Labour ministers. On average 64 per cent of Conservative ministers have previous ministerial experience when entering government (the average experience of a Conservative minister being three years). This compares with 53 per cent of Labour ministers who have previous experience (the average experience of a Labour minister being two years).

Other features revealed the slightly falling level of public school education for both Labour and Conservative ministers over time, and the slight fall in average age. Average age of an incoming administration with new party colours is, unsurprisingly, lower than the average age of an administration that has been in power over several terms. But these differences are marginal to say the least. The average experience in years of ministers also varies from a low of 1.03 years for the incoming Attlee administration in 1945 to a high of 5.47 in Major's first administration.[6] There is no trend discernable here, and experience varies largely with how long each party has been in or out of power.

How long do ministers last?

Our main variable of interest is the length of time that ministers serve in post. Table 4.3 presents mean length of observed tenure and other average characteristics of our sample of ministers by the rank of the minister.[7] The mean observed tenure is longer the further up the ministerial ladder you climb but these differences are not very pronounced. On average a cabinet minister serves two and a half months longer than does a government whip. However, there are larger differences in the personal characteristics of ministers at different ranks. Cabinet ministers are older on average, some nine years older than junior ministers, indicating that seniority brings its rewards in the British system of government. There are also differences to be found in the level of education at each ministerial rank. There is a positive correlation between rank and education; higher-ranked ministers are more likely

---

[6] Major's second administration drops to 3.88 years which is still on the high side overall.
[7] See note 2.

Table 4.3. *Average tenure and characteristics of ministers by ministerial rank*

Variables	Cabinet ministers		Ministers of cabinet rank		Junior ministers		Whips and members of HM Household	
	Mean	Std.D.	Mean	Std.D.	Mean	Std.D.	Mean	Std.D.
Observed tenure in months	28.67	16.39	28.31	16.41	27.56	15.67	26.80	16.42
Public school	0.66	0.47	0.61	0.49	0.54	0.50	0.47	0.50
Oxbridge	0.56	0.50	0.50	0.50	0.43	0.50	0.36	0.48
Age	55.15	7.17	51.04	7.68	46.49	7.85	47.60	9.57
Female	0.06	0.24	0.08	0.26	0.10	0.30	0.10	0.30
Some experience	0.88	0.33	0.72	0.45	0.47	0.50	0.36	0.48
Experience in years	6.08	4.03	3.34	3.37	1.31	1.87	0.78	1.56
Noble	0.18	0.38	0.24	0.43	0.12	0.33	0.33	0.47
Observations	414		779		944		510	

Note: See Table 4.1 for the definition of variables.

to have been educated at public school and to have gone to Oxbridge. It is also noticeable that the average level of previous experience is six and a half years for a cabinet minister, three and a half years for a minister of cabinet rank, one year and four months for a junior minister, and less than one year for a whip. Finally, our data show that nobles are overrepresented at lower levels of government in comparison to higher posts. This is due to government needing representation for departments in the upper house but being reluctant to have peers as full cabinet ministers.

The focus solely on exogenous attributes fixed at the time of a minister's appointment might to some extent be misleading. Of course ministers enter government (usually) having a well-developed political career. In terms of attributes attained during the minister's political career, we focus attention on the experience of being in government that each minister brings with him.[8] Much of the literature on

---

[8] We coded for experience in two ways. First, an experience variable measuring the years of ministerial experience in previous governments at the start of a spell. Second, a variable (some experience) coded 0 on first appointment and 1 for subsequent appointments in any later government term. The 'experience'

ministerial turnover highlights experience as an indicator of ministerial quality and this might lead one to expect that experienced ministers have a greater capacity for survival. It has long been noted that the average level of experience amongst British ministers is lower than that in other countries (Dogan and Campbell, 1957, pp. 313–45; Williams, 1964, p. 206; Herman, 1975). The reasons given are usually that the unstable coalitional politics of multi-party government means that factions must be kept happy and prime ministers have less control over whom to select and deselect for their cabinets. The British prime minister must also select to keep factions in her party happy and may be forced to choose powerful colleagues for major positions and to choose some of their allies for junior positions in their departments. But the British prime minister still has much greater control than her foreign counterparts over the selection and deselection process, and can certainly seize upon difficulties a minister has faced over time to usher him discreetly to the door. Commentators have often bemoaned the fact of lower experience amongst British ministers in comparison to other countries, though Huber and Martinez-Gallardo (2004, pp. 46–7) make the crucial point that experience is not everything, and certainly we would not find an unchanging cabinet desirable. Nobody has yet modelled the optimal level of cabinet experience. Dewan and Dowding (2005) have demonstrated that getting rid of ministers is a way of weeding out bad ones – at least ones that detrimentally affect government popularity. But other factors may be at work.

One might expect that MPs with experience would be more welcomed into government than ones without. Controlling for age and experience might surely demonstrate the credentials of prospective ministers. The only reasons not to take into account experience might be that a prime minister prefers softer hitters, or discounts those who have had jobs at junior levels but did not progress to higher office because of a lack of skills. Rank within government should therefore be a mark of ability and indeed we find that higher ministerial rank increases a minister's durability. We do, however, find one surprising result. We find evidence that ministers with previous experience

variable was insignificant when the 'some experience' variable was included, so when we refer to experienced ministers we mean those who have served a spell in a previous government. Newly appointed ministers are those appointed in the current term of government.

of government have higher hazard rates than ministers without such experience. Whilst this finding may simply be a reflection of some 'natural' wastage – the longer one has been a minister the more likely one is to go – it is not age-related and such a finding does not fit well with the argument that British government suffers from having less experienced ministers.

Hazard rates and survivor functions

The precise question addressed in our statistical analysis is 'what is the likelihood at any point in time that a ministerial spell will end, given the time elapsed since the minister's appointment?' Whilst our unit of analysis is then a ministerial spell, similar questions have been asked about how long governments survive once they are inaugurated in office. The techniques we use are the same as those used to analyse those questions (see King, Alt, Burns and Laver (1990)). The key question in that literature is whether the fixed attributes of governments influence how long they last when considering the random shocks that may affect them. As in that literature it is useful to draw a distinction between the duration of a ministerial spell and a minister's durability. The former is a direct measure of how long the minister serves, the latter refers to inferences we can draw about the expected length of a ministerial spell once we take account of the minister's background characteristics. The key factor which concerns us is, relatedly, to account for the stochastic element of ministerial tenure – a minister's career is subject to unforeseen shocks – whilst considering that a minister has some attributes, such as age and/or experience, fixed at the time of his entry into government, that may make him more durable.

To see why an analysis that did not simultaneously account for both attributes and events might lead to misguided inferences being made consider a situation where we observed two subsequent but different administrations: in the first ministers were predominantly male, whilst in the second ministers were predominantly female. If the average chance of survival were found to be higher in the first administration it would be tempting to conclude that, upon appointment, a male member of cabinet has a higher chance of survival. But such a claim could be erroneous. For one (and as we explore more fully below), gender difference may relate to group effects – if male members of cabinet are more likely to serve alongside male members – rather than to individual effects. However, an additional factor that we need to take into consideration is not only how long ministers survive but also the events that provide the context for their tenure. A minister who serves in an administration that has to deal with an economy affected by a major international financial crisis may be more vulnerable than one serving when the economy is less affected by international events (we explore similar claims in Chapter 7). Luckily, however, the class of statistical models known as duration models, introduced by Cox (1972) and now widely used in political science, allows us to deal with these claims. The basic idea, which we elaborate on below, is to take into consideration a baseline hazard rate of termination (which we also define below) that incorporates the stochastic element of the length of a ministerial career that may be due to unforeseen shocks. The shape of this duration function may be unknown. For example, it may be that the arrival rate of shocks that may lead to the premature end of a ministerial career is constant, or it may be increasing or decreasing over time, and at different rates at different points in time. The statistical model we use, known as the Cox proportional hazards model, allows us to abstract from this issue. The assumption we make in implementing this model is that a baseline hazard, whatever its shape, shifts proportionally according to the fixed characteristics of ministers and the governments they serve. Later we will provide some evidence to support this assumption.

There are a number of features which one would wish to take account of in such analysis. Our first and primary concern is to analyse the effect of individual characteristics, such as educational background and ministerial experience, upon the length of time which a minister serves. We treat these features as fixed at the time when a minister enters a government. Thus our first set of ministerial characteristics are those which ministers attain prior to embarking upon their political career or which are unrelated to anything done during that career. In addition we estimate the effects of characteristics which ministers attain during their political career such as experience in government and ministerial rank. There are different channels via which these background characteristics can influence ministerial tenure. We can think of these characteristics as having both a direct and an indirect effect upon ministerial tenure. The direct effect comes through the fact that ministerial characteristics are related to the options which ministers have outside of politics. If a minister is under stress or pressure to resign, the value of his 'outside options' might influence the decision whether to stay or to quit. Higher education and a network of acquaintances in high places may then lead to greater opportunities outside of government, and a minister who is under pressure, but who has career opportunities outside of politics, may not wish to stick around. On the other hand, educational background may help a minister to survive. Informal networks based upon acquaintances made at school and university may provide some protection for a minister during times of trouble.

The indirect effects are due to the relationship between ministerial characteristics and ministerial performance. What it takes to be an able minister is open to much debate,[9] but it is likely that ability is related to ministerial characteristics. For example, better-educated ministers may be more able at handling their civil servants or even the dispatch box. There is no better tuition for facing the House of Commons than debating at the Oxford Union: Edward Heath when first elected was not awestruck, recalling later 'when I first went to the House of Commons, in 1950, I felt I was coming home' (Walter, 1984, p. 11, cited in Paxman, 2002, p. 53). Experience may also relate to an ability to perform one's job. We elaborate more fully on this particular channel, linking attributes to tenure via performance, in Chapter 7. Here we concentrate on establishing an empirical relationship between characteristics of ministers fixed at the time of their entry into office and the duration of their subsequent service.

Our analysis focuses upon the effects of ministerial attributes and political factors upon the length of time a minister serves in government. We analyse the length of time that elapses from when a minister enters government until he leaves or the government terminates. A minister leaves the government following an individual resignation or following a reshuffle. We treat the end of a government term as occurring when there is either an election or a change of prime minister. We treat the starting day for each minister as occurring two weeks from the day the government is formed, thus allowing for a period during which the prime minister might shuffle her cabinet.[10] Similarly

---

[9] See Headey (1974a, 1974b) for discussion of what makes able ministers.

[10] These days the post-election shuffle rarely takes more than a couple of days but in the past shuffling the cabinet was a more leisurely affair.

we censor everybody two weeks before the end of government just to avoid problems generated by coding errors either in the end or beginning of governments. The unusual events of the pre-election period and immediate aftermath are thus excluded in order for us to analyse the systematic effects on ministerial duration.[11]

Due to the censoring problem, the statistical approach used in duration analysis proves useful. The Cox proportional hazards model assumes that the duration function may take any form, so excluding the beginning or end of government is unlikely to bias our analysis as long as the proportionality assumption is correct.[12] The hazard rate is the ratio of the probability that a ministerial spell of duration T is terminated within the interval between t and t' conditional upon it not occurring previously, to the length of the relevant time interval. It is useful to explore the hazard rate, which we write as $\lambda(t)$. This is obtained by taking the limit

$$\lambda(t) = \lim_{t' \to t} \frac{Prob(t \leq T < t'|T \geq t)}{t' - t}.$$

A related concept is the survivor function which is minus the logarithm of the integrated hazard rate. Writing the survivor function as $G(t)$ we obtain

$$Log\ G(t) = -\int_0^t \lambda(\tau)d\tau \Leftrightarrow G(t) = exp\left(-\int_0^t \lambda(\tau)d\tau\right).$$

This expression provides a useful way of graphically illustrating and exploring the relationship between individual characteristics of interest and the observed tenure of ministers.

To begin, it is useful to explore the whole sample. Despite the common perception that ministerial tenure is precarious, we find that a typical ministerial spell will be rather long, with 75 per cent of

---

[11] We chose this rule since Butler and Butler (2000) report different end dates for ministers following a new government forming with its usual reshuffle. Some are given as ending just before the new government forms, some with the reshuffle. Some whips resign before the election. However, all these are on a par. We believe there are no cases of genuine resignation other than as part of the general clear out and reshuffle during the last two weeks of government and our results are not affected at all by taking all ministers' spells up to their reported duration.

[12] In fact, we cannot reject the null hypothesis that this is the case.

ministerial appointments lasting over 35 months.[13] We also present Kaplan–Meier survivor functions for ministers with different individual attributes.

Education effects

In Figure 4.1 we explore whether the education of ministers affects how long they serve in government. Recall from Table 4.2 that the number of those educated at public school is significantly higher in Conservative administrations than in Labour ones. Do these educational effects influence the expected tenure of these ministers? In Figure 4.1a we explore the survivor function for those who did and those who did not go to public school. At a glance it is clear that, in terms of their survival, nothing much distinguishes the cohort of ministers who have attended public school from those who have not.

What about other bastions of educational privilege? Does having been to Oxford or Cambridge have an effect on a minister's ability to survive? Figure 4.1b shows the survival function for those who have been to either of these universities in the heavier line. Here the effects are more pronounced. After the first eighteen or so months in office have passed, those with Oxbridge backgrounds appear to be more durable. For example, evaluated at 40 months in office, around 75 per cent of those who have been to Oxbridge are still in office, whereas just over 60 per cent of those who have not been to these universities remain. This provides some evidence that those who have received an elite education prosper for longer. However, here we cannot distinguish whether this is due to their education, their underlying ability, or other factors such as socialization. Moreover, as we have seen, and as investigation of Table 4.2 reveals, the percentages of ministers with Oxbridge backgrounds in Conservative and Labour government differ. They are around 30 per cent for most Labour administrations and at least double that in most Conservative ones. Furthermore there are also differences within Labour governments and within Conservative governments. For example 65 per cent of Churchill's post-war administration had Oxbridge educations, while only 48 per cent of John Major's government attended these universities. Thus whilst the graphical evidence suggests the existence of educational effects, we will need to explore this more deeply in subsequent analysis.

---

[13] This picture of ministerial stability prevails if each government is analysed separately, though we do not report these results here.

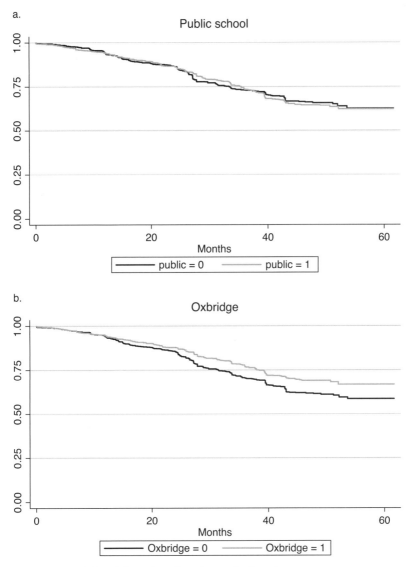

Figure 4.1. Ministerial survivor function and education

Effects of gender and other characteristics

In Figure 4.2 we look at the effect of gender. As we saw in Table 4.2 the ratio of female to male ministers has been very low in the post-war era, and only recently, under the Blair governments, have we seen a

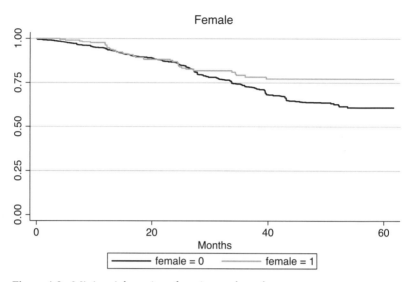

Figure 4.2. Ministerial survivor function and gender

more representative government. Of course this is just one measure of existing political inequalities. Such an effect would be compounded if, in addition to having fewer women in office, those women who attain office also serve shorter spells as ministers. The evidence does not suggest, however, that this is in fact the case. Beyond roughly two months in office, female ministers have a higher chance of survival than their male counterparts. Whereas 75 per cent of women who serve in government survive a full five-year term, just over 60 per cent of their male colleagues do likewise.

Another variable of interest reflects the level of experience that a minister brings to office. As a direct measure we use whether ministers have previous experience of government when entering office. Here the effects, displayed in Figure 4.3a, are somewhat surprising. Those who upon entering government have previously served in office have a higher hazard rate than those who enter government without such experience. Whereas 75 per cent of those without prior experience survive 40 months in office, the figure is closer to 60 per cent when evaluating the cohort without previous experience. In the remaining panels of Figure 4.3 we look at other effects that are due to a minister's past service. In Figure 4.3b we find that a first-term minister returned to office in a new administration has a hazard rate

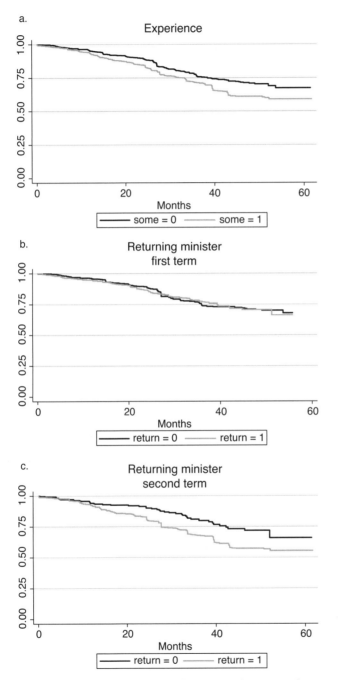

Figure 4.3. Ministerial survivor function and ministerial experience

comparable to a minister without this defining characteristic. However in Figure 4.3c we observe that a second-term minister returning to office (for a third spell) has a significantly higher hazard rate. Just over half such ministers have served a full term.

Thus, at first glance, these pictures appear to show evidence that ministerial characteristics acquired before entering a political career have some effect upon length of ministerial tenure.

Political effects

In Figure 4.4, we look at some of the political effects. We look first for partisan differences in the survivor function but such effects are not evident in these graphs. We also look for the impact of majority size. Serving in a government with a high majority, defined as having more than 55 per cent of the seats, does not affect the probability of surviving in any distinguishable way. We do, however, observe differences in the effect of the government term.

Separating the effect of individual characteristics

Although these analyses are strongly suggestive that fixed attributes of ministers are related to length of ministerial tenure, this conclusion is not watertight. In particular they do not take into consideration that ministerial tenure might be related not only to characteristics of individuals, but also to attributes of the government in which these ministers serve. To see this, suppose that, taking these effects into consideration when observing the failure of ministers, the impact of different traits were modelled linearly: we might then estimate the following equation:

$$T_{igf} = \alpha + X_{ig}\beta' + Z_{igf}\gamma' + B_g\delta' + P_{gf}\lambda' + \varepsilon_{igf}$$

where T_{igf} is the spell of minister i, in government g, at the time of failure f; Xig is the set of fixed individual characteristics (such as educational background) that a minister brings into government at the start of his job; and Z_{igf} is a vector of performance of the minister which includes his performance at different points in time in his job and his performance at the time of failure. B_g is a vector of characteristics of the government that the minister serves in; for example, the party

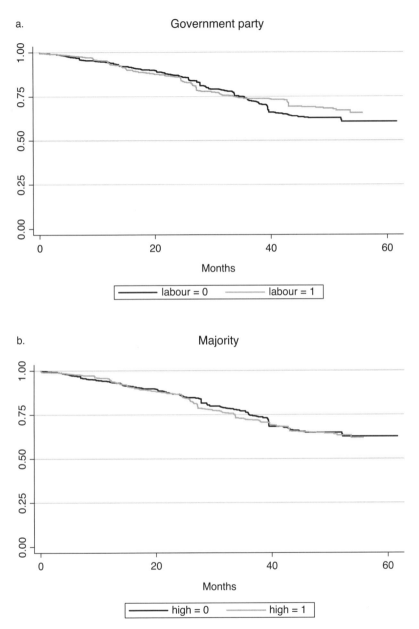

Figure 4.4. Ministerial survivor function and parties

in power or its majority.[14] P_{gf} is a vector of factors that capture the overall performance of the government up to time f.

Of course, Z is implicitly a function of X. A minister's performance is related to the characteristics which a minister brings to government. Similarly P_{gf} is also related to Z. Thus the characteristics of ministers are likely to have an effect on performance through various channels: directly, through the effect of the coefficient β; and indirectly through the effects on Z and P_{gf}. If MPs were randomly allocated into government then a simple comparison of means of T_{igf} between ministers with different characteristics would measure the causal effect of these characteristics on tenure. This parameter would capture both the direct and indirect effects of ministerial characteristics and it is this parameter that we attempt to identify here.

Obviously, however, MPs are not randomly selected into governments. When we look at the effect of X_i on T_{igf} we may well be confounding characteristics of the government with those of individuals. For example, the educational backgrounds of Conservative and Labour MPs differ systematically and the effects of educational background or the colour of one's party may be confounded. We tackle this problem by using models which add government characteristics to the set of variables, and in some of our models we also use government fixed effects (see Table 4.4). One of the key findings of this chapter is that the effects of ministerial characteristics upon tenure are surprisingly robust to these controls.

The determinants of ministerial hazard rates

In the previous section, we have presented some interesting contrasts in the survival probabilities of ministers who differ either in their personal characteristics or in the characteristics of the governments in which they serve. In this section, we try to disentangle the contribution of each of these factors to a minister's hazard rate using a multivariate regression analysis. A standard way to approach this task is using a

---

[14] In fact we only code for majority at the start of the government's term of office. Its majority at any point thereafter is highly correlated with its majority at the start of its term. To code each time an MP dies, switches parties or a by-election is held would require a new entry for each minister on each occasion.

Cox proportional hazards model which expresses the hazard rate for minister i in government j as

$$\lambda_{ijt} = \lambda(t) \times exp(X'_{ijt}\beta)$$

where $\lambda_0(t)$ is the minister's baseline hazard at t and X is a vector of characteristics which may affect a minister's durability including individual characteristics and characteristics of the government in which he serves. From this expression, the baseline hazard is the hazard rate when all measures of characteristics which may affect a minister's durability are recorded as zero.

In Tables 4.4 and 4.5, we present the impact of individual attributes on ministerial hazard rates. In column 1 of Table 4.4, we condition only on individual attributes. We find that public-school-educated ministers have a hazard rate some 17 per cent higher than those ministers without a public school background. The hazard rate is lower for those who have been to Oxbridge (22 per cent).[15] Only the Oxbridge effect is statistically significant at standard levels. The educational credentials of a minister, as represented by attending a public school or Oxbridge, may capture some inherent characteristics of the minister such as acquired skills, latent ability or access to social networks. *A priori*, these factors may contribute to either a decrease or an increase in the minister's hazard rate. On the one hand, these characteristics could be correlated with better on-the-job performance but this, in turn, may increase the value of a non-ministerial career. Our results, however, suggest that, on balance, these factors lead to a decrease in a minister's hazard.

Although we have shown the existence of seniority effects as measured by age and its relationship to ministerial rank, we find that conditioning upon rank and, as expected, age has a positive effect on ministerial hazard. An additional year in age increases the hazard rate of a minister by 4 per cent.[16] Finally, we find that the hazard rate for female ministers is around 33 per cent lower than that of their male counterparts.

Ministers who come to government with some ministerial experience have a hazard rate some 40 per cent higher than those without

---

[15] We also included dummy variables for highest level of education attained which proved to be statistically insignificant.

[16] We included a squared term in age which was not statistically significant.

Table 4.4. *The determinants of ministerial durations. Hazard ratios from Cox models*

Variables	(1)	(2)	(3)	(4)
Public school	1.175	1.078	1.052	1.044
	(0.115)	(0.118)	(0.117)	(0.115)
Oxbridge	0.776***	0.773***	0.781**	0.777***
	(0.076)	(0.075)	(0.076)	(0.076)
Age	1.042***	1.045***	1.045***	1.043***
	(0.006)	(0.006)	(0.006)	(0.006)
Female	0.666**	0.654**	0.646**	0.651**
	(0.113)	(0.112)	(0.113)	(0.114)
Some experience	1.395***	1.236**	1.271**	1.486***
	(0.134)	(0.131)	(0.141)	(0.178)
Noble	0.95	0.942	0.934	0.93
	(0.103)	(0.102)	(0.101)	(0.101)
Ministers of cabinet rank	1.144	1.122	1.129	1.135
	(0.137)	(0.135)	(0.136)	(0.136)
Junior ministers	1.517***	1.455***	1.465***	1.515***
	(0.195)	(0.188)	(0.190)	(0.197)
Whips and members of HM Household	1.859***	1.748***	1.825***	1.893***
	(0.288)	(0.273)	(0.287)	(0.298)
Majority		1.002	1	
		(0.010)	(0.016)	
Labour		0.830*		
		(0.087)		
Second term		1.273**	1.197	
		(0.125)	(0.143)	
Third term		1.334*	1.530**	
		(0.199)	(0.273)	
Prime minister fixed effects	No	No	Yes	No
Prime minister × term fixed effects	No	No	No	Yes
Observations	4495	4495	4495	4495

Notes: Standard errors in parentheses. *significant at 10 per cent; **significant at 5 per cent; ***significant at 1 per cent. See Table 4.1 for the definition of variables.

previous experience.[17] This finding, whilst consistent with evidence that British ministers on average are less experienced than ministers in other countries, is somewhat counterintuitive. One would perhaps expect experienced ministers to have greater durability, especially if experience is correlated with ability. One reason why experienced ministers have shorter duration is that, whilst at some point the marginal gains from remaining in office diminish, the corresponding risks do not. A minister who has served a long and valuable career, and with his eye on a lucrative position upon leaving political life, may be less willing to stick around when the going gets tough. At some point a concern for preserving an established reputation which may be useful outside of politics may take precedence over the desire for further political service. Or perhaps these ministers simply get tired of the game. This finding may suggest that rather than British ministers being suboptimally inexperienced, the British cabinet is closer to optimal experience than that seen in other countries. The pressures in the UK are more on the 'objective' features that reveal the abilities of ministers to run departments and deal with parliament, the media and the public. By contrast, in other systems factional coalitional politics may allow ministers revealed as incompetent to stay in power.

In this model the hazard rate is decreasing with the rank of the minister. Government whips have a hazard rate some 86 per cent higher than that of cabinet ministers; junior ministers have a hazard rate some 52 per cent higher; and ministers of cabinet rank a hazard rate some 14 per cent higher than their colleagues in cabinet. Whips are something of a special case. To resign as a whip does not necessarily affect one's future advancement, and whilst time as a successful whip can enhance one's future career, being a successful whip is not thought to be an important indicator of ministerial quality. Higher rank should, one expects, correlate with latent factors such as quality picked up in the promotion process. So, whilst British prime ministers reshuffle more often and more easily than the prime ministers of coalition governments the result of that shuffling ought to lead

---

[17] As is traditional in the analysis of employment duration, we included experience measured in years and it is squared in our estimations. These variables were not statistically significant once the indicator variable for experience was included.

to the most able ministers remaining in the game. According to this view the prime minister uses her power of patronage to reward the most able of her ministers, and the ability of the minister should be reflected in terms of longer tenure. Of course, promotion may also indicate other aspects of the relationship between the prime minister and minister, such as friendship or loyalty, but again the expected effect of these latent factors should be to increase the durability of the minister.

A mitigating factor, however, is that higher-ranking ministers also face greater levels of scrutiny in parliament and the press. The actions of full cabinet ministers are subject to more scrutiny than those of lower-ranking ministers, though junior ministers and ministers of cabinet rank are often associated with particular policies where failure may lead to close scrutiny. Where there is major departmental failure, lower-ranked ministers will sometimes resign along with the full cabinet minister (as happened over the Crichel Down affair in the 1950s or the Falklands War in the 1980s). Cabinet-ranked ministers may also face greater scrutiny of their personal lives, though the press now seems to think that junior ministers are fair game for intense media scrutiny too. On balance, our results show that ministers appointed to jobs of a higher rank are more durable.

The last individual attribute we include is a dummy variable for members of the government who are nobles. Being in the House of Lords might have various effects. On the one hand, peers do not face re-election pressures, and thus may have greater durability. A reinforcing effect is that the Lords face less media attention and may receive less hostile scrutiny – though again the Lords is often thought to have more careful debate. On the other hand, governments might find it difficult to identify competent peers to represent them in the Lords. On balance, we find that nobles are as durable as any other ministers in our sample.

One might suspect that all these results are due to the fact that ministers' characteristics are correlated with systematic features of the governments in which these ministers served. For example, we have seen in the previous section that Conservative ministers are more likely to have been to public school and Oxbridge. To disentangle these effects, in columns 2–4 of Table 4.4 we condition on different sets of government characteristics. We start in column 2 with a set of obvious factors such as which party is in government, the size of the party majority and the term of the prime minister.[18] In column 3 we condition upon prime minister fixed effects as well as government term and size of the party majority. The estimates from our most restrictive specification, including a dummy variable for each government, are presented in column 4. Surprisingly, the effects we found in column 1 are robust to these different specifications.

The political effects we have estimated could work in two ways: (1) they could shift up or down the baseline constant λ_0; (2) they could affect the magnitude of the coefficients of the ministerial characteristics. In Table 4.5 we break down our sample according to government characteristics to study these effects. In column 1 we restrict the sample to ministers serving under a prime minister in the first term, in column 2 to those serving under a prime minister in her second term, in column 3 to ministers serving in Labour administrations and finally, in column 4, to ministers serving in Conservative administrations. All in all, the estimates of the impact of individual characteristics are of a similar magnitude to those presented in the previous table. However, in these model specifications these effects are less precisely estimated.

Conclusion

In this chapter we have introduced our data set of all ministerial movements in the UK between 1945 and 2007 and have examined ministerial duration using a set of variables that capture both the individual characteristics of each minister and the political features of the government in which the minister was a member. Exploring these data provides us with some understanding of how background characteristics shape political careers. Although differences in ministerial duration will reflect not only the problems each individual minister faces, but also the specific historical events shaping each administration and the particular style of each prime minister, we have found that there exist key systematic indicators of duration. In particular, background variables such as education and gender affect a minister's capacity to survive, with female ministers and those with an Oxbridge

---

[18] We find no statistically significant majority effects. Ministers who are serving in the second term of a prime minister have 27 per cent higher hazard rates relative to those serving in the first term of a prime minister, whereas those in a third term have a hazard rate 33 per cent higher.

Table 4.5. *The determinants of ministerial durations for selected sub-samples. Hazard ratios from Cox models*

Variables	(1)	(2)	(3)	(4)
Public school	0.872	1.227	1.016	0.996
	(0.158)	(0.193)	(0.166)	(0.154)
Oxbridge	0.724**	0.757**	0.841	0.761**
	(0.116)	(0.106)	(0.145)	(0.091)
Age	1.056***	1.037***	1.060***	1.035***
	(0.010)	(0.008)	(0.010)	(0.007)
Female	0.536*	0.677	0.747	0.515**
	(0.173)	(0.169)	(0.157)	(0.168)
Some experience	1.224	1.716***	1.279	1.604***
	(0.230)	(0.306)	(0.257)	(0.242)
Noble	1.026	0.796	0.779	1.005
	(0.176)	(0.126)	(0.143)	(0.138)
Ministers of cabinet rank	0.963	1.347*	1.085	1.190
	(0.184)	(0.234)	(0.195)	(0.194)
Junior ministers	1.335	1.632***	1.245	1.832***
	(0.283)	(0.305)	(0.243)	(0.323)
Whips and members of HM Household	2.229***	2.020***	1.344	2.628***
	(0.521)	(0.469)	(0.321)	(0.557)
Prime minister fixed effects	Yes	Yes	No	No
Prime minister × term fixed effects	No	No	Yes	Yes
Observations	2,022	1,967	2,053	2,442

Notes: Standard errors in parentheses. *significant at 10 per cent; **significant at 5 per cent; ***significant at 1 per cent. Column (1) has only ministers serving in the first term of a prime minister. Column (2) has only ministers serving in the second term of a prime minister. Column (3) has ministers serving only in Labour governments. Column (4) has ministers serving only in Conservative governments. See Table 4.1 for the definition of variables.

background having lower hazard rates. The former effect does not correspond with the evidence from studies of Italian mayors cited earlier. The latter effect is consistent with the notions of elite theorists that privileged elites have greater access to political power.

Attributes of a minister relating to political performance also have an effect. Higher-ranking ministers have a greater durability. We also find that experience increases ministerial hazard rates. These effects are robust to the inclusion of a large set of variables pertaining to the political characteristics of the government in which the minister serves.

Perhaps worth additional comment is the robustness of the effect of experienced ministers. The fact that experienced ministers have lower durations may provide some insight into the low levels of experience of ministers in government in the UK, as highlighted by previous studies of cabinet turnover. Many commentators and politicians have bemoaned the relatively low levels of experience and quality of ministers in British government. Objectively assessing such claims is difficult. The ministerial job market is unlike most others, which show increased durability with experience until a worker retires at some (usually fixed) age. That is not the case with ministers, and perhaps this is simply because being a minister is a stage in a career rather than a career itself. Choosing the point to leave, given one's prospects in the ministerial job market, as opposed to one's prospects outside, is a fine point of judgement. If one's ministerial career appears to have reached its zenith, then taking one's experience elsewhere may begin to look attractive.[19] More junior ministers return to the back benches to serve their time out on committees and in the House, less constrained by loyalty to their party. More senior ministers tend not to remain on the back benches in the Commons for very long after they leave office (though of course there are many notable exceptions) but rather pursue careers outside of politics, often with the sinecure of the back benches in the Lords. Either way, our findings suggest the diminishing marginal returns of a ministerial career in the structured context of single-party rule where one's route to the top is more clearly ordained than in the less predictable rough-and-tumble of coalitional politics. It is this very predictability that may lead to less experienced ministers in the British one-party government system than are found in coalitional states. However, rather than suggesting that this is a problem for the British system of government, it may well be an indication that without the internecine political intrigues of coalitional states that keep possibly incompetent ministers in their jobs, the duration of senior ministers in Britain approaches

---

[19] Chief executives may have similar hazards. Someone might work their way up through the management team of a company, but once at the top have a high hazard for that company, choosing to move to another such post sooner rather than later, perhaps while their company is doing well rather than when it fails.

optimality. We might ask, what other indications of optimality could we ask for?[20]

With the exception of Alt's 1975 study, previous commentaries upon ministerial tenure have focused almost exclusively on the role of the prime minister in directing the cabinet. This is largely due to the fact that, whilst power is concentrated in the hands of a modern British prime minister, each prime minister has used that power in different ways. One would suspect that the personal characteristics of the prime minister and differences in the government will be a key determinant of ministerial tenure. Our results are important since they indicate the existence of systematic features of ministerial tenure related to ministerial characteristics which are independent of the aspects of the government.

As well as offering a specific contribution to understanding the mechanics of British cabinet government our analysis contributes to the broader literature on ministerial careers and on key aspects of government duration. The literature examining legislative careers has not looked systematically at ministerial durability (for example Best and Cotta (2000)). The duration literature examining the forces and stresses of government break-up or cabinet instability has concentrated upon multi-party coalitions (though some comparative studies include countries with single-party majorities). Whilst there is a growing literature on government durability, relatively little has been written about the durability of ministers themselves and, as noted by Huber and Martinez-Gallardo in their study of ministerial tenure in the French Fourth Republic, high rates of government turnover need not imply high rates of ministerial turnover (Huber and Martinez-Gallardo, 2004). However, strong single-party government also faces stresses which can be examined through ministerial turnover. There is an increasing interest in the systematic analysis of such ministerial turnover (Dewan and Dowding, 2005; Dowding and Kang, 1998; Dumont, De Winter and Dandoy, 2001).

---

[20] We might note the finding from Table 4.2 that Attlee's 1945 administration was the second-least experienced of the period, but most commentators see it as an efficient whilst enterprising government; and Major's first administration was the most experienced of the entire period, and his second highly experienced, but they were seen as tired and inefficient.

5 | The prime minister and cabinet

In the previous chapter we have shown, perhaps surprisingly, that the length of time that a minister serves in British politics is related to personal characteristics that are fixed at the time of their appointment. This relationship holds even when we consider aspects such as prime ministerial style that might confound it. Whilst these results might inform us about important power relations in British society and politics, the aim of this book is to go beyond this analysis in exploring the political relationships that define ministerial careers in the UK, and to use our analysis to draw wider inferences about the nature of accountability in parliamentary democracies. Perhaps the most important relationship that defines a ministerial career is that which the minister maintains with the prime minister. As we have already noted, the prime minister is responsible for the hiring and firing of ministers. She thus directly controls our key variable of interest: ministers care about the length of their service; and the length of their service is thus reflective of the minister's relationship with the chief of the executive.

The importance of this relationship is not lost in the analysis of ministerial turnover that takes place in the British press and in much of the academic literature on the subject. When a minister resigns and is replaced, the gossip that fills Whitehall and filters through onto the front pages is about how this event shapes the balance of power within the government: has the prime minister been strengthened or weakened by the resignation? Will the incoming minister prove as valuable a servant? Numerous biographical and autobiographical accounts tell us of the different managerial styles that prime ministers have deployed while in office. If these accounts are to be believed then there is little else of importance in determining how long a minister serves other than the personal relations he enjoys with the prime minister. But how important are these factors in determining a minister's tenure? In this chapter we provide an overview of different British prime ministers, their personal style of cabinet management, and how events of the day affected their premiership.

One view, long argued by commentators on British politics, is that prime ministers move ministers around too much. Indeed, in comparison with other parliamentary governments in western Europe in the post-1945 period, ministers in Britain do not stay in their posts very long (Herman, 1975; Keman, 1991, pp. 114–16). In Keman's (1991, p. 115) table only Ireland and Italy of Western European cabinets have similar low rates of persistence (the cumulative time in one post accrued by a single minister) and mobility (the number of different ministries held by one person), which suggests both that Britain's ministers do not stay long in particular posts, and do not stay so long as ministers overall. The link between the empirical evidence (that ministers in Britain are reshuffled relatively frequently) and the normative claim (that this is undesirable) is tenuous at best. There are many reasons why a prime minister would wish to replace ministers, and the fact that in some countries, where perhaps there are greater constraints upon the prime minister, ministers serve for longer is not necessarily an indication of better governance there.[1]

As we have mentioned, there are two potentially rival accounts of why the prime minister might replace ministers. One is due to selection – ministers are replaced relatively quickly because they prove to be unreliable – and the prime minister judges she can replace them with someone more to her liking as an agent. The second is to try to overcome the tendency of ministers to allocate less than optimal (from the prime minister's perspective) effort to their government tasks. Ideally, we would be able to distinguish these hypotheses which refer to general features of a prime minister's firing rule from the specific style of cabinet management that each prime minister brings to the job. But what are these individual styles? Here we can extract a number

---

[1] For example, prime ministers in coalition governments might be happy to see bad ministers from rival parties in their coalition failing if it will give the prime minister's party a comparative advantage in the next general election. In other words, and as we have already argued, for coalition governments the strategic nature of cabinet formation and reshuffling is much more complex than in Britain (see Dowding and Dumont, 2009b). This is particularly so when we consider, as we have argued, that turnover can act as an accountability mechanism. Allowing the prime minister to remove ministers who are deemed to have failed, or replace ministers when a better candidate is available, might enhance good government.

of vignettes, that are based upon various sources and designed to give the general impression of each prime minister and administration from qualitative judgements made by historians and commentators on their individual style in dealing with their cabinets. We then examine our data to see whether the patterns we find are supportive or otherwise of these claims.

Prime ministerial styles

The relations between prime ministers and their cabinets are shaped largely by circumstance. Prime ministers are constrained by the circumstances of their elevation to power – some have large majorities and can appoint colleagues who share their worldview, whilst others are less free – and by the events that shape their administration. Moreover, given these circumstances, different prime ministers bring to office different styles of cabinet management. As we shall see, some are more collegial than others, using the cabinet as a forum for discussion, whilst others are dictatorial. Some prime ministers seek to micromanage their government, whilst others are more trusting of those whom they appoint to office. We examine the style of the prime ministers in dealing with their cabinets, along with a few of the major events that characterized their administrations, and explore the effects of these individual styles upon the turnover of individual ministers.

Clement Attlee – 26 July 1945 to 26 October 1951 (two administrations)

Main issues of the day
Attlee's administrations were characterized by the necessities of the post-war period. These included getting British troops home, beginning the process of breaking up the British Empire and introducing democratic government to its dependencies, and post-war reconstruction. Britain remained a country at war, with troops fighting communist forces in South East Asia, and with troops in Palestine dealing with terrorism and the problems of the setting up of the state of Israel. Unbeknownst to parliament and most of the cabinet, Attlee's government embarked on Britain's independent nuclear weapons programme. Despite these heavy imposed external constraints, the efficiency of his government is demonstrated by the massive and unprecedented

amount of legislation enacted between 1945 and 1951; every item in the 1945 manifesto was put on the statute book. These items included major nationalizations of the railways, coal, and iron and steel industries; the setting up of the National Health Service; and continued reforms of the education system. In the 1950 election the Conservatives won a majority of the votes but a minority of the seats and Attlee's second administration stumbled on with a six-seat majority, ending in 1951 when Labour gained the most votes but lost to the Conservatives. Nevertheless, the vast majority of Labour's legislation remained unchanged by the incoming Conservatives.

Cabinet style

Attlee has the reputation of being one of the most efficient and effective prime ministers of the post-war period, whose premiership can be seen as a model for others. Cabinet discussion was brisk and organized, with Attlee determined to get through business as quickly as possible. On major issues he would ask the opinion of Herbert Morrison (Deputy Leader, and Attlee's rival for the leadership) first and then work round the cabinet finishing with Ernest Bevin (Foreign Secretary); Attlee would then sum up the decision without a vote. Attlee disliked unnecessary discussion and was impatient with the rambling, discursive cabinets he suffered in Churchill's wartime cabinet meetings.

It is generally agreed that Attlee had a very talented cabinet; he used an informal 'inner cabinet' consisting of Bevin, Morrison, Dalton and Cripps to discuss issues. It is often suggested that prime ministers need to be good 'butchers' and get rid of ministers not up to the job, and in this regard Attlee is often considered a model for later premiers.[2] He was loyal to those doing their job, but did not hesitate to get rid of those seen as ineffective or inefficient (Thomas, 1998, pp. 7–8).

Winston Churchill – 26 October 1951 to 5 April 1955 (one administration)

Main issues of the day

Churchill's government had a very quiet time. Despite Churchill's attacks on Attlee at the 1945 election, accusing Labour of communist

---

[2] For example, Macmillan (1969, pp. 50–2), who thought Attlee was a good chair in the wartime cabinet, described him as a 'good butcher'.

sympathies, his government did little to try to undo the major welfare or nationalization programmes of the Attlee governments. In the main these programmes were popular and the Conservatives were aware of their small majority. One major domestic programme was house building, which they had promised during the election campaign.

Churchill himself was almost exclusively interested in foreign relations. On the whole the Conservatives were lucky in government. At first a rapidly deteriorating balance of payments deficit meant their first budget cut food subsidies and government spending, though with some tax cuts and increased welfare spending. But the budget was unpopular and the government lost a by-election in Scotland, having done badly in local elections there. However, the ending of the Korean War saw the terms of trade increase sharply for the better and led to better economic times throughout the 1950s.

Cabinet style

Churchill ran his post-war administration rather like his wartime government. He did not need to know everything that was going on, and gave little leadership in economic or domestic policy, maintaining a moderate and non-doctrinaire look to his cabinet, with most right-wingers either kept on the back benches or if in office under tight control. Although he made several highly successful appointments and, in some cases on the advice of his Chief Whip, brought able younger men into his government (such as Macmillan), he also kept through loyalty or lack of care some whose performance was substandard. Churchill did not fully trust his cabinet, however, as evidenced by his keeping the Defence portfolio to himself, and his constraining of the Chancellor of the Exchequer from freedom of initiative (Childs, 1992, p. 71). Churchill has been accused of 'government by cronies', largely because he enjoyed the company of a coterie of trusted friends and colleagues. However, he did not operate an inner or 'kitchen' cabinet and few people had a sustained influence on him. He attempted to coordinate the activities of government and provide more strategic vision and direction through 'overlords' overseeing the work of several departments. The 'overlord' process had worked well during wartime but failed here, with those given these roles unsure of what their job was supposed to be. Thomas (1998, p. 11) suggests 'On the whole, once he had appointed a minister he left him alone to get on with the job, and in general backed them regardless of his own ideas on policy.'

The exception was foreign policy, where Churchill still felt he was one of the few people who could deal effectively with world leaders; in this regard he worked well with his Foreign Secretary, Anthony Eden, though the latter was increasingly frustrated with Churchill as time went on.

Cabinet meetings were rambling affairs that did not always follow the agenda, and non-cabinet ministers might wait for long periods to be called in to report. Churchill, seventy-seven years old on becoming prime minister again, suffered ill health, as did Eden his deputy, and at times Harry Cruikshank, Leader of the House, and later in the administration R. A. Butler would chair cabinet meetings. Churchill resigned as prime minister at the age of eighty-one having suffered several strokes, though the true nature of his illness was kept from the public for some time and the government had in effect been led by his successor Eden for several months.

Anthony Eden – 5 April 1955 to 9 January 1957 (two administrations)

Main issues of the day

Eden waited a long time (from 1942 (Avon, 1960, p. 302)) as heir apparent to Churchill, taking on the premiership in April 1955. He made few changes to the cabinet and immediately went to the nation at a favourable time, following a tax-cutting budget and with an opposition split over the issue of rearmament of Germany and nuclear weapons, while a tired Attlee was leading his party campaign for the last time. Eden, with an increased majority of 58 seats over all other parties and a good economic and international outlook, might have been a successful prime minister. However, that was not to be. The economy faltered and a supplementary budget added sales taxes to many items, and cut housing subsidies.

Eden's administration is marked by the Suez crisis. Suez involved secret negotiations between Britain, France and Israel for the latter to invade Egypt to take control of the Suez Canal recently nationalized by Egypt. Israel's justification was Egypt's continued interception of ships in the canal in contravention of the Security Council resolution of September 1951. Britain and France, keen not to be seen as invading Egypt but simply as returning the canal back to their own commercial interests, would use Israel's action as justification. The plan was for them to tell both Egyptian and Israeli forces to withdraw to enable Britain and France to secure this strategic resource for the world's shipping. Few in the cabinet had been consulted, and nor, crucially for the plan's success, had the USA. Several ministers resigned (see Chapter 4) and eleven Conservative backbenchers wrote a letter asking the purpose of the policy, while Walter Monckton, then Paymaster General, criticized the policy in public though he did not resign. The public at first seemed to support the Suez action, but the weight of views in the opinion-forming classes and the lack of support from key foreign nations such as the USA ensured the policy failed. Eden subsequently resigned following illness, breaking down in tears at the cabinet saying 'You are all deserting me, deserting me' (Childs, 1992, p. 91).

Cabinet style

Despite his long apprenticeship and occupation of high office during the wait, the consensus is that Eden was a complete failure in dealing with his cabinet. He was seen as nervous and tense, frequently losing his temper, and he tried to get involved in the detail of policy rather than allowing ministers to run their departments. He often saw principal colleagues alone, leading to problems of communication and coordination across the government. He did not like opposition to his plans, or plans that he had not agreed to. Outside cabinet he was hopeless with his colleagues, but he was considered to be a good chair of the cabinet itself (Thomas, 1998; Childs, 1992). He had not been well even before the Suez crisis and the ill health that led to his resignation in January 1957 had dogged him for years. Of course, Suez defines our attitudes to him as premier and we do not know how he might have settled down as prime minister without it, but the early signs were not good. He had little time to shuffle his cabinet to any great degree, or show his strategic awareness of governmental needs.

Harold Macmillan – 5 January 1957 to 18 October 1963 (two administrations)

Main issues of the day

The first task of Macmillan's government was to get the economy moving, helped by the Suez Canal opening up on 7 April 1957 which allowed petrol rationing to end in May of that year. It was also in May that Britain tested its first hydrogen bomb in the Pacific. Macmillan also announced early on that compulsory military service would end after 1960. All these policies seemed to have popular support. The big issue facing government, though less in the popular mind, was Britain's relative decline as a world power both politically and economically. However, the economy seemed to be doing well and it was in July 1957, just a few months into his premiership, that Macmillan made his famous 'Most of our people have never had it so good' speech. The working week had been reduced, relative earnings increased dramatically, and the extension of hire purchase enabled many new consumer goods from washing machines and refrigerators to television sets to enter into modest households. The major problems that were faced were abroad, with British forces engaged in fighting in Malaya, Cyprus, and British Guiana, whilst independence for many African states was being promoted and promised against a background of conflict between the black majorities and white minority settlers. However, economic prosperity ensured Macmillan romped home in the 1959 election, with the Labour opposition in some turmoil over policy on nuclear weapons and foreign policy. He took on the title 'Supermac' with relish, a title given in scorn by a *Daily Mirror* cartoonist.

Following the 1959 victory, Macmillan took up the challenge of promoting independence in Africa, giving his 'wind of change' speech; he started the process of applying for Britain's admittance to the European Union, the House of Commons agreeing to seek membership after a two-day debate in July 1961 where one Conservative and four Labour MPs voted against and twenty-five Conservatives and the Opposition abstained. The application was vetoed by De Gaulle in January 1963. The process had generally been approved by industry and the public. Macmillan's government started losing popularity at about this time as the economy slowed and an unpopular budget in July 1960 increased various taxes and cut public expenditure to control the budget deficit. Following the budget the IMF granted Britain credit. From June 1961, Labour led the Conservatives in the polls and the Conservatives lost a series of by-elections.

Cabinet style
R. A. Butler had been expected to take over from Eden: he had acted as his deputy and been responsible for clearing up some of the mess of Suez in Eden's absence through illness. However, his moderation

over Suez probably cost him the job as two Suez hardliners (Salisbury and Kilmuir) organized the consultation process which resulted in the recommending of Macmillan. Macmillan had had a variety of senior posts including a few months as Foreign Secretary and then Chancellor of the Exchequer (1955–7). Macmillan kept Eden's Foreign Secretary, Selwyn Lloyd, to keep the Suez hardliners happy, and Butler accepted the Home Office (though he would have liked the Foreign Office). Macmillan's first cabinet was designed to keep all factions happy. What was noted at the time was the extent to which his government was a family affair, the magazine *John Bull* pointing out that 35 of the 85 members of his government and 7 of the 19 members of his cabinet were related to him by marriage.

Macmillan liked to give the impression that he did not work too hard, but he was highly nervous and prone to deep depression. He introduced Prime Minister's Question Time much as it now is into parliament, but was physically sick before entering the House on those days. Unlike Eden, he did not overtly interfere in departmental business, but he used the network of Private Secretaries and the Cabinet Office to keep in touch with events. He was not interested in detail but in the grand sweep of policy. He would let others air their views in cabinet and avoid showing his own hand until he had heard them, and he was skilful in summing up. According to Thomas (1998, p. 16):

Macmillan's skill in appointments meant that he was outstanding in the way he got people into the jobs he wanted. He was especially skilled in balancing the various factions within the party, especially in the wake of Suez, and he did not bear grudges. He showed considerable judgement in giving opportunities to younger men such as Heath, MacLeod and Maudling. He was good at managing his ministers, mainly securing affection and devotion. Generally he would back his colleagues; one mistake did not mean the end of a career, although his reputation has been tarnished by the panic sacking of the 'night of the long knives'.

This famous event occurred on 13 July 1962 when eight cabinet ministers were sacked; three days later nine junior ministers departed. This was a reshuffle unprecedented in British history. Macmillan announced he was resigning on 13 October 1963 due to ill health (he was convinced he was dying but did not die for another 24 years at the age of 92). Historians vary in their judgements. Some see him as one of the most successful post-war premiers; others concentrate on the

failures of his administration which by the end faced economic problems and was suffused with scandal and corruption. Its problems
included not only the Profumo affair involving a cabinet minister,
but also a number of spy and security scandals; scandals of develop-
ers helped by three pieces of 1950s Conservative legislation, and the
notorious Great Train Robbery that stood as a paradigm of the rise of
organized crime in the post-1945 period.

Alec Douglas-Home – 18 October 1963 to 16 October 1964 (one administration)

Main issues of the day

Douglas-Home was not prime minister for very long and in the main
continued the policies of his predecessor. There was one piece of controversial legislation, pushed through by Edward Heath as Secretary of
State for Trade and Industry, that abolished resale price maintenance
(many Conservatives abstained at the vote), and the government continued the expansion of higher education. The Conservatives lost a
close election despite being ahead on eve-of-election polls (their first
poll lead for three years).

Cabinet style

The Peerage Act which became law on 31 July 1963, allowing peers to
renounce their titles and become commoners, enabled Douglas-Home
to become prime minister. Lord Home (Alec Douglas-Home) read out
Macmillan's letter of resignation at the Conservative Party conference and Lord Hailsham announced he was renouncing his peerage to
stand for the leadership. There were several other contenders including
Reginald Maudling and Butler. There were no elections for leadership of the party; rather, 'soundings were taken'. It is not clear
how Douglas-Home emerged as victor, though it appears Macmillan switched his support from Butler to Douglas-Home, and despite
Maudling and Hailsham withdrawing in favour of Butler and mount-
ing disquiet in the cabinet, Macmillan recommended Douglas-Home
to the Queen. Two cabinet members, MacLeod and Enoch Powell,
refused to serve under him and his qualities as a politician if not a
man were questioned in the media. So Douglas-Home took over a
divided cabinet and party facing economic problems and difficult foreign affairs. There is a general consensus among his ministers that he

did not run his government in an overbearing manner and did not interfere in the way Eden did, but he was not in the post long enough to develop a definitive style or show how he would manage problems.

Harold Wilson – 16 October 1964 to 19 June 1970 (two administrations)

Main issues of the day

The big problem of Wilson's first years was the balance of payments deficit, but then Rhodesia's unilateral declaration of independence to secure white minority rule, as well as decisions over nuclear weapons, caused him problems within his own party. He called an election in 1966, winning an improved majority over the Conservatives now led by Edward Heath. However, the next four years were no less troubled. A Selective Employment Tax introduced by Callaghan was universally condemned, industrial relations were very troubled, and the economic crisis of 1966 where the government tried to hold off devaluation of the pound but finally accepted the inevitable was damaging. Wilson did manage to persuade the Trades Union Congress to abide by an incomes policy. His foreign policies were also problematic, failing to resolve the Rhodesian problem, continuing trade with South Africa against the demands of many in the Labour Party, and failing to stop civil war in Nigeria. His attempts at joining the EEC also failed with another De Gaulle veto. The government was forced to cut defence expenditure, ruining relations with Australia and New Zealand as British forces withdrew east of Suez. Then in 1969 violence erupted in Northern Ireland.

Wilson attempted reform of the civil service. The 1968 Fulton Report recommended changes but these were watered down in implementation by the very civil servants who were supposed to be reformed (Fulton, 1968; Fry, 1993). Promised reform of the House of Lords also came to nothing. Wilson called an election for June 1970 but was defeated by Heath's Conservatives.

Cabinet style

Wilson entered parliament in 1945. After two years as a junior minister he entered cabinet (at thirty-one the youngest cabinet minister since 1806), resigning in 1951 over a policy disagreement. He became leader of the Labour Party in February 1963 and with the likelihood of an election the left and right factions within the party mobilized behind him. His first cabinet rewarded many powerful people and set the scene for the way Wilson ran his government. He gave Callaghan, one of his rivals for the party leadership, the Treasury, but created a new Department of Economic Affairs for long-term economic planning, giving it to another rival in Deputy Leader George Brown, ensuring Brown and Callaghan were at loggerheads for several years. Wilson did not show particular loyalty to friends in his cabinet composition. George Wigg, the architect of Wilson's leadership campaign, counted in Wilson's first cabinet eight members who had voted for Callaghan, seven for Brown and six for Wilson. He said, 'From the moment of his election as Leader of the Opposition until the day he ceased to be Prime Minister in 1970, Wilson seemingly forgot the existence of his enemies within his own Party. Indeed, the more violent and loud-mouthed the opponent had been, the better was his chance of being included in the Wilson administration' (Wigg, 1972, p. 259, cited in Childs, 1992, pp. 161–2).

Wilson had a tiny four-seat majority in parliament, which made life difficult. Despite the talent in his cabinet, it was also inexperienced and so Wilson took many decisions himself or with the advice of Brown and Callaghan, though they never formed an inner cabinet in the mould of Attlee's. He was a good manager who generally got his way, using the cabinet to establish priorities and reconcile differences, but he was a stickler for procedure, and at times let ministers talk themselves to a standstill at cabinet meetings, a habit that infuriated Callaghan. However, on some difficult issues he would go round the cabinet and something akin to a vote would take place. It was said that his greatest influence was his political secretary Marcia Williams, and he held a 'kitchen cabinet' of advisors including Williams, George Wigg, Professor (later Lord) Kaldor, Professor (later Lord) Balogh, Peter Shore (then a journalist, later an MP), Gerald Kaufman, and later a few others. This kitchen cabinet caused consternation in the cabinet and the civil service alike, and led to some scorn in the press.

Overall Wilson was perhaps constrained more than his Conservative predecessors in his choice of cabinet, needing to satisfy different factions in the Labour Party which was split along left–right lines, and he needed to use simple patronage to ensure loyalty and support in parliament and on Labour's National Executive Committee (NEC) and to keep the trade unions who bankrolled his party happy. Wilson was accused, like Churchill, of running a government filled with his cronies, and it might be that he attempted to keep his government together by neutralizing opponents by keeping them in government. Thomas (1998, p. 22) describes Wilson as 'a reluctant butcher'. Simple statistics on the durability of his ministers might obscure the fact that he shuffled and moved his ministers around a great deal.

Edward Heath – 19 June 1970 to 4 March 1974 (one administration)

Main issues of the day

Influenced by the Republican right in the US, one of the first acts of the Conservative government was to cut public expenditure and attempt to break the post-1945 consensus on the welfare state. It cut council house subsidies and encouraged councils to let tenants buy their houses. House prices increased, fueling inflation. In opposition the Conservatives had opposed Wilson's prices and incomes policy, but in government they soon introduced their own. They introduced the Industrial Relations Act in 1971 and reformed local government with the Local Government Act of 1972. They faced continuing violence in Northern Ireland, while government policy towards Rhodesia and South Africa continued to cause the government problems with black Commonwealth nations. The one policy Heath pursued with success was Britain's entry into the EEC. Economic problems grew with the oil crisis which followed Egypt's attack on Israel on 6 October 1973. Even without the oil crisis the British economy was not in a good state. The miners had struck against the incomes policy in 1972, forcing the government to back down. With oil shooting up in price, coal became an even more important power commodity. In 1973 the miners' work-to-rule protesting against their dangerous working conditions (three pit disasters had killed 42 men the previous year and 40,000 miners were suffering incurable pneumoconiosis) reduced output, but this time the government wanted to face them out. On 2 January 1974 with the country facing a power crisis and enduring regular electricity blackouts, the government declared a state of emergency and introduced the three-day working week. On 4 February the miners voted to go on strike. Heath was forced to go to the electorate. The Conservatives won slightly more votes than Labour but fewer seats, and after attempting to form a coalition with the Liberals, Heath stood down. Wilson formed a minority government.

Cabinet style

Edward Heath was rather enigmatic as prime minister. He had been Chief Whip for a number of years, a job which involves talking to backbenchers, persuading waverers to vote with the party line. Those who hold that position often gain the respect of their MPs, and indeed this role certainly helped Heath become the first elected leader of the Conservative Party. However, as prime minister he was seen as aloof and distant, not only from backbenchers but also from his cabinet colleagues. He was more interested in the administration of government, and desired to restructure Whitehall with much larger departments. He wanted a small full cabinet consisting of just 16 people, but could not go under 18 (itself below Wilson's 21 on departure) without offending too many people.

He brought back the former prime minister Sir Alec Douglas-Home to the Foreign Office, and Iain MacLeod went to the Treasury but died of a heart attack a month later, being replaced by Anthony Barber. There was no great controversy in Heath's cabinet – no one resigned over policy disagreements – though, for example, Margaret Thatcher blamed him for a U-turn in economic policy during his second year in power. He tended to leave ministers alone to get on with their departmental duties and yet gained the reputation as a dominant and autocratic prime minister, possibly because he relied on the advice of his officials rather than party colleagues. Some said he would have been happier as a senior civil servant than as a politician.

Harold Wilson – 4 March 1974 to 5 April 1976
(two administrations)

Main issues of the day

Wilson formed a minority government that all realized would attempt no major legislative programme until another election was called, some six months later. However, he ended the miners' strike and allowed the incomes policy to run its course. There was continued terrorist activity in Northern Ireland. The October election was narrowly won by Labour with a three-seat overall majority. The Conservatives were in some disarray, with Heath losing several prominent members who announced they would stand down at the next election and some of his party openly saying he too should resign.

The inactivity of that caretaker government continued through Wilson's second term. An unprecedented referendum on whether to stay in the EEC was held, designed to shore up splits within the Labour Party, the 'renegotiated conditions' being largely cosmetic.

Cabinet style

In many ways Wilson ran his cabinet along similar lines to those of his earlier administrations, though he did not direct so much, allowing his ministers to run their own departments. He said that whilst he 'played centre forward' in his first administration, he took up the role of centre half in the second, and that from 1974 ministers ran their own departments with Wilson as a 'sweeper', a 'deep-lying centre-half'. He thus allowed ministers more room to make their own decisions, but as a result his government seemed to lack direction, perceived as a party trying to keep in power rather than a government trying to do things. Wilson was seen as a manipulator, and his second period of government was racked with splits and controversy, so much so that for the EEC referendum he suspended the normal rules of collective responsibility, allowing his colleagues to canvass on opposite sides. In truth the UK was in economic crisis, and the government did little more than react to events, trying to prop up industry and reduce unemployment and inflation simultaneously. Wilson's resignation shocked and surprised many people; it was probably due to the early onset of Alzheimer's disease from which he was later known to have suffered.

James Callaghan – 5 April 1976 to 4 May 1979 (one administration)

Main issues of the day

James Callaghan was seen by the public as an affable uncle figure, but he perhaps took this image too far. His government faced high inflation and returned to an incomes policy, trying to keep public sector wages down. Despite high unemployment and industrial problems, the pound rose against other currencies at this time as confidence grew abroad, due to Labour's expenditure cuts which reduced borrowing and to the discovery of North Sea oil and its promising revenues. Callaghan surprised his cabinet as well as the nation by not going to the polls in autumn 1978, but was eventually forced to by losing a vote of confidence on 28 March 1979, the first government to do so since 1924. He almost certainly soldiered on in order to complete a fourth year of wage restraint, but failed. Public sector workers struck during that 'winter of discontent', leaving waste in the streets and bodies in mortuaries as state cemeteries were closed. At the general election high unemployment and a powerful Conservative campaign ensured a decisive loss for Labour.

Cabinet style

Wilson's resignation had come as a major surprise to many, though he had confided in Callaghan, giving him a chance to work quietly towards succeeding Wilson. He had to contend with a minority in parliament virtually the whole of his premiership, as Labour lost seats in several by-elections. Callaghan had a clear view of what he wanted and guided cabinet discussion. He was more relaxed than Wilson, and there was less conspiracy in the air. He regularly consulted all 22 members of his cabinet – Hennessy (1986b) suggests this period was the high-water mark of cabinet government. On the whole he had good relations with his cabinet and offered ministers support when they needed it. After a nervous start he was an efficient manager.

Margaret Thatcher – 4 May 1979 to 28 November 1990 (three administrations)

Main issues of the day

The early years were dominated by rising unemployment and industrial discontent. Her Chancellor Howe's first budget raised indirect taxes and cut public expenditure. Unemployment shot up and in the summer of 1981 riots occurred in major British cities. The Falklands War changed perceptions of her as a prime minister and together with a strengthening economy ensured victory at the 1983 election. Thatcher's first term was dominated by the monetarist economics her Treasury team pursued with cuts in many areas of expenditure, though with rising unemployment the welfare bill continued to increase. Carrington, her Foreign Secretary, had success in the negotiations over Rhodesia, forcing a settlement for black majority rule, though he fell on his sword over the Argentinian invasion of the Falklands Islands (or Malvinas) in 1982. Thatcher was also helped by the Labour Party tearing itself apart internally, the right factions eventually seceding to form a powerful third party, the Social Democrats, making an electoral pact with the Liberals. This split the opposition vote at the 1983 election, ensuring a massive majority for her second term.

In her second term Thatcher set about further reform, of the civil service, attempting to break up its hierarchical form and bring efficiencies (Dowding, 1995). She introduced a massive programme of privatization of state industries, forced contracting-out on local councils and the civil service, and allowed council tenants to buy their council houses. She developed a form of popular capitalism by enabling ordinary people to buy undervalued shares in newly privatized companies, ensuring profits on quick sales. The second term, however, was dominated by a miners' strike. It had been the miners who derailed Heath, and Thatcher was determined to break them. In an earlier skirmish she had backed down, judging the time was not right. This time, however, she manoeuvred the miners' leader, Arthur Scargill, into a strike which for the unions was at the wrong time: in the spring with lower coal demands ahead and up to a year's supply of coal stockpiled at major power stations. The unions were split and after violence amongst miners and between them and the police, eventually the strike was broken. Once again Thatcher had shown strength and resolution.

Her third term continued her privatization policies and reform of the civil service. It also saw the introduction of the policy that probably brought her down: the poll tax. The Community Charge was a tax per person to replace property tax for raising local revenue. An inefficient tax to collect, it also ensured more people lost than gained and was therefore deeply unpopular. The Conservatives were also deeply split over the European Union. Unlike the leading members of her cabinet, Thatcher was no Europhile, while her backbenchers were split. During her third term she also introduced a major Education Bill, faced a series of prison riots and suffered security scandals. Football hooliganism was also a significant problem.

Cabinet style

Margaret Thatcher is recognized as one of the most important British prime ministers of the twentieth century. Along with Attlee's government which constructed the welfare state from 1945, her government probably affected the nature of the British state more than any other. She was one of the most divisive premiers of the period: loved and hated in equal degree. She became leader of the Conservative Party in 1975 and made it plain from the first that she was a conviction politician. Her first cabinet reflected the ideological spectrum in the Conservative Party, though she cleverly ensured that most of the key economic posts were held by those she trusted and that none attempted the economic U-turn she blamed Heath for. However, her cabinet was divided, with many leaks and semi-open dissension, and she was not at first seen as an effective prime minister. Inside two years there were suggestions that she might not last the full term and insinuations of women's incapacity for the top job. The Falklands War changed these perceptions, and Thatcher's steadfastness and determination enabled her to dominate her cabinet subsequently.

Apart from her war cabinet, Thatcher never operated an inner cabinet, but effectively used the cabinet committee system to ensure most issues were not discussed at full cabinet. She often spoke to ministers on a one-to-one basis and was famous for her lack of patience if they or civil servants did not get to the point quickly. She favoured a few ministers for advice, largely those who shared her policy aims (though William Whitelaw, of somewhat different tenor, was a 'rock' sustaining her through her first government. Thomas (1998, p. 37) says:

Margaret Thatcher did not leave ministers secure in their posts. By the end of her term in office she was the only remaining member of the original 1979 Cabinet. The changes she made were not primarily on the grounds of competence but in order to shift the ideological balance within the government. Her stamp upon every area of government policy was immense.

Ideology must be understood broadly; her question 'is he one of us?' is important. Heseltine, who later famously resigned, was always more of a social conservative than Thatcher, but was seen as 'one of us' because of his 'can do' dynamism, whereas for example Mark Carlisle was moved on from the post of Education Secretary despite effectively steering though the first piece of legislation of her government, probably because he was perceived to have 'gone native', defending the civil service line rather than a more radical one. He was not a go-getter and not radical.

Importantly, under Thatcher the Treasury gained power, first through the 'star chamber' where ministers had to defend spending plans against a committee chaired by the Chancellor, which then evolved into a more detailed policy defence against the Treasury with the Chief Secretary to the Treasury acting as a prosecutor and the Chancellor as judge and jury.

Thatcher stated her opinions at the beginning of discussions and dared others to challenge her. She almost certainly lost power because she forgot that her power was based upon the tacit consent and support of her cabinet and her party (Jones, 1995; Smith, 1994). When the disastrous poll tax looked likely to lose the Conservatives the next election, her party was prepared to dump her. Challenged for the leadership and having failed to secure enough votes to win on the first round of the ballot she sounded out her cabinet one by one. Most failed to encourage her to carry on, and she resigned to allow her cabinet colleagues to put themselves forward.

John Major – 28 November 1990 to 2 May 1997 (two administrations)

Main issues of the day

Major entered parliament in 1979. He held several junior posts before entering cabinet as Chief Secretary in 1987 and then rose rapidly: promoted to Foreign Secretary in July 1989, then three months later becoming Chancellor of the Exchequer after Nigel Lawson's resignation. He became leader of the Conservative Party in November 1990 when Heseltine challenged Margaret Thatcher. Major stood in the second round, just failing to get an overall majority but all the other candidates stood down. One of his first acts was to start dismantling the deeply unpopular poll tax. The economy went into recession in Major's first year, and for many commentators his victory at the 1992 general election against a slick Labour campaign was surprising. His majority was small at 21 but workable. Five months in, the course of his entire second term was changed by Black Wednesday on 16 September 1992 when billions of pounds were spent trying to defend sterling. In one day the Conservatives lost their reputation as the best party to deal with the economy. Major remained loyal to his Treasury team, largely because he supported their policy. It later emerged that Major was as close to resigning over Black Wednesday as drafting a letter of resignation to the Queen.

Major presided over a Conservative Party riven over the issue of the European Union. This was seen most dramatically when his government lost a vote in the House of Commons on ratifying the Maastricht Treaty by 23 votes. Major called another vote the following day, making this a vote of confidence, which he won by 40 votes. The continuing split between the Europhiles and Eurosceptics in his party ensured that Major was constantly having to fight not only backbenchers but his cabinet colleagues. He tried to reinvigorate his government with a 'back to basics' campaign which was was supposed to be directed towards central issues like the economy, education and crime, but was immediately interpreted by the press as being about morality. His government was rocked by a series of financial and sexual scandals involving ministers and backbenchers, making 'sleaze' a major issue. Constant threats to his leadership which never culminated with an actual challenge led him to resign as leader of the Conservative Party in June 1995, stating he would then re-stand for the leadership. This flushed out a challenger: John Redwood. Major won the contest, portraying it as a decisive victory. He furthered the Thatcherite privatization programme, though this was proving less popular, with the privatization of the railways particularly disastrous. One policy success was Northern Ireland. The Downing Street Declaration of 15 December 1993, followed by an IRA ceasefire the following year, can be seen as an important step in bringing peace to Northern Ireland. Major tried to relaunch his premiership time and again, and sometimes wrong-footed opponents with clever political moves, such as his resignation from the party leadership. At the end he led a party that had been in power for eighteen years and seemed weary of it, embroiled in scandal after scandal, in many ways resembling the Conservatives during Macmillan's last years and Douglas-Home's tenure.

Cabinet style

Major's rise was rapid, he presided over a deeply split party and was seen, perhaps unfairly given those divisions, as a weak prime minister. He was much more collegial than Thatcher. He was dependent upon cabinet heavyweights such as Heseltine and Clarke, though relations with the latter cooled as Major moved to the right to hold his party together. He sought consensus. He was accused of not being a good butcher, unable to sack ministers when necessary – for example Norman Lamont after the fiasco of leaving the European Exchange Rate Mechanism – and of letting personal friendships get in the way, for example hanging on to scandal-mired Mellor for too long. Major appeared loath to sack ministers unless absolutely necessary, yet he shed them at an alarming rate. He was criticized for dithering, though on becoming prime minister he quickly disposed of the poll tax and introduced the council tax to replace it. His public indecisiveness was aptly summarized in Lamont's resignation speech: 'We give the impression of being in office, but not in power.' Again in autumn 1994 eight Eurosceptic Conservative MPs had the whip removed, but they were soon brought back: Major needed their votes as his majority was disappearing following by-election losses. Major himself said that his premiership was 'too conservative, too conventional. Too safe, too often. Too reactive. Later too often on the back foot' (Major, 1999, p. xxi).

Tony Blair – 2 May 1997 to 27 June 2007 (three administrations)

Main issues of the day

Blair was elected leader of the Labour Party in July 1994 following the death of John Smith. Gordon Brown, one-time mentor of Blair, stood aside so that they would not split the vote of the 'modernizers'. (The 'modernizers' in the party wanted extensive organizational and policy changes.) On gaining power Blair allowed Brown sweeping powers within the Treasury and it was their frictional relationship that characterized much of his premiership. For the first two years Brown kept a tight rein on expenditure, and gave the Bank of England greater independence. From that beginning Blair presided over a booming economy. There were not many significant policy initiatives, despite his long tenure. There was constitutional change with the House of Lords Act 1999 that expelled all hereditary peers bar 92 making it a predominantly appointed house (Shell, 2000). Promised further constitutional reform never took place (McLean, Spirling and Russell, 2003). The government increased expenditure on education and then health, and announced that their aim was better public services, which they attempted through higher expenditure and various initiatives such as introducing quasi-market and market practices and opening up choice in public services. Blair secured close relationships with the US, being hawkish on foreign policy in the Balkans and then after 11 September 2001 aligning with the US on the 'war on terror' and the invasion of Iraq. The latter took much government effort both in trying to justify the war and to maintain public popularity. Blair won a second term in 2001 still a popular prime minister, but his 2005 victory was due more to the continued divisions in the Conservative Party than good will towards his government. He did have policy success in Northern Ireland with the Good Friday Agreement leading to power-sharing and the chance of a long-lasting peaceful settlement.

Cabinet style

Like Churchill and Wilson before him, Blair was accused of cronyism. In part these accusations, from early on in his premiership, came as he ennobled close friends and confidants: Derry Irvine to Lord Chancellor; a one-time flatmate Charlie Falconer; Larry Whitty for years of service as General Secretary of the Labour Party; Liz Symons having run the First Division Association for senior civil servants, and so on. However, Blair was only following previous precedents in creating lords, and after eighteen years of Conservative rule he felt the need to find people outside the Commons who could do jobs for him and not fully trusting former Labour ministers already in the Lords. Nevertheless, an air of suspicion around his appointments and behaviour grew even as he proclaimed his 'pretty straight sort of guy' image. The role of press and media advisors also became a major issue. A key fact of Labour's latter-day success in opposition, their handling of the media and general 'spin' around government business created a 'sleaze' problem equal to that faced by Major.

Blair further downgraded the importance of the cabinet, preferring one-to-one meetings with ministers in his famous 'sofa government'. He made effective use of cabinet committees, putting in those he trusted as chairs. Like Thatcher before, in issue areas he became interested in, he dominated policy; however, he allowed Gordon Brown at the Treasury to take on enormous powers in domestic social policy as the Treasury became increasingly involved in policy formation and implementation through its line-by-line examination of the spending power of departments – utilizing and strengthening the scrutiny system originally set up by Thatcher. Blair, like Thatcher, was a policy outlier in his own government and, similarly, suffered from a constant leakage of ministers unhappy with policy and interference. Blair was still seen as a potential winner of elections, however, and the Labour Party seemed more reluctant to let him go than the Conservatives had Thatcher. He was very loyal to his ministers, and was the only prime minister of

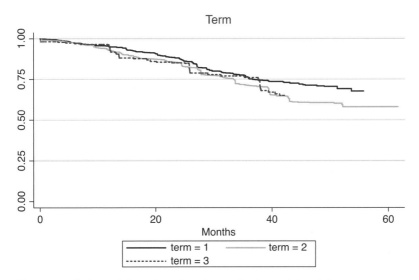

Figure 5.1. Ministerial survivor function and prime ministerial terms

the modern period to bring back a full cabinet minister he had himself sacked. However, the conflict with Gordon Brown that defined his premiership led to speculation over every cabinet reshuffle about whether he would remove Brownites and impose his own people.

Survivor functions for different prime ministers

Having recounted the conventional wisdom of how different prime ministers have managed their cabinets, we are now in a unique position, given our detailed data, to explore whether these data in fact support these traditional accounts. To so so we look at the survivor functions for different ministers serving under different prime ministers. A note of caution is warranted when interpreting these figures. Some governments lasted longer than others and the reasons for this may well be correlated with the survival prospects of individual ministers in these administrations. Nevertheless we can ask whether, conditional on the overall length of government, ministers who served under some leaders were more vulnerable than those who served under others. As a basic overview of the terrain we plot the survivor functions by prime ministerial term in Figure 5.1. At a first glance we observe

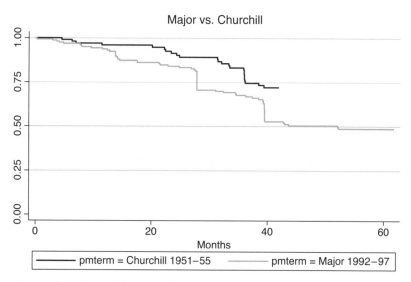

Figure 5.2. Ministerial survivor function: Churchill versus Major government

key differences in the survival paths of ministers serving in different administrations.

We can gain more insight by using carefully selected comparisons that help illustrate these differences. In Figure 5.2 we compare the second Major administration from 1992 to 1997 with that of Churchill from 1951 to 1955. Evaluated at the 40-month period only 50 per cent of those serving under Major were still in post. By contrast, in Churchill's government, which lasted just over 40 months in all, 75 per cent of those appointed at the start of the term were still in government 40 months later. This comparison may then suggest that there are key differences in prime ministerial style, and that correspondingly ministers are more vulnerable when serving under one prime minister rather than another. But of course such a conclusion might be misleading since the events that shaped the premierships of Major and Churchill were very different. As we have already noted, Churchill was somewhat 'lucky' during his premiership, whereas Major led a party deeply divided over the European issue.

Since to a large extent we can treat the events that shaped these different premierships as exogenous to the different styles that different leaders deployed, it may be more instructive to compare the same prime minister at different points in time. Here we can draw

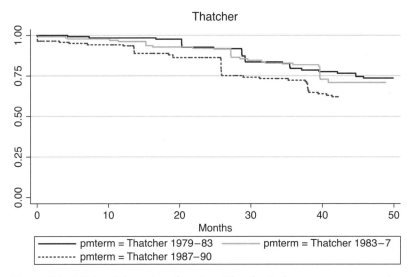

Figure 5.3. Ministerial survivor function: Thatcher's three governments

useful comparisons between prime ministers in their first, second, and third terms. Doing so reveals interesting insights. In Figure 5.3 we contrast the survivor function for ministers in the Thatcher administration: each of Thatcher's three terms lasted between 40 and 50 months and in the first two terms 75 per cent of ministers lasted the course of her government; the hazard rate of ministers in her final term was somewhat higher, with around 60 per cent of ministers seeing out the 40-month term. Here, the figures do not correspond with conventional wisdom that sees Thatcher as gradually imposing herself on her government. Indeed, if this were true, then we would expect that once she had a loyal coterie of ministers in place then those ministers would be more likely to survive. In fact, if anything, those serving in the last Thatcher administration were less likely to survive in office.

Similarly we can compare the three Wilson administrations in Figure 5.4: in the first, 1966–70, roughly 75 per cent of ministers saw out the first 40 months and roughly 60 per cent lasted until the end of the administration. By contrast the survival chances in subsequent administrations were higher, although the term lengths were far shorter. In 1974 and between 1974 and 1976 very few ministers lost their positions.

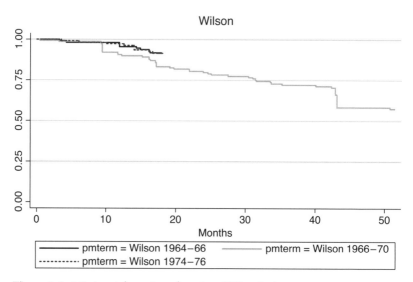

Figure 5.4. Ministerial survivor function: Wilson's three governments

We can also see how the particular reputations of ministers are shaped by the events of a specific administration. As illustrative examples, in Figure 5.5 we look at the different administrations of Attlee, Macmillan, Wilson and Major. In the first column we look at their first adminstration and in the second column we look at one other administration of the same prime minister. The first row compares Attlee's first administration with his second. We see that Attlee's reputation as an effective butcher is supported by observing the survivor function for his ministers during the 1945–51 administrations: there is a steady turnover during his first term, with a bigger shuffle around the twenty-second month. Furthermore, we observe that Attlee's reputation as an effective butcher is entirely due to his treatment of ministers between 1945 and 1949.

Similarly when comparing the Macmillan government of 1957–9 and that of 1959–63 we observe that the brutality of the 'night of the long knives', which occurred just over midway through his second term as prime minister, is out of sync with his treatment of his cabinet earlier in the same administration and in 1957–9.

The graphs also perhaps indicate a slightly more nuanced view of the administrations of John Major (last row). His reputation is supported by the graphs during his second term as prime minister. Only

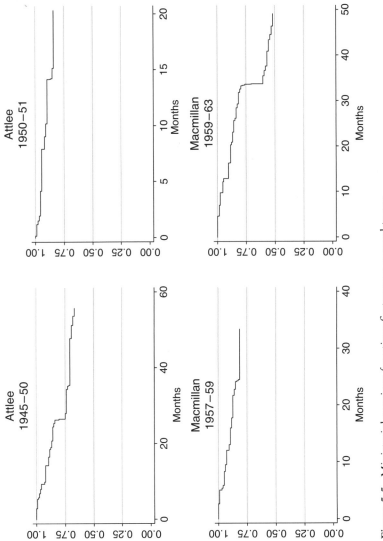

Figure 5.5. Ministerial survivor function: first versus second terms

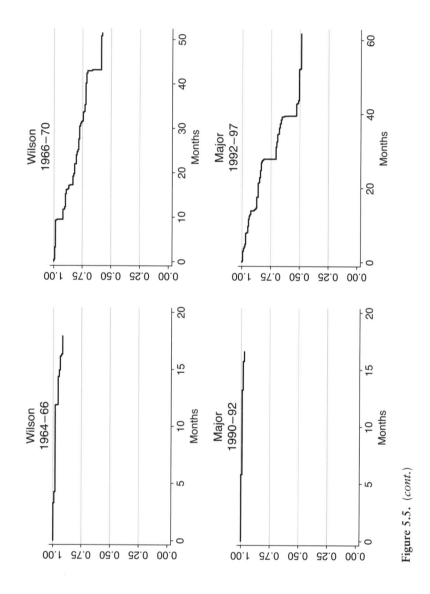

Figure 5.5. (*cont.*)

50 per cent of ministers survive beyond forty months. However, he had a low turnover in his first administration leading to his election victory in 1992 and a low turnover in the final twenty months of his second administration with only two ministers departing in that period leading up to the election of 1997. Despite continued warring within the Conservative Party, the government managed to remain largely intact in the twenty-month run-up to the 1997 election.

Conclusion

This chapter has discussed common perceptions of the leadership styles of different prime ministers. Using these vignettes combined with our data, we have sought to establish whether the historical record, built up largely through anecdotal evidence and biographies, is consistent with what we find when evaluating our data. The picture is some-what mixed, as one might expect. In some situations the established reputations of prime ministers are consistent with what we find when observing the plots of survivor functions for ministers grouped by prime ministerial term. In comparison to other prime ministers, min-isterial life under Attlee was short (though not necessarily nasty or brutal). However, structuring our data in this way also revealed that sometimes the overall picture is more nuanced than previous accounts allow: Attlee, and also Macmillan, established their reputations as a result of specific episodes that occurred in a particular administration. Otherwise, the tenure patterns observed under Macmillan or Attlee are not particularly remarkable. And sometimes also our analysis chal-lenges conventional wisdom. For example we observe that turnover rates were fairly consistent across the Thatcher administrations.

The overall picture that emerges is, however, one in which the indi-vidual style of prime ministers, and their response to the events of the day, matters in determining the length of ministerial tenure. As we have already seen, conditioning on these individual styles, the background characteristics of ministers also affect length of tenure. But we want to push further and to provide a more systematic account of the relations between the prime minister and her ministers, an account that does not rely on the idiosyncracies of event or style, but that instead pro-vides some understanding of the strategic considerations that inform the prime minister's actions and thus determines the (average) length of ministerial tenure. Another way of asking the same question is, how much of what we might consider to be due to individual style of a prime minister can actually be accounted for by the strategic considerations faced by *all* prime ministers? In particular our focus, which we elaborate upon in the following chapters, is on the way in which prime ministers use information in their hiring and firing decisions.

6 | Performance measures and forced exits

Introduction

In this book we are analysing the length of ministers' spells in office based upon characteristics that are fixed at the time of their entry and what happens to them in government. We ask what effect political events, such as resignation calls, have on ministerial tenure. Such calls, whilst subject to the noise associated with adversarial British politics and a mass media increasingly hunting for controversy, provide a measure of ministerial performance. In Chapter 7 we will be examining in detail the effects on ministerial tenure of calls for resignation. In this chapter we introduce our performance measure and examine one aspect of the measure – when a minister is forced to leave government following a call for his resignation.

A forced exit is a ministerial resignation which occurs without the planning of the prime minister. It might occur because a minister decides to quit – perhaps in consequence of personal conflict with the prime minister or with other ministers, or because of his disagreement with some aspect of government policy. These cases fall under the rubric of resignation due to collective responsibility: the minister no longer feels able to take on part of the collective responsibility for government policy. More often, however, forced exits occur because of some specific issue: a controversy or a scandal that embroils the minister. These cases are ones of individual ministerial responsibility. Either way round we call such problems – whether they actually lead to resignation or not – 'resignation issues'. Such resignation issues might arise and go away quickly, either because the minister swiftly realizes that his position is or will become untenable and and so resigns quickly or because the prime minister moves to force the exit. Such was the case of Keith Speed, Under Secretary of State for Defence for the Navy, in May 1981. Speed had made a controversial speech, which had not been cleared with Conservative Central Office, over the government's proposed defence cuts. He warned against running down the navy at a time when his own secretary of state was looking into cost-cutting. Speed had many backbench supporters and felt confident of his position on 17 May when he told reporters that he was not considering resignation in protest at the government's policy. The defence review caused Thatcher many problems and on 18 May she dismissed Speed for going ahead with his controversial speech without consulting anyone and for disloyalty to the Defence Secretary, John Nott. In a Commons debate Mrs Thatcher said that Speed had breached collective responsibility by making a departmental debate public. In another famous case Hugh Dalton, Chancellor of the Exchequer, resigned even before the issue became public. He resigned in November 1947 after admitting giving information away about the Budget to a lobby correspondent before his budget speech in the House of Commons. The opposition asked for an investigation into the leak, but Dalton had already offered his resignation to the prime minister.

More often, however, ministers try to weather the storm and fight to retain their post. They look for support to their ministerial colleagues, backbenchers and, of course, the prime minister. They may go the rounds on TV and radio and talk to newspaper journalists. Home Secretary David Blunkett resigned in December 2004 after an exhaustive investigation over two weeks into claims that his office had intervened in fast-tracking a visa application of his former lover's nanny. In such cases, when it is clear the issue will not go away, the minister will offer his resignation and the prime minister will decide whether or not to accept it. The prime minister might reluctantly decide that the minister 'has to go', perhaps losing a key ally, or might accept the resignation more willingly. Sometimes the prime minister will tell the minister that he has to resign when the minister wants to fight on – such was the case in Peter Mandelson's second resignation in January 2001. It was suggested that Mandelson had phoned Home Office minister Mike O'Brien on behalf of Srichand Hinduja who was seeking British citizenship. The Hinduja family was a major sponsor of the Millennium Dome for which Mandelson had had some responsibility. At the time the Hinduja brothers were under investigation by the Indian government for alleged involvement in the Bofor Scandal. An independent inquiry later concluded that Mandelson had done nothing wrong (Hammond, 2001), but this second scandal, given Mandelson had been reappointed only two years after having first resigned over a financial scandal (see below), led the prime minister, urged by his press secretary Alastair Campbell as part of their media management (Kuhn, 2002, pp. 55–7), to act swiftly. Mandelson (2010, p. 311) later believed that he had made a mistake in doing a series of interviews in order to try to strengthen his position.

Occasionally the prime minister will let it be known that he sacked the minister but more often an amicable exchange of letters occurs allowing at the least the appearance that the minister offered his resignation voluntarily and honourably.

Sometimes a minister avoids quitting after a resignation call despite the story running and running. We discuss several such cases below. Often however, the resignation issue is relatively trivial, or actions by the minister save him and public attention turns elsewhere. For example there were calls for Edith Summerskill, Minister of National Insurance, to resign in May 1950. She had been president of a women's organization, the Six Point Group, which had openly criticized the government's policy on Korea and Formosa (now Taiwan), potentially breaking collective responsibility. Summerskill stated that she had not attended the group for 'at least a year' and had no prior knowledge of the group's statement. She immediately resigned the presidency of the Six Point Group, and in reply to questions from Conservative MPs, Prime Minister Clement Attlee stated that he accepted that Summerskill had not been associated with the group's criticism of the government. The issue ended there.

This chapter provides some basic descriptive statistics over such forced exits. It examines the issues that proximately cause a minister to go and we see that historically some issues are more likely to cause resignations than others. We also see that the annual number of forced exits has increased in the post-war period almost certainly as a result of the number of 'resignation issues' similarly having increased. We examine some of the reasons why the number of resignation issues has risen so rapidly. Our main aim in this chapter, however, is simply to frame the number and type of such forced exits in order to put into context the structural features that lead to ministerial turnover and durability which is the subject of Chapter 7.

Resignations and non-resignations

There are many case-study articles on specific resignations or sets of resignations suggesting that the minister 'had to go' for this or that reason (Chester, 1989; Doig, 1989, 1993; Finer, 1956; Ganz,

1980; Hennessy, 1986a; Nicholson, 1986; Oliver and Austin, 1987; Pyper, 1983; Wheare, 1975). However, one can only make such causal inferences if we examine the class of all resignation issues. When considering what causes a forced exit we should not select on the dependent variable only and discuss where ministers have resigned. In one sense, just as any day that a given minister resigns is a resignation for that minister, any day on which he does not resign is a 'non-resignation' day for him. When we examine ministerial durability through hazard analysis that is precisely how we consider non-resignations. In this chapter, however, we define a 'non-resignation' more narrowly in terms of cases where ministers do not resign despite there being a resignation issue. A 'resignation issue' is defined as any case of forced exit or where there is a call for a resignation (sometimes given in 'code', such as 'the minister must consider his position') that comes from a serious source but following which the minister does not resign. Serious calls include those from the opposition front bench, the back benches (excluding ritual catcalls), some reputable outside organization such as a professional association or trades union, or contained in an article or editorial in a national newspaper. A 'non-resignation' is then thought of as any case where there is a resignation issue but no resignation occurs.

The data have been collected over many years using the following method. First, they cover all individuals who have served as full cabinet ministers, ministers of state, junior ministers or whips. The data have been collected from Butler and Butler (2000, 2006, 2011) and official sources. For the years 1945 to 1991 collected prior to online sources being available, *The Times* index was consulted year by year, noting all references to departments, ministers by job and ministers by name. These are cross-referred to events to build up a comprehensive picture of the major political events of each year. All potential resignation issues were then consulted in *The Times* on microfiche. For the years 1996 to 2007 the individual ministers were identified through *The Times* online by cross-referencing name with 'Resign*' and the other newspapers were consulted. For the years 1991 to 1996 both methods were used to ensure comparability across methods. All the issues which are resignation issues are collected for the file. Cross-references to other newspapers, Hansard and through biographies, autobiographies and other historical sources try to build a more comprehensive view of the events. (During the period of non-publication of *The Times* due to strike activity *The Daily Telegraph* was used.) The data thus collected are then categorized according to the coding frame described below. A resignation is easy to observe, but non-resignations are also required. The method for identifying a 'non-resignation' is simple. If someone in the House of Commons or the press, or from some non-political organization (understood broadly) suggests that the minister should resign, or the press suggests that the issue is 'seriously damaging' or some similar phrase then it is defined as a 'potential resignation issue'. We coded various elements not used in this analysis, and describe only the codes as we use them. These are the reasons which led to a call for the minister's resignation, or have been coded as the proximate cause of the resignation. Resignation cases were coded in nine categories: personal error – in which the minister made a serious mistake for which he or she is personally accountable, either in his role as a minister or some other incident not otherwise coded; departmental error – a serious mistake occurs in the minister's department; sexual scandal; financial scandal; policy disagreement – in which the minister publicly criticizes government policy; personality clash – where the minister clashes with the prime minister or other cabinet colleagues; performance – ministers may be called on to resign by backbenchers or the press when they are seen to be performing badly over a long period of time (usually this is through policy failure or lack of decisiveness over important issues); 'other controversy' is a residual category where the issue does not fit the other categories; 'retirement and reshuffles' where there is no proximate event that leads to the resignation. Often, of course, various reasons are involved. Performance is related to policy, and both personal and departmental error may occur. In such cases secondary reasons are coded too, but judgements have had to be made at times over the correct categorization and some debate may remain about the coding in some cases. We only analyse the primary proximate cause in this chapter.

During the period of our analysis from the beginning of Clement Attlee's government in 1945 to the end of Tony Blair's government in 2007 there have been 346 resignation issues, leading to 91 forced exits. Of these, 46 are due to collective responsibility (the minister chooses to go due to disagreement with government policy or there is a clash between ministers of a more personal nature) and 45 are due to some controversy or issue that has arisen, including questions concerning the minister's overall competence. Often when a minister resigns over policy there are no prior calls for resignation. Occasionally there are calls for a resignation when it is widely believed that a minister is unhappy with some aspect of government policy. Sometimes a minister resigns over individual ministerial responsibility without there being any prior call and the issue is only revealed with the resignation.

Ignoring turnover caused by changes of government following a general election, there have been 574 non-forced resignations during the course of this period. These are planned exits which occur as the prime minister shuffles her cabinet. Sometimes these reshuffles result from changes caused by forced exits, as a few months later the prime minister decides to reinvigorate the government team. Some are 'mid-term' reshuffles which have become the norm since Margaret Thatcher (though they did occur prior to her term of office as well). Prime ministers in the UK do shuffle their cabinets more often than in other Westminster-style governments. The up-to-five-year cycle allows more time than the three-year cycle in Australia or New Zealand (see, for example, Dowding and McLeay, 2011; K. Dowding, C. Lewis and P. Packer, 'Ministerial Exits in the Australian Commonwealth Government', unpublished paper, 2011), enabling prime ministers to give their government a new look as they begin planning for the general election. Indeed, reshuffles are almost forced upon British prime ministers at times, as newspaper speculation over which ministers are to be moved in the 'forthcoming reshuffle' destabilizes the government.

So, of the 665 resignations during the period under consideration, 574 (86 per cent) either occurred through cabinet reshuffles or retirement without undue controversy at the time. Of course, some of those ministers who were moved during a reshuffle might have been involved in previous resignation issues, and we consider how these affect the underlying durability of ministers in Chapter 7. The remaining 91 resignations, at an average of 1.4 per year, have been coded into our set of categories mentioned above. The analysis conducted allowed for each resignation to be coded into one of the eight categories as the proximate cause of the resignation. Non-resignations as we define them here have been similarly coded.

Figure 6.1 shows the total number of resignations per year, both reshuffles and forced exits. There is no obvious pattern in total resignations though the peaks largely appear in mid-cycle, with numbers tailing off as the date of the general election approaches. Peaks occur in 1947 (1946–9 government), 1957 (1955–9 government), 1962

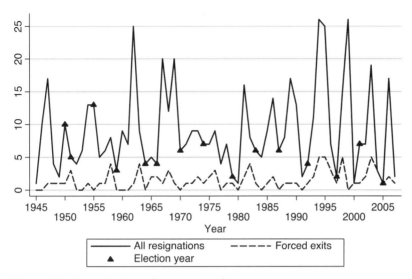

Figure 6.1. Forced exits and resignations by year

(1959–64 government), 1967 and 1969 (1966–70 government), 1976 (1974–9 government), 1989 (1987–92 government), 1982 (1979–83 government), 1986 (1983–7 government) 1994 (1992–7 government), 1999 (1997–2001) government, and again mid-term in 2001–5 and just after the 2005 election. All these reflect cabinet reshuffles, the 1976 reshuffle also reflecting a change in prime minister. There are some peaks at election time however (where the triangles are), notably 1951 and 1956, and peaks occur at other times too. There are high levels of resignations from 1967 to 1969, reflecting various problems, scandals and controversies in the Wilson government. The Thatcher decade also has an almost regular trough–peak pattern, which seems to be continued in the Major and Blair eras, reflecting the 'normal politics' expectation of a mid-term reshuffle that has grown in the past thirty years or so. The forced exits in Figure 6.1 at times mirror the overall resignations reflecting larger reshuffles caused by forced exits (for example in the mid-1990s) either at the time or just later as the prime minister strategically reshuffles the cabinet.

For the Thatcher decade certain events can be picked out to explain this pattern: the 1981 recession crisis with a cabinet reshuffle, and the 1985 reshuffle cemented her control over her cabinet following the election victory two years earlier (when she had also brought in new

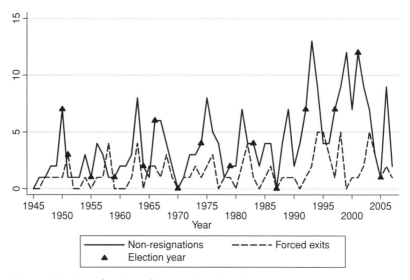

Figure 6.2. Forced exits and non-resignations by year

faces), and the controversies in the cabinet in 1989 which eventually led to her downfall. Similarly the troughs occur during the year of an election or the following years: 1952, 1964, 1970, 1980, 1984, 1987, 1993, 2001 and 2005, though again there are exceptions. The regular or cyclical patterning is thus much as would be expected, with ministerial turnover largely dependent upon mid-term reshuffles and with few changes following an election victory.

Figure 6.2 gives forced exits only along with non-resignations. We see from Figure 6.2 that the number of resignations and resignation issues varies widely year by year. Election years are marked with bold triangles and we can see that fewer resignation issues and resignations occur immediately after an election. The 'honeymoon period' usually has fewer controversies, and ministers have not had time to make the sorts of mistakes that lead to calls for them to resign. The pattern here seems fairly regular and it is not so obvious that the numbers of both have increased over time. Figure 6.3 smooths the resignations into five-year cycles. Whilst there is still a clear up-and-down pattern, we can see that the number of forced exits has increased over the period. The peaks and the troughs both tend to be higher as the half decades pass.

Why has there been such an increase in resignation issues? There are several possible explanations. The number of ministerial

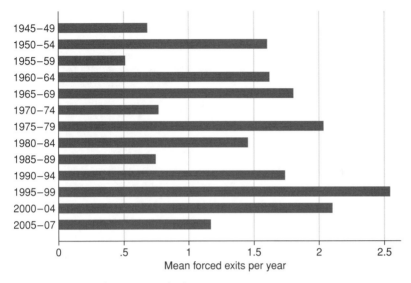

Figure 6.3. Forced exits smoothed

appointments has increased, particularly in the junior ranks. Junior ministers often take on a much higher profile than they once did, particularly if their responsibilities include issue areas which attract controversy (Theakston, 1987, 1999).[1]

It seems that the big increases in both calls for resignation and forced exits has occurred in the past twenty years. If we split the sample into roughly two halves, the first of 336 months (up to the end of Harold Wilson's second spell) and the second of 374 months (Callaghan to the end of Blair), we find 36 forced exits in the first half compared to 55 in the second: not that much more than we might expect from the increase in the number of ministers. However, the non-resignation cases show a massive increase from 87 to 168, and as we can see from Table 6.1 and Figure 6.2 the really big increase comes from the 1980s with Margaret Thatcher's government (though Wilson's government in the 1960s also saw a high level). We examine these figures more closely in Table 6.2. The first column shows the number of resignation issues averaged on

---

[1] Controlling for size of the payroll does not have an effect, leaving the average number of calls for resignation at around 2–3 for most of the period (both Wilson administrations having higher averages at 5 and 6) before taking off to 7 under Major and continuing at the higher level under Blair.

Table 6.1. *Forced exits and non-resignations by prime minister*

| Prime minister | Tenure | Events | | |
		Forced exits	Non-resignations	Total
Attlee	75	7	14	21
Churchill	41	1	5	6
Eden	21	1	5	6
Macmillan	81	10	20	30
Douglas-Home	12	0	2	2
Wilson 1	67	9	19	28
Heath	44	4	8	12
Wilson 2	25	4	14	18
Callaghan	37	4	8	12
Thatcher	138	13	41	54
Major	77	16	41	57
Blair	122	22	78	100
Total		91	255	346

Table 6.2. *Annual resignation issues by prime minister*

| Prime minister | Events | | |
	Total	Forced exits	Non-resignations
Blair	9.84	2.16	7.67
Major	8.88	2.49	6.39
Wilson 2	8.64	1.92	6.72
Wilson 1	5.01	1.61	3.40
Thatcher	4.70	1.13	3.57
Macmillan	4.44	1.48	2.96
Callaghan	3.89	1.30	2.59
Eden	3.43	0.57	2.86
Attlee	3.36	1.12	2.24
Heath	3.27	1.09	2.18
Douglas-Home	2.00	0.00	2.00
Churchill	1.76	0.29	1.46

an annual basis. We see the highest number under Tony Blair, closely followed by John Major and Harold Wilson's second government, then Wilson's first government, then Margaret Thatcher, and so on down. The rise in the numbers of calls for resignation almost certainly demonstrates the increased scrutiny by the press of governments, and the increasing lack of respect paid to politicians by the mass media.

The mass media take a much bigger interest in the private lives of politicians (Deacon, 2004), as indeed they do with other public figures, than they once did and report on scandals that they once ignored (see footnote 2). They also treat politicians with much less respect than they once did. This phenomenon is worldwide (Corner and Pels, 2003; K. Dowding and C. Lewis, 'Culture, Newspaper Reporting and Changing Perceptions of Ministerial Accountability in Australia', unpublished paper, 2011) and leaves politicians more exposed than they ever were in the past. The increasing number of resignation issues has less to do with changing standards of ministerial behaviour and rather more to do with changing standards of what the media choose to report upon. Partly in response to these changing reporting standards, ministerial codes of conduct have been strengthened, increasing expectations from the public about ministerial behaviour. For example, some of the financial scandals we mention below would not have been considered scandalous in the past (see below).

Differences between prime ministers and parties in power

Figure 6.4 shows the number of cases by each parliament and Figure 6.5 by each prime minister. They also reveal the striking increase in cases, especially when we take into account the annual rates of resignation per prime minister. The highest rate of resignations is from the Major government with sixteen in total, a rate of 2.5 per year, with Wilson 2 and Blair equal second with a rate of 1.9 per year. The number of non-resignations is also high for Major but not as high as for Wilson or Blair.

Another way of looking at these figures is suggested in Table 6.3. Here the 'honour ratio' measures how often ministers resign when faced with a resignation issue. The 'honour ratio' is calculated by the number of resignations per administration divided by all resignation issues, giving a score between 0 and 1: the higher the score the more 'honourable' the administration. We do not make much of the 'honour ratio' since it takes no account of the seriousness of the calls for resignation; nevertheless it might tell us something about how the public view politicians and governments. We see at the beginning of the period about 1 in 3 calls for resignation leading to a forced exit; by the end

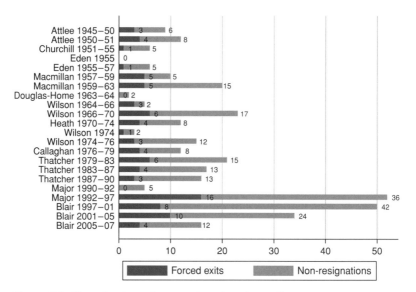

Figure 6.4. Forced exits and non-resignations by parliament

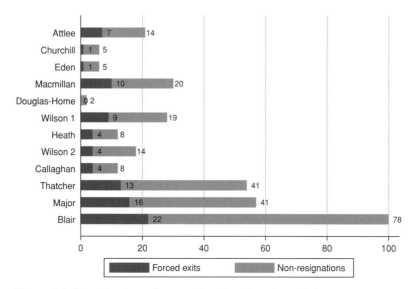

Figure 6.5. Forced exits and non-resignations by prime minister

of the period this is down to 1 in 5. Eden stands in the early period as having the worst 'honour ratio' along with the second Wilson administration. However, the trend is down, with Thatcher, Major and then Blair all having ratios between 1 in 4 and 1 in 5. Despite the fact that

Table 6.3. *Honour ratio*

| Prime minister | Events | | |
	Forced exits	Total	Honour ratio
Attlee	7	21	0.33
Churchill	1	6	0.17
Eden	1	6	0.17
Macmillan	10	30	0.33
Douglas-Home	0	2	0.00
Wilson 1	9	28	0.32
Heath	4	12	0.33
Wilson 2	4	18	0.22
Callaghan	4	12	0.33
Thatcher	13	54	0.24
Major	16	57	0.28
Blair	22	100	0.22

many calls for resignation are of such a nature that politicians them-selves think that the minister should not go, the sheer number of such calls relative to the number who resign must affect public attitudes to the wholesomeness of politicians.

It is well known that trust in politicians and government has fallen in the UK, as it has in other countries. One reason might be the sheer number of criticisms and calls for resignation that befall major politi-cians in the modern age. This is despite the fact that prime ministers respond to those calls in roughly the same manner.

Figure 6.6 charts the reasons for forced exits by party. Policy dis-agreements are much more likely in the Labour Party – with 51, almost two a year – than in the Conservative Party at 30, about 0.85 per year. (In the Labour Party they are also more likely to lead to resignation (57 per cent leading to resignation) than in the Conservative Party with only 47 per cent leading to resignation.) This supports the view that the Labour Party has traditionally been more split than the Conserva-tives. When ministers do go it is less likely to be directly as a result of policy disagreement (even if that is an underlying cause). We note that the Conservatives seem more prone to sexual scandal both in total numbers and on an annual basis (indeed sexual scandal leading to calls for resignation was unknown to Labour until Blair's government). Are Labour ministers unattractive, do they not get caught, or have they stronger family values than Conservative ministers? We cannot judge,

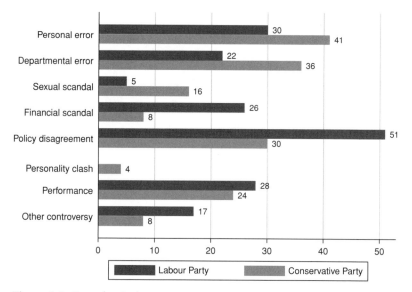

Figure 6.6. Forced exits by party

but certainly John Major's 'back to basics' campaign undoubtedly led to closer scrutiny of his ministers, which probably explains the high number in the past few years, as does the media packaging of various issues under the title of sleaze (Dunleavy, Weir and Subrahmanyam, 1995). It must also be recognized how much more interested newspapers are in the personal lives of ministers than once they were. This trend which has grown steadily from the 1970s has become more pronounced from the mid-1980s. Until the 1970s the newspapers showed little interest in ministers' or MPs' private lives.[2] In the post-war period

_____

[2] A mention in a divorce case would lead to a resignation, as suggested by the example of Charles Parnell (not a minister but the Leader of the Irish Parliamentary Party) way back in 1889. But otherwise, as far as newspapers ever reported the private affairs of government ministers, the stories generally appeared in coded form in the social columns or in *The Times* court news. Yet we know from the many biographies and secondary accounts that, in the past, ministers certainly were involved in events that today would trigger cries for resignation. Indeed 'the first Prime Minister' Robert Walpole openly had a mistress, Molly Skerrett, who bore him a daughter (Plumb, 1960, pp. 112–15). William Gladstone had a penchant for visiting prostitutes and scourging himself afterwards because of his unclean thoughts (Crosby, 1997, ch. 4; Matthew, 1997, ch. 4). In his case newspaper editors protected him both in 1853 (Crosby, 1997, p. 66; Matthew, 1997, pp. 89–90) and thirty years later when they felt there

there were no sexual scandals involving ministers until 1958, and sexual behaviour only really became an issue in the 1970s. In 1958 Ian Harvey was forced to resign after he was charged with gross indecency. However, he only resigned, and newspapers only reported the case, after it had already gone to trial and the charge had been dropped. The much-vaunted Profumo affair in 1963 is certainly remembered as a sex scandal (and of course that is what sold the story), but it involved a genuine concern about national security and Profumo resigned because he misled parliament (we code the issue as a non-resignation sex scandal in March 1963 following a story in *The Times* that he had offered his resignation over his relationship with Christine Keeler, but code his resignation in June as personal error since that was a result of his admitting to the Chief Whip that he had given misleading statements to parliament about that relationship) (see Gastor, 1988 for details of the Profumo affair). So Lords Lambton and Jellicoe, who stepped down in 1973 after admitting to casual affairs with prostitutes (though the official explanation given at first for Lambton's resignation was 'personal and health' reasons), may be regarded as the first ministers pressured to resign over sex alone (rather than following legal cases), without some other substantive political issue attached. Conservative regimes continued to be dogged by sexual scandals in the 1980s. Until Blair took office, sexual scandals appeared to be a Conservative problem, since up to 1997 newspapers did not expose Labour ministers' sexual misdemeanours. Robin Cook was the first Labour minister to be implicated in a sex scandal.[3]

was no hard evidence of wrongdoing (Matthew, 1997, pp. 541–3; Parris, 1995, p. 49). In the twentieth century Prime Minister H. H. Asquith had an obsessive infatuation with a young woman, Venetia Stanley, to whom he wrote letters during cabinet meetings including details of government policy (Brock and Brock, 1982) whilst Lady Dorothy Macmillan's long affair with Conservative MP Robert Boothby would today surely have affected her husband's premiership. More recently, until he stepped down in 1974, Tom Driberg survived thirty-four years as an MP (never a minister) without his sexual exploits being reported, despite being apprehended by police several times for sexual solicitation in toilets and parks; he did receive some protection due to his position as a journalist as well as an MP (Wheen, 1990). Newspapers are now reporting the private lives of ministers and their families in ways they chose not to previously, and over issues that are not nearly so scandalous.

[3] Robin Cook ended his first marriage on 2 August 1997 with a statement at Heathrow airport that he had been having an affair, a story about to be broken by the newspapers, and under pressure from the prime minister's office to deal with the problem swiftly.

Labour ministers are more prone to financial scandal, averaging almost one a year (though Blair's government has by far the most), with Conservatives averaging one every four years. We can only speculate whether this has anything to do with social backgrounds of ministers from the different parties.

Proximate causes of forced exits

Whatever the ultimate reason for forced exits there is always a precipitating event which constitutes the proximate cause, and we have coded these proximate causes into nine categories. By far the most cases of forced exits are those over policy disagreement. These concern collective rather than individual ministerial responsibility, and include such famous cases as Michael Heseltine marching out of the cabinet following disagreement over the Westland affair in 1986 (Hennessy, 1986a; Heseltine, 2000), Robin Cook's resignation in March 2003 over the Iraq War (followed quickly by those of four non-cabinet ministers), and a few months later Clare Short's over what she saw as broken promises about Iraq reconstruction (Cook, 2003; Short, 2004). Most, 29 of the 43 cases of policy disagreement forced exits, are not full cabinet ministers however. Our data include government whips as well as ministers proper; whips and junior ministers find it much easier to resign over disagreement with policy than do full cabinet ministers who will only go over major questions of policy, such as war, economic policy, or, as in Heseltine's case (arguably), over an issue he felt was his area of responsibility. Junior ministers have less invested in the government than more senior ones. If they are at the beginning of their careers they can resign, especially over an issue that is controversial, and come back to have successful careers. Three prime ministers, Eden, Churchill and Wilson, all resigned over issues about which they felt strongly and received kudos from their respective parties to come back and lead those parties and the government. Older junior ministers might realize their career is going nowhere and take the easy exit by resigning over an issue that they feel strongly about. Whips can come and go, and resigning as a whip might have some short-term career effects but is unlikely to affect one's career in the long term.

We have also coded 38 cases of non-resignation over policy disagreement. In the main these are cases where a minister is known to be unhappy with policy, often through selected leaks via friends. The press or opposition suggest that the minister concerned ought to come out and support the government or resign. We also have three cases of resignation due to 'personality clash', the first two being MacLeod and Powell who refused to serve under Sir Alec Douglas-Home when he replaced Macmillan. The category is used sparingly since personality, faction and policy can be hard to disentangle. The third case exemplifies the difficulty. We coded Norman Lamont's resignation, in 1993, as a 'personality' clash, though it might as easily have been coded 'policy disagreement'. We did not code it as the latter since others in that category are clearly disagreement with a specific policy. Whilst Lamont in his resignation speech did suggest some disagreement over economic policy, he clearly did not resign because of any specific disagreement. Rather, at least as suggested in his resignation speech, Lamont disagreed with the manner in which Major's government was being conducted, saying:

There is something wrong with the way in which we make our decisions. The Government listens too much to the pollsters and the party managers. The trouble is that they are not even very good at politics, and they are entering too much into policy decisions. As a result, there is too much short-termism, too much reacting to events, and not enough shaping of events. We give the impression of being in office but not in power. Far too many important decisions are made for 36 hours' publicity. (Lamont, 1993)

It is also clear that although they had once been quite close as colleagues, the relationship between Lamont and Major had broken down at a personal level. His resignation speech, as he must surely have realized, damaged the prime minister.

There are many other cases of personality clash being reported in the press, but rarely with resignations or threats of resignation being explicitly discussed; hence they do not enter into our database.

Some resignation issues have traditionally been more likely to lead to a resignation than others. Figure 6.7 and the associated Table 6.4 chart resignations and non-resignations in the categories coded. By far the largest category for both resignation and non-resignation is policy disagreement with 81 cases, of which 43 (53 per cent) led to resignation. Policy disagreement is an unusual category in relation to the others for a number of reasons. As noted, it concerns collective rather than individual responsibility. Secondly, policy disagreement sometimes only emerges when the minister resigns. To be sure, Westminster insiders

Table 6.4. *Proximate reasons for resignation issue by party*

	Labour		Conservatives	
Reasons	Forced exit	Non-resignations	Forced exit	Non-resignations
Personal error	4	26	10	31
Departmental error	0	22	4	32
Sexual scandal	1	4	8	8
Financial scandal	6	20	4	4
Policy disagreement	29	22	14	16
Personality clash	0	0	3	1
Performance	4	24	0	24
Other controversy	2	15	2	6
Total	46	133	45	122

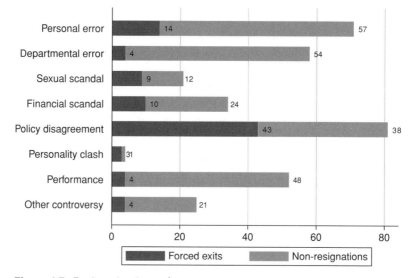

Figure 6.7. Resignation issues by category

and the politically acute might be aware that a particular minister is unhappy with aspects of government policy, but the majority of the public might only learn of such disquiet when a minister resigns. If we were able to collect data on disagreements that do not emerge in newspaper reports, or ones that spill out to lead to calls for a minister to resign, or even where ministers consider resigning without this ever emerging publicly, then a much smaller proportion would lead to actual resignation. To some degree the fact that most policy disagreements lead to resignation stems from the fact that disagreements only really emerge as 'resignation issues' when a minister is highly likely to go. It is worth noting therefore that the fact that so many policy disagreements lead to resignation is a factor dependent upon our data collection methods and coding. When disagreement within government has become so notable that the press discuss a minister's plight and suggest he might resign over the issue, it has already become serious enough that he is likely to go. Government in recent years (and the Blair government was particularly notable for this fact, having learned the lessons from the highly fractious Major administration) is always keen to demonstrate that they speak with one voice, and there is little conflict within the government machine. Whether this is healthy for government or for accountability is another matter. If the press was less keen to highlight dissension and suggest this is problematic for government, more open and greater discussion of difficult issues might be more possible.

The next largest category is personal error, which reflects the fact that it is an error directly attributable to a minister that constitutes the heart of retributive accountability – although only 19 per cent of cases lead to resignation and a high proportion of those are due to the cardinal sin of misleading parliament.

The third-highest category of resignation issue is departmental error. There are often calls for a minister to resign due to policy failure or implementation failure by departments. Until the 1990s any major prison break-out would bring a call for the Home Secretary to resign, but none ever did. Such calls are based on the great myth of sacrificial ministerial responsibility, where a minister is supposed to carry the can for all those who work under him. We have coded four resignations as being due to 'departmental error'. This is out of 58 resignation issues where departmental error has been coded (or about 7 per cent). The first one is coded thus in deference to the myth of sacrificial responsibility – Sir Thomas Dugdale's resignation over Crichel Down in 1954. This is the case upon which the myth of sacrificial ministerial resignation for actions of their civil servants is so often based (Chester, 1989; Mackintosh, 1977, pp. 530–1; Delafons, 1982, p. 256; Boyle, 1980). In fact Dugdale was implicated far more deeply than was widely realized at the time; Nicholson (1986) argues that departmental error had little to do with Dugdale's resignation. The other three cases in this category concern one incident: the Argentine invasion of the Falklands, which produced the forced exits of Lord Carrington and his juniors Richard Luce and Humphrey Atkins (Pyper, 1983; Jordan, 1983; Woodhouse, 1994, pp. 87–106).[4] These three resignations had more to do with saving the prime minister Margaret Thatcher than errors by the Foreign Office. The Secretary of State for Defence (John Nott) and the prime minister herself were more implicated in the signals that led to the invasion, that is cuts in the defence budget (over which a junior minister Keith Speed had resigned, see above) than the ministers in the Foreign Office. However, Carrington, being the loyal servant, offered to resign to save his prime minister.[5] Indeed, as Jordan (1994, pp. 224–6) has pointed out, in both the Crichel Down and Falklands cases the ministers were praised not only for their chivalry but also for the fact that resignation was unnecessary. There are other cases where departmental error can be coded as an auxiliary reason but in all such cases personal error is the main coding. Neither Crichel Down nor the Falklands invasion is convincing as an example of the doctrine of sacrificial ministerial responsibility for departmental error.

There are 52 resignation issues over performance. When ministers perform poorly either in parliament or when there is a perceived policy failure, the opposition or the media often call for resignation. When the economy is doing badly there are calls for the Chancellor of the Exchequer to go (5 calls), or the Home Secretary (4 calls), but most calls are for the prime minister to leave over the performance of the government as a whole (11 calls, with Harold Wilson garnering 5 calls during his first administration (1964–70). Only 5 have resulted in actual resignations. That there are so few (and two of them very much special cases: prime ministers resigning) underlines the fact that ministers do not forcibly exit over poor performance. However, as we shall see in Chapter 7, poor performance does lead them to exit

---

[4] The junior minister, Lord Carrington, who offered to resign at the same time as Dugdale over Crichel Down is the father of the Lord Carrington who resigned over the Falklands conflict. Perhaps the sacrificial myth is encoded in the genes of Britain's hereditary rulers.

[5] Had the Leader of the Opposition, Michael Foot, provided a more coherent and robust attack in the emergency debate in the House of Commons following the initial invasion, the prime minister might have had to resign in any case.

sooner than they would have if they had shown stronger performances. Prime ministers do not always sack at the time of criticism of ministers but wait for an appropriate time to get rid of weak ministers through reshuffles.

Although they are not included in the counts it is interesting to discuss the cases of Anthony Eden and Margaret Thatcher. We have coded Anthony Eden's and Margaret Thatcher's resignations as performance-related (though Eden's officially was due to his health). Thatcher resigned as prime minister as John Major became leader of the Conservative Party. In fact four different codings could be appropriate for this case: personal error, policy disagreement, personality clash and performance. Her personal errors were to forget how much she ultimately relied on her party and her cabinet for her power (Alderman and Carter, 1991; Jones, 1995), and losing her grip on the issues as she became personally identified with some of the government's most unpopular policies, notably the poll tax (Butler, Adonis and Travers, 1994). Policy disagreement, partially over the poll tax, but more over economic policy and the European Community, saw her lose several cabinet ministers. These errors also involved underlying personality clashes as her domineering attitude became overwhelming. All these are coded as auxiliary reasons however; ultimately she lost the premiership because her cabinet deserted her when she failed to gain victory in the first round of the leadership ballot, which occurred because her backbenchers feared they would lose the next election under her. A case can be made that she went because she was unwilling to accept the doctrine of collective ministerial responsibility (Jordan, 1994, pp. 208–9).

We have coded three ministers as forcibly exiting because of performance. Tom Fraser (Minister of Transport) resigned in December 1965 after he had been criticized within his own party for failing to make visible progress with the party's commitment to produce a plan for the integration of road and rail transport. Stephen Byers resigned in May 2002 after a series of problems plagued him and his Department of Environment, Transport and Regions (we have coded seven non-resignations for Byers in the previous three years (4 personal errors, 3 departmental errors). There had been no specific calls for him to resign just prior to his resignation, though a parliamentary report had labelled his ten-year transport plan 'incomprehensible'. In a press conference he admitted making mistakes and said his continued presence would damage the government. Estelle Morris resigned as Secretary of State for Education in October 2002 stating in her resignation letter that she did not feel up to the job, especially in managing a department.

We then come to the scandal categories – financial and sexual scandal. Until the 1980s sexual scandal virtually always led to resignation. Profumo is a counter-example, but only because he at first denied he had an inappropriate relationship with Christine Keeler, a statement he later retracted, then resigning because he had misled parliament. It is clear that he would have had to resign originally had he not lied. The first case of admitted sexual liaison which did not lead to resignation immediately was Nicholas Fairbairn, Solicitor General for Scotland (December 1981). The prime minister asked the Chief Whip to investigate the story of a woman, who had been a House of Commons secretary, who was found hanging from a lamppost outside Fairbairn's London flat. She was cut down and resuscitated in hospital. Fairburn's marriage had been dissolved in 1979, and it had been thought that he might have married the woman, Miss Milne. Many Tory MPs believed that Fairbairn would have to resign because of the scandal, although there was no evidence of Fairbairn having done anything wrong. Thatcher left the matter as a private affair and made it clear that she would not ask for Fairbairn's resignation, and Fairbairn made it clear that he would not offer it. The fact that he had had many affairs emerged in the press at this time. The second case was David Mellor, Secretary of State for National Heritage (July 1993), who also did not resign over press stories concerning affairs. Nevertheless, both resigned soon afterwards, Fairbairn just one month later in January 1982 and Mellor two months later in September 1993.

Whilst in both cases the proximate cause of the later resignation is different, there is no doubt that the ministers had lost political capital through the earlier revelations, which were important in their final resignations. Fairbairn resigned a month later, a resignation which we coded as personal error. Fairbairn was heavily criticised for telling a Scottish newspaper of the decision not to prosecute in a Glasgow rape case before making a statement to the Commons. MPs were angry at this insult and also because Fairbairn had talked about a case which could still come before the courts as a private prosecution. Fairbairn did not convince MPs about the soundness of the decision. At first he said that the woman was not capable of giving evidence because of her psychological condition. Later the woman said that she would give evidence and the psychiatrist treating her said that he had not told the law officers that she should not give evidence. The debate came at a time when there was growing disquiet over the prosecution of rape cases as evidenced by the government's willingness to accept an amendment to the Criminal Justice Bill compelling judges to jail rapists or send them to psychiatric hospital. Fairbairn's earlier problems were undoubtedly significant in this resignation, as was the fact that he was a flamboyant personality who had a tendency to shoot his mouth off. His backbenchers saw him as a liability.

The David Mellor case is significant for it reveals the importance of the press with regard to the increasing number of resignation issues over time, and also signals a period when the press conducted veritable witch-hunts of ministers.

David Mellor's attempted overhaul of the popular press a few years earlier formed a catalyst for the press attacking ministers. Mellor had steered through parliament the 1990 Broadcasting Act, ending what many Conservatives regarded as a lack of accountability of private TV companies by subjecting them to a bidding process for franchise renewal. He then turned his attention to the popular press and concerns that their non-statutory self-regulating body, the Press Complaints Commission, did not adequately prevent press intrusion into people's private affairs. Mellor antagonized the press by remarking that they were 'drinking in the last-chance saloon' and calling for curbs on the 'sacred cow' of press freedom. The Sunday newspaper *The People* responded to Mellor's jibes by launching an investigation into Mellor's own private life – a move widely acknowledged as a warning shot to politicians about press freedom: 'the exposé by *The People* was seen by both sides as an attempt to underline the consequences of tighter restriction on what the press could publish' (Doig, 1993, p. 73). Shadowing Mellor, using wire taps and financial inducements to his mistress, *The People* exposed a lurid tale of Mellor's affair with the actress Antonia de Sancha. To justify what was otherwise simple gossip about the private life of a minister *The People* used the 'public interest' defence suggesting his comments during a taped conversation with her that their liaison made him 'absolutely exhausted' and 'seriously knackered' affected his abilities as a public servant (Doig, 1993). Mellor survived in July due to the support of the prime minister – demonstrating that Major was no sexual prude – (indeed it emerged later that whilst a minister under Thatcher he had

had an affair with another minister, Edwina Currie (Currie, 2002) – and discreet official briefings making clear that legislation on privacy and press freedom were unlikely.

However, the press did not let up on Mellor and for two months he endured press speculation. He finally resigned on 25 September 1992 following what we code as a 'financial scandal'. *The People* had headlined a story 'Top Tory and the PLO paymaster' suggesting it had been unwise of David Mellor to go on a family holiday with Mona Bauwens, the daughter of an official of the Palestine Liberation Organization. Bauwens sued *The People* for libel, claiming that her reputation had been impugned by the suggestion she was not a fit person for decent people to associate with; during the trial it turned out she had paid for the Spanish villa and flights for Mellor and his family.

The Mellor episode set the template for future relationships between the press and politicians. No longer did the press simply report pertinent political events or broadcast the opinions of opposition leaders; instead they began actively to pursue 'difficult' politicians on personal or other grounds, raising a range of allegations until one stuck and the minister resigned. There are notable examples of this kind of ministerial 'witch-hunt' during both the Major and Blair administrations. Between September 1992 and May 1993, the press accused Chancellor of the Exchequer Norman Lamont of misconduct on seven occasions and three counts: performance (five occasions), financial scandal (one occasion) and personal error (one occasion). Lamont finally resigned for his handling of the economy, rather than over the press disclosure that he had used taxpayers' money to pay the legal bills incurred in his evicting of a 'sex therapist' who rented his London home.

Blair's government suffered various sex scandals, but their relatively minor nature and changing public attitudes meant that only one minister (Ron Davies in October 1998) tendered his resignation. Davies's was rather different to the other sex scandals in two regards. First, whereas the others involved long-time affairs, Davies was robbed by a man he met on Clapham Common, a well-known area for gay liaisons. Secondly, and perhaps more important, the details emerged very slowly as Davies did not tell the whole truth to the prime minister.[6] Davies

---

[6] Given that fact this could be coded as 'personal error' but Davies did not mislead parliament and the incident was quickly regarded by the press as a sexual scandal.

stood down citing 'an error of judgement', later acknowledging both his bisexuality and his psychiatric treatment for a personality disorder leading him to pursue risks.

Financial scandals also come in varying degrees of severity. Financial scandal leads to forced exit in about a quarter of all cases: John Belcher, stepping down October 1948 (though not formally resigning until December); Reginald Maudling, July 1972; Lord Brayley, September 1974; Tim Smith, October 1994; Neil Hamilton, December 1994; Peter Mandelson and Geoffrey Robinson, December 1998; David Blunkett, October 2005; and Lord Sainsbury, November 2006.

John Belcher, Parliamentary Secretary to the Board of Trade, resigned on 13 December 1948. The resignation came after he gave evidence to the Lynskey tribunal investigating corruption in the government. He had requested leave from his duties in October when the inquiry was being set up. The allegations concerned proposals over an application to import amusements machinery; an application for a building licence; permission to issue capital on the formation of a football pool company; the withdrawal of a prosecution against a firm of football promoters; and representations made by that firm for an allocation of paper. Attlee told the House of Commons that the President of the Board of Trade had been informed by officials that allegations had been made against the Parliamentary Secretary and other ministers and officials. Belcher admitted receiving gifts from people in a position to benefit from the activities of the Board of Trade and resigned for this indiscretion. He denied both being influenced by these gifts and any allegations of corruption. Lynskey's findings centred around Sydney Stanley who had acted as an intermediary between businessmen and government ministers and officials. The report said Belcher had received lavish hospitality from Stanley, and had used his ministerial position to help Stanley's clients or the givers of the presents. An official at the Bank of England, George Gibson, was also criticized for allowing his judgement to be influenced by the hope of favours from Stanley (Cmd, 7617, 1949). The report cleared all civil servants and several other ministers of any suspicion, though arguably it remains one of the biggest corruption scandals of post-1945 British government (Robinton, 1953; Gross, 1963; Doig, 1996; Roodhouse, 2002).

Maudling's is a strange case, involving John Poulson. During his public examination for bankruptcy, Poulson said Maudling had been chairman of an associated company and had told Poulson to pay a deed of covenant to his wife's charity rather than pay him a salary. Payments of £22,000 were made, according to Poulson. As allegations of corruption in the Poulson case were made, Maudling's position came under scrutiny. There were no calls for his resignation from politicians, but the *New Statesman* said he should resign for his indiscretion, even though it was not committed while he was in office. When it was announced that the Metropolitan Police were to investigate Poulson, Maudling resigned, saying it would be impossible to remain as Home Secretary while the investigation took place. (Unlike other police forces in the UK, the Metropolitan Police at that time were overseen directly by the Home Office.) The resignation was purely Maudling's decision; Heath offered him another post in the government but he declined. Members of both parties were shocked at the announcement in the Commons. The changes in the government after Maudling's resignation were makeshift – suggesting the possibility of his being brought back at a later date. Maudling denied any fault in taking the chairmanship of Poulson's subsidiary, resigning because of his responsibility for policing in the metropolis. The shadow Home Secretary, James Callaghan, argued that this did not amount to a resignation issue. A *Times* leader said Maudling was right to resign because of the Home Secretary's responsibilities towards the police – though, as Marshall (1989, p. 198) points out, this is a misapprehension of the duties of the Home Secretary. *The Times* went on to say there was no evidence of Maudling having done anything wrong, but he had failed to make sure his business associates were totally above board. The nature of what Maudling thought his departmental duties were led to his resignation as much as the scandal itself, but the proximate cause is the financial scandal.

Lord Brayley, Under Secretary of State for Defence for the Army, resigned on 25 September 1974. Investigations into the accounts of Canning Town Glass revealed that Brayley owed the company £16,000. Brayley had been a director of the company until his government appointment. A *Sunday Times* article claimed the sum being investigated could be up to £213,000. Wilson, who was a personal friend of Brayley and had surprised many Labour members with his appointment, denied he had ordered an investigation into Brayley's affairs. But ten days later Wilson informed Brayley that the Department of Trade was to investigate the companies with which he had been associated and Brayley resigned, saying that while he believed the investigation would not reveal anything improper he could not remain as a minister while it went ahead.

Tim Smith and Neil Hamilton both resigned over the 'cash for questions' affair in which it was alleged they accepted money to ask questions in the House of Commons on behalf of Mohammed Al-Fayed, the owner of Harrods. Smith went after accepting he had asked questions without declaring the connection in the Register of Members' Interests; Hamilton hotly disputed the claims but was asked to resign by the prime minister when new allegations emerged from an alleged former mistress (Doig, 1998; Woodhouse, 1998). Mandelson and Robinson also resigned because of a failure on Mandelson's part to register an interest after Robinson lent lending him £373,00 interest-free to purchase property in London. Robinson also resigned over the affair, though perhaps more because he had been under pressure for months from opposition MPs, having apologized to the House for not properly declaring various business interests (Mandelson, 2010).

David Blunkett resigned after failing to declare an interest in DNA Bioscience where he took a directorship several months before being reappointed as a minister. The company was preparing to bid for government contracts, and whilst the investigation by the cabinet Secretary Gus O'Donnell decided Blunkett had not broken the Ministerial Code of Conduct it found that he should have consulted the Advisory Committee. Indeed it emerged that the Chair of the Advisory Committee had three times suggested Blunkett should seek their advice; and further that Blunkett held other paid positions he had not declared. Given that Blunkett had just returned to cabinet following his first forced exit the prime minister decided Blunkett had to go, summoning him to Downing Street just before Blunkett was due to appear before a House of Commons select committee.

Lord Sainsbury, a major donor to the Labour Party, was implicated in the honours scandal, being interviewed by the police as a potential witness, when it was alleged that businessmen were donating to the Labour Party and being rewarded with honours. Sainsbury insisted he resigned for 'personal reasons' unconnected to the scandal, but also said he was 'fed up with his name being dragged through the mud'.

We will not describe all the non-resignations as some involve quite trivial issues. Jonathan Aitken's is worth mentioning since it was coterminous with the Smith and Hamilton cases. It concerned a bill for his stay at the Ritz Hotel in Paris debited to the sixth-floor suite of Arab businessman Mr Ayas. Aitken's case has to be understood in the light of a series of allegations against MPs and ministers of taking money for helping businesspeople. The *Sunday Times* had exposed several Conservative MPs as willing to take money to ask questions in the House, but more serious for Aitken were the resignations of Tim Smith and Neil Hamilton discussed above. Just two days after Hamilton had been cleared of wrongdoing by the Cabinet Secretary Jonathan Aitken found himself denying similar charges. The *Guardian* claimed that it had documents demonstrating that Ayas paid at least half Aitken's hotel bill. Aitken survived partly because of the support of his backbenchers who attacked the *Guardian* for the 'cod fax' purporting to be from the House of Commons it sent to the owner of the Ritz, Mohammed Al-Fayed. Al-Fayed was aware the fax was from the *Guardian* but wanted to be able to deny helping the paper in its pursuit of Aitken. It was thought by many parliamentarians that a fax on House of Commons headed paper sent to a person who knew it was fake was a much more heinous crime than the Chief Secretary to the Treasury receiving gifts from an arms dealer. Aitken was probably helped by the previous resignations, as his backbenchers felt compelled to rally round lest the Major government lose all its second-rank ministers. Aitken was later jailed for contempt of court as it emerged he had lied in his testimony in a libel case about the affair (Harding, Leigh and Pallister, 1999).

In all other resignation issues forced exits are less likely to occur. Personal errors led to resignation fourteen times, only 17 per cent of cases, and there were only four or 16 per cent over 'other controversy'. The resignations because of personal error are Hugh Dalton, November 1947; Tom Galbraith, November 1962; Charles Fletcher-Cooke, February 1963; John Profumo, June 1963; Nicholas Fairbairn, January 1982; Leon Brittan, January 1986; Edwina Currie, December 1988; Nicholas Ridley, July 1990; Michael Mates, June 1993; Allan Stewart, February 1995; Peter Mandelson, January 2001; Beverley Hughes, April 2004; and David Blunkett, December 2004.

Hugh Dalton's resignation on 13 November 1947 is one of the most famous. As already mentioned, it followed his admission that he had revealed information about the Budget in a conversation with a lobby correspondent before he entered the House of Commons to make his budget speech. Whilst the opposition had asked for an inquiry into the leak, Dalton had already offered his resignation and on the 13th he explained to the Commons what had happened. Two leaders in *The*

Times (15 and 19 November) said Dalton was unfortunate but had to resign because of the trust placed in the Chancellor. The opposition praised Dalton's conduct in resigning so swiftly but did not conceal their satisfaction at the resignation of a Chancellor whose policies they so bitterly opposed. An inquiry reported that Dalton had made an unpremeditated disclosure but had had no way of knowing it would be published before his speech in the Commons. He returned to the cabinet six months later in May 1948 as Chancellor of the Duchy of Lancaster.

Galbraith, Under Secretary of State for Scotland, resigned on 8 November 1962 after the committee of inquiry into the Vassall spy case published an interim report which included letters received by William Vassall from Galbraith and his wife. These letters had been the subject of considerable press speculation. The report cleared Galbraith of any wrongdoing. But he felt he had to resign because 'it is apparent to me that my long accustomed manner of dealing with officials and others who serve me has in the circumstances become an embarrassment to the Government'. He offered his resignation to the prime minister who accepted, saying that he believed it to be the right thing to do because criticism could be made of his judgement. Whilst somewhat obscure, this case has been coded by us as personal error which is how Galbraith and the prime minister publicly viewed it.

Charles Fletcher-Cooke, Joint Under Secretary of State at the Home Office, resigned on 22 February 1963 after a man to whom he had lent a car was alleged to have committed a motoring offence. Fletcher-Cooke had been involved with the aftercare of delinquents, and decided in this case he had made an error of judgement. He also wanted to be free to take legal action if necessary.

Fairbairn has been discussed above; his is a case where his earlier problems were at least as much a cause of his resignation as the error he actually made. Leon Brittan has also been coded with personal error as the proximate cause, but the issues surrounding this resignation are complex. Brittan was Secretary of State for Trade and Industry and resigned on 24 January 1986 over the Westland affair. Heseltine had resigned only thirteen days earlier, when he left a cabinet meeting over a dispute over the minutes of a cabinet committee and a refusal to clear all speeches on the matter with the Cabinet Office. Thatcher herself was under pressure over this resignation as public opinion suggested more voters wanted Heseltine as leader of the Tory party than Thatcher, and two-thirds also believed he was right to resign. A *Times* leader and the *Economist* criticized her approach to cabinet government. Brittan's troubles began when Heseltine asked in the Commons on 13 January if Brittan had received a letter from British Aerospace seeking clarification of its position over the Westland bid. Brittan denied this at first but later apologized to the House for misleading it. Further complications arose over Brittan's dealings with industrialists in this matter and the leaking of a letter from the Solicitor General. A public opinion poll showed most voters believed Brittan was lying and should resign and, following an inquiry into the leaked letter, on the 23 January the prime minister stated that Brittan had authorized the leak after consultation with officials at Number 10. Brittan came under increasing pressure from his colleagues and backbenchers and resigned the following day. There was a great deal of speculation about how much the prime minister knew, and suspicion that Brittan was a scapegoat to save her.

Edwina Currie, the Health Minister, resigned on 16 December 1988. She is perhaps the only minister ever to have resigned for telling the truth to the public. The National Farmers' Union mounted an extensive campaign against her after she suggested in an ITN television interview that most egg production was contaminated with salmonella. This was widely reported as the claim that most eggs were contaminated with salmonella. There were many articles sympathetic to her, arguing that although her remark was unguarded it was essentially true and she had pinpointed a serious problem the industry and the Department of Agriculture had been trying to keep quiet. She was defended strongly by the prime minister, but eventually was forced to resign in the face of opposition from the powerful Conservative backbench 1922 Committee and because of the growing number of writs for damages issued by egg producers. In the hostility of many Conservative backbenchers there were suggestions of anti-Semitism – as there had been with Brittan – and a great deal of resentment over her attention-grabbing style. Labour, anxious to score political points after a recent poor by-election performance, also pressed hard for her resignation, saying she had threatened jobs with her careless remarks.

Nicholas Ridley, Secretary of State for Trade and Industry, resigned after an interview published in the *Spectator* where he had described proposed European monetary union as 'a German racket designed to take over the whole of Europe', suggesting giving up sovereignty to

Europe was as bad as giving it up to Adolf Hitler. Outcry abroad and at home led to his resignation.

Michael Mates, Under-Secretary of State for Northern Ireland, resigned on 25 June 1993 after a month's battle to ride out his links with the fugitive businessman Asil Nadir, who had skipped the country before trial for corruption. It was revealed that whilst Nadir was under investigation by the Serious Fraud Squad, Mates had sent him a watch engraved with the words 'Don't let the buggers get you down'. Despite being supported by the prime minister, Mates eventually resigned. Most of the press and many of his own backbenchers felt he had acted very foolishly, though there were also many who had not forgiven him for his previous sniping at Margaret Thatcher over the poll tax and defence cuts.

Allan Stewart, a Scottish Office Minister, resigned on 8 February 1995 after he had allegedly brandished a pickaxe in a confrontation with anti-motorway campaigners in Glasgow. This incident occurred when Major's government felt beleaguered by scandals and problems, and the resignation was deemed necessary atonement for participation in an undignified fracas.

We have coded Peter Mandelson's second resignation in January 2001 a 'personal error' though, as discussed above, it is not clear he did anything wrong at all. An inquiry later completely exonerated him, but he was asked to step down by a Blair anxious to draw a line under increasing 'sleaze' accusations against his government. Beverley Hughes, Minister of State for Citizenship and Counter Terrorism, committed the cardinal sin of misinforming the House of Commons: the issue was over her knowledge of procedural errors concerning the granting of visas to certain categories of Eastern European workers. David Blunkett's first resignation is similar in form to that of Mandelson's: he was accused of interfering in the visa application of the nanny of his former lover. The claim almost certainly came to light because Blunkett was pursuing a paternity claim through the courts against his pregnant former lover.

The four resignations in the case of 'other controversies' are Patrick Gordon-Walker in January 1965, Jeremy Bray in May 1969, David Mellor in September 1992 and the Earl of Caithness in January 1994. The latter involved a personal problem, following his wife's suicide and criticism of his behaviour by her relatives. Gordon-Walker was made Foreign Secretary despite having lost his seat at the general election. He was made Labour candidate for the theoretically safe seat of Leyton but lost the by-election narrowly. Having him go to the Lords would have been too embarrassing for the government. Bray, Joint Parliamentary Secretary at the Ministry of Technology, was forced to resign by Wilson when he announced he wanted to write a book on the machinery of government. Bray said that he did not wish to leave the government. He had been involved with the changes Labour had made and his only difference with the prime minister was on the issue of publication.

Conclusions

We have given some descriptive statistics on the proximate causes of forced exits, that is, the issues that arose that led to ministers feeling they could no longer serve in the government. We have put these resignations in the context of 'non-resignations', that is, similar issues where the minister did not feel obliged to resign. Such counterfactuals are always problematic. With regard to forced exits due to policy disagreement, we cannot code such disagreements where they have been kept within government circles, or the minister did not feel so strongly that his disquiet moved beyond a relatively small circle of friends or advisors; nor indeed any case which was not brought to press attention and led to calls for the minister to resign. Perhaps all that can be said about such proximate causes of forced exit is that ministers will resign only when they feel strongly enough about an issue or, perhaps, where they can see strategic advantage to their careers from resigning over a particular issue. Forced exits due to policy disagreement stand out in another way: they concern the issue of collective rather than individual ministerial responsibility.

Within the other categories we can see that there is some variation surrounding the likelihood that an issue will lead to a resignation. Traditionally sex scandals have tended to lead to resignation. This factor has been reduced since the mid-1990s, partly as a result of changing moral standards – husbands leaving wives for lovers is now considered a less heinous crime; homosexuality is more accepted – but also perhaps reflects the fact that the public has become more immune to the stories the press have chosen to report. The pursuit of sex stories was a 1980s phenomenon and perhaps after thirty years they make less impact (and perhaps their publication in itself helped change public attitudes). Certainly stories about ministers (and MPs and celebrities) have been carried in newspapers in the past twenty years that would not have appeared twenty years earlier, let alone sixty years ago.

Similarly, financial scandals such as those which brought down Blunkett the second time would not have been considered heinous thirty years earlier, as scrutiny of ministers' financial interests is far greater now than in the past. Even over policy and performance concerns, politicians and newspapers seem quicker to demand resignation than they once did. The one issue that has not changed much is personal error in the form of misleading parliament. If a minister is caught doing so, only a very rapid apology may avert resignation. It is also clear when examining cases of resignation and non-resignation that the specific facts of the case are not the only concern with regard to the probability of resigning. To be sure, the more serious the issue, the more heinous the perceived crime, the more likely it is that a minister will have to resign. However, other factors are important. Both Mandelson and Blunkett might have survived the second time they were forced to exit if each had not already had such a recent previous resignation. In many ways what is unusual in those cases is that Blair was quicker to bring back ministers who had been forced to go than any previous prime minister of the modern era.

In other examples a minister might be saved by others' resignations. Arguably Jonathan Aitken survived his financial scandal precisely because Smith and Hamilton had resigned and the complications about the newspaper's behaviour enabled his party to rally behind him. There might be advantages to a prime minister's accepting resignations (Dewan and Dowding, 2005) as we see in the next chapter, but they cannot keep losing ministers, and at times might need to face out criticism. Ministers falling like ninepins only encourages the opposition and press to scream for more, as John Major found at the height of his problems. We examine these issues more carefully in Chapter 7. Here we have concentrated upon the proximate causes of forced exits, there we focus upon more underlying factors and ultimate causes that lead to ministerial turnover or survival, not only immediately over a given issue or scandal, but over the longer term.

7 | *Ministerial performance and tenure*

In Chapter 4 we demonstrated that the background characteristics of ministers help explain the length of their ministerial service. For example, observable traits (gender, age) and verifiable facts about the background of those taking office (experience, education level) allow us to predict the length of their ministerial spell relative to others with different characteristics. The fact that we observe and measure these traits before ministers enter office, and that we include a range of measures that capture fixed characteristics of the governments that ministers serve, allows us to be reasonably confident that the parameters of interest are well identified. That is, we can be confident that the effects we observe are causal: some ministers serve longer than others because of their characteristics and not, for example, because they served as part of a particular administration or because specific incidents determine tenure. To be sure, some ministers leave office due to specific events occurring, but our fixed effects control for those factors allowing us to see the effects of ministerial characteristics outside of those other influences.

Our micro-level data on British cabinet ministers has thus allowed us to provide some answers to fundamental questions in British politics. Attaining ministerial office is the pinnacle of a political career. Therefore we can assume that upon attaining high office, ministers desire longer rather than shorter spells. It might then be seen as surprising that fixed characteristics should affect the length of service, and yet, as we have noted, careful investigation of executive service elsewhere has produced similar findings. However the analysis is not yet as tight as one would like. For one, we would like to know why these background characteristics matter. Can we use our data to rule in or rule out different hypotheses about the mechanism that links individual traits, fixed at the time of entry, to ministerial survival? Might it be, for instance, that these traits are correlated with the ability of a minister to perform the tasks expected of him?

Moreover, knowing that ministerial characteristics are determinants of the length of ministerial tenure, whilst providing useful information about the nature of representative government, does not tell us much about cabinet relations. And this is what we set out to understand. As we described in Chapter 5, cabinets have had different sets of members and prime ministers have different styles and some have been more willing to fire their cabinet colleagues than others. To derive our estimates we controlled for the style of different prime ministers. Thus, by including these fixed effects, we obtain estimates that allow for these differences. These are, however, elements of a prime minister's style, documented in Chapter 5, that whilst interesting for the historical record tell us little systematic about the strategic interaction between the prime minister and her ministers. Understanding these aspects is the task we have set ourselves.

In this chapter we begin to get at some of these more thorny issues concerning how the prime minister manages her cabinet. To do so we utilize some of the data introduced in previous chapters that allow us to gain a better understanding of cabinet relations. In particular we are interested in the performance of ministers. Many factors of course go into judgements about how well a minister performs, and the prime minister in her role as the principal with oversight over ministers will be in one of the best positions to make such judgements. However, the public and parliament also can see how well ministers perform in terms of how they behave in public, how their private behaviour becomes known publicly, and how well their departments and the policies they originate and implement operate. We have collected data, as described in Chapter 6, on calls for ministers to resign. In this chapter we use these resignation calls as performance measures. They provide information to the prime minister about how parliament and the public view the performance or competence of a minister in a manner that was not available at the time of his appointment. Such calls are an important oversight procedure not only for parliament but also for the prime minister. The prime minister will have private information about the performance and competence of a minister, and will also have strategic and political incentives to respond differentially to such calls with regard to different ministers. We described these strategic considerations in Chapter 6. Overall, however, controlling for such effects will allow us to see whether prime ministers do generally respond to calls as performance measures. In this chapter we provide a theoretical and empirical framework for assessing this question. Before continuing, we recap and expand on our assumptions laid out in Chapter 2 and discuss how they relate to our analysis.

Our assumptions

Ministerial motives

We assume that ministers are career politicians. In a parliamentary system, attaining ministerial status represents the peak of a political career. Whatever motivates entry to parliament – a desire for office in itself, the perks that come with office, policy influence or social standing – achieving these goals means attaining ministerial status and maintaining it. Ministers leave office for a variety of reasons, but when they leave, even voluntarily, it is because they realize they are unlikely to progress further or will soon be asked to leave; when their stated reason for exit is a desire to spend more time with their family, few political commentators give such views much credence. Moreover, in the UK government ministers are rarely deselected by their constituents. Exit from ministerial life comes either when the government the minister serves is defeated (either by a vote of no confidence in parliament or election of the opposition) or when a minister is fired because of perceived negligence or incompetence on his part. Adopting the parlance of King (1981) and Diermeier, Keane and Merlo (2005), government ministers in parliamentary democracies are 'career politicians': they desire government service, and once appointed wish to remain in office for as long as possible. This assumption is important since it means that ministers will never willingly jeopardize their career through unwise actions. More precisely, we assume that a minister never willingly attracts a resignation call in order to terminate prematurely his political career and that the prime minister knows that.

Misalignment of incentives

Whilst serving country and party is an important source of (intrinsic) motivation for a minister it does not preclude the existence of an incentive problem between the prime minister and her ministers. The objectives (or payoff functions) of ministers and prime ministers are not necessarily perfectly aligned. Relative to the concerns of the prime minister, a minister may place more weight on tasks that are uncorrelated with government performance. For example, relative to what the prime minister would have him do, a minister may wish to allocate more time to building relations within the party or with outside interests and less to developing government policy. A minister might have different policy objectives from the prime minister. Some ministers might be interested in building networks for post-ministerial careers, and so on. An incentive problem arises because the prime minister does not directly observe the effort of her ministers which determines the outcome of a ministerial task. Instead, she observes a variety of performance measures which include inside information provided by other colleagues, backbench MPs, civil servants and so on, but also more public measures such as, for example, the success or failure of the minister's policy initiatives and media evaluations of his performance.

Imperfect information

We assume that the prime minister can observe the characteristics of her ministers when appointing them. All of the variables we have documented, and others we have been unable to obtain data on, form part of the prime minister's decision to appoint someone to cabinet. Thus, at the time of the appointment the prime minister observes aspects of a minister's career to date, including education and experience, for example, and forms a judgement as to whether he should be included in the cabinet. Thus we might consider that at the time of the appointment the prime minister forms a judgement as to the executive competence of her potential employee based on what she knows about his career thus far; this includes knowledge of the fixed traits that we measure, and observations of the minister's performance on the back benches and on committees on which we do not have measures. As we have seen, some of these factors are also causally related to how long a minister will serve.

We suppose, however, that these factors do not alone determine the length of a minister's service. In particular a minister is subject to performance evaluation: when he is the subject of a resignation call then the prime minister may re-evaluate her decision to include him in her cabinet. This is because the prime minister might now infer that the minister is not as competent as she assumed when appointing him, that is, he is simply not up to the task; alternatively, the prime minister might infer that the minister did not perform well because he did not allocate enough time and effort to his government task. Empirically, this means that there is a now a time-varying variable, namely whether a minister is subject to a resignation call or not on a particular day, that may determine whether he remains in office or not.

Performance and tenure

Our question is: how does the prime minister use the instruments at her disposal to align ministerial incentives with her own, when the information she receives about the minister's performance (or competence) is imperfect? The prime minister has a blunt but powerful weapon at her disposal: she can fire the minister in question if his performance is not to her liking. The instrument is blunt, because it is an all-or-nothing affair: either the minister stays or he goes. It is powerful, nonetheless, because ministers have the objective, so we assume, to remain in office.

An immediate question is: how does the prime minister wield this instrument and how does its exercise depend upon the information that is available to her? The theory of incentives says that the principal should reward or punish an agent using any performance measure that (conditional on the other measures of performance used) has a positive informational content (Gibbons, 2005; Baker, Gibbons and Murphy, 1994; Holmstrom and Milgrom, 1991; Holmstrom, 1979, 1982). The weight these performance measures should receive in the reward scheme will depend on the responsiveness of these measures to the effort and quality of the agent, their degree of alignment with the objectives of the principal, and the level of risk they involve. *Ceteris paribus*, the more responsive, the higher the degree of alignment; the lower the risk involved, the more weight the reward scheme should place on those measures.

Resignation calls as performance indicators

We can consider the relationship between ministers and their principals as a contract which specifies tenure as a function of a set of observed indicators. For example, we might believe that a resignation call is more likely to occur when the performance of a minister falls below some threshold. It signals that the minister is not performing as expected. He might be allowing other objectives – such as his own political preferences or his private life – to interfere with his performance. Or he might simply not be up to the job despite apparently having had the qualities when a backbencher. Importantly, a resignation call may provide information to the prime minister that was not available when she appointed her minister. As such, a resignation call serves as a discrete indicator of ministerial performance and, intuitively, we would expect the relationship between it and observed tenure to be negative; a call for a minister to resign leads to shorter tenure, since a prime minister will sometimes accede to that call.

We note of course that a prime minster cannot always accede to a call for a minister to resign. That would encourage the opposition to call more often. We also note that the prime minister ought to have some private information to judge when to accede to a call and when not. Furthermore, no performance measure is perfect and the prime minister will recognize that fact. A resignation call is a noisy signal of the minister's performance, compounding features for which he is rightly responsible in his capacity as minister with subsidiary factors, or random shocks, beyond his control. To illustrate, consider the issue of riots or inmates escaping from prison. Such activities by high-security prisoners in British jails in 1991, 1994 and 1995, for example, have demonstrated systematic failures within the prison service during that decade (Barker, 1998). These events have often resulted in a call for the Home Secretary to resign since ultimately prisons fall within his responsibility. Such events may reveal problems within the prison service, or within particular prisons. But whether an attempted break-out is successful can rely upon chance factors as well as on the preparedness of the prison service. Individual prison policy is in the hands of prison governors, and even systemic failures within the prison service might be more to do with policies and policy implementation that were in place prior to the incumbent minister being in charge. Furthermore, a problem such as prison escapes, serious though they are, is only one aspect of the Home Secretary's responsibilities. Failure in one (small albeit high-profile) area does not mean failure in others. Such factors make the problem and the call for resignation noisy signals on the Home Secretary's competence.

Since a resignation call is a noisy signal of the minister's performance, the theory of incentives tells us that the prime minister will likely include additional measures in her reward scheme. Random shocks which might affect the performance of a particular minister are likely to be correlated across government departments: an economic downturn caused by a change in oil prices can lead to a tightening of the budget and to pressures on service delivery across departments; a health scare, such as a virulent new flu strain, could affect health services, transport, and education, amongst other things. Whereas different ministers are responsible for these areas, their performance is conditional on a common shock and the evaluation of that performance should reflect this common cause.

One measure which might be used in addition to an individual performance measure is the performance of other ministers: if a minister is seen to fail at a time when others falter also, his performance may not be judged so harshly; conversely, if a minister is seen to succeed when others around him flounder, then his performance will be judged more positively. Indeed, to the extent that the performance of others can help eliminate noise in any individual measure of performance, it may be a good idea to include it in the reward structure of an agent.

In theory these shocks may be observed by a prime minister when deciding whether to fire or to retain a particular minister. In practice, and in order to test this theory, we would require measures for every possible common shock but this is not feasible. Nevertheless we can use a single measure which encompasses many of these common causes. As our measure we use the cumulative number of resignation calls over a government's life span. We think that our cumulative, rather than an instantaneous, measure of collective performance might be a natural way for a prime minister to aggregate the relevant information. For example, whereas the performance of health and emergency services could be immediately assessed in light of a flu outbreak, the effects on educational performance (such as test scores) would be felt some time thereafter.

Our framework allows us to explore the relationship between the length of ministerial tenure and the performance of government ministers, when controlling for the individual characteristics such as ministerial experience, educational background, and gender, which we have seen are strong predictors of the length of ministerial tenure. Here, however, we can more closely identify how the arrival of information about the performance of the minister and the government he serves affects length of service. This provides us with leverage on two questions.

Firstly, we can better assess the channels via which the individual attributes we identified earlier affect ministerial tenure. In particular we can assess whether the relationship is due to the minister's superior performance, which is perhaps related to a given set of skills that are associated with these background characteristics. If this is so then we would expect that, once we include our additional measures, then the effect of a minister's background characteristics will wash away in the analysis.

Secondly, we can now explore our hypothesis about how the prime minister uses information to shape her cabinet. If our hypothesis is correct we should then expect that a minister's hazard rate is increasing with a call made for his resignation. However, the hazard rate for any individual member should be *decreasing* the greater the cumulative number of scandals within the cabinet as a whole. We examine how these factors interact and provide a full description of the empirical framework we use to test these claims below. Before moving on to that framework we provide some descriptive analysis of our claims.

Descriptive analysis

Figure 7.1 explores the effect of our individual performance measure on ministerial tenure. It provides a graphical representation of the survival probability of a minister during his first five years in office, breaking down the sample according to those ministers who have not faced a resignation call ($r = 0$) at time t and those who have faced at least one such call ($r = 1$) at time t. As one would expect, the survivor function falls more sharply for ministers experiencing one or more resignation calls. In governments which see out their term of office, 70 per cent of ministers who have not been involved in a resignation call survive; in contrast only 30 per cent of ministers who have faced one or more resignation calls see out their term.

Figure 7.2 distinguishes between ministers who have been subjected to just one resignation call and those who have received more than one. Doing so reveals that the likelihood of surviving a second call is far lower than that of surviving a first.

Our main hypothesis is that a minister's prospects for survival are driven not only by his own performance, but sometimes also by the

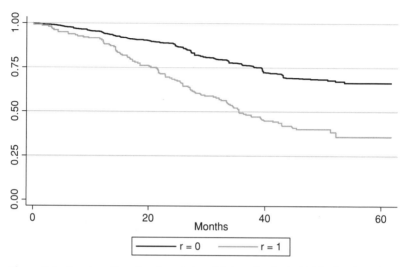

Figure 7.1. Survivor function for ministerial duration by individual resignation calls

Note: r = 1 when one or more individual resignation calls have been received and 0 otherwise.

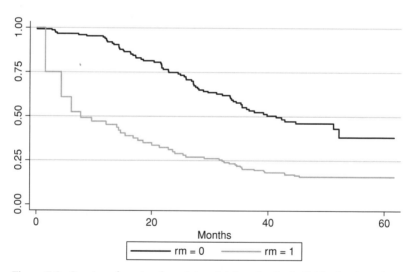

Figure 7.2. Survivor function for ministerial duration by individual resignation calls for minister with at least one resignation call

Note: rm = 1 when two or more individual resignation calls have been received and 0 when only one has.

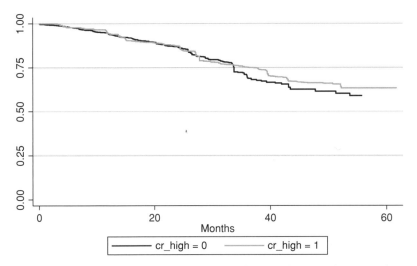

Figure 7.3. Survivor function for ministerial duration by cumulative number of government resignation calls below or above the median
Note: The median number of resignation calls is 11. cr_high=1 if the number of cumulative government resignation calls is bigger than the median and 0 otherwise.

performance of the government as a whole. To explore this hypothesis we look at the effect of our measure for government performance. Figure 7.3 illustrates the survivor function evaluated at different levels of our cumulative resignations index. In particular, we look at the survivor function of ministers in governments where this cumulative index is less than 11 at time t and more than 11 at time t, with 11 being the median number of resignation calls during all our spells. Ministers serving in governments that experience more cumulative calls than the median tend to survive longer, although the difference seems small.

A key message illustrated in these graphs is that a minister's probability of survival depends not only on his own performance but also on that of his colleagues. This is as we expected. The evidence suggests that the prime minister uses all of the information that is available to her when retaining or firing her minister: relative performance matters.

However, indicative though they are, these graphs do not pin down these effects. If we are to identify the effects of our performance indicators, we must also take account into account the characteristics of different ministers in our sample. The likelihood of a resignation call may reflect observed personal characteristics of a minister that were known to the prime minister when she formed her government. Our hypothesis, recall, is that resignation calls provide additional information to the prime minister that was not available at the time of appointment. So, in order to distinguish the effect of additional information that a prime minister receives, we need to factor out the effect of these characteristics on a minister's hazard.

Of course it might also be that the cumulative number of resignation calls may simply reflect fixed characteristics of the government in which a minister serves. Some governments may be comprised of a less able set of ministers, or may be more prone to resignation calls than others. Little wonder then that the survival rate of ministers is lower. To extrapolate from such cohort effects we need to follow a similar empirical design to that used in Chapter 4. We want to estimate the effect of an increase in the cumulative number of resignation calls on a minister's tenure when controlling for the fixed characteristics of the government in which he serves.

In order to get to grips with these issues we return to the framework that we used in Chapter 4. We develop the empirical strategy used there in order to disentangle these effects.

Empirical strategy

As before we define t_{ig} as the spell of minister i in government g where an individual starts a new ministerial spell every time he enters government independently of having had spells in previous governments. Therefore, expressed in the proportional hazards format, we adopt the following empirical specification:

$$h_{igt} = \lambda(t_{ig})exp\left[\psi_1 r1_{igt} + \psi_2 r2_{igt} + \beta cr_{gt}\right], \qquad (7.1)$$

where $\lambda(t_{ig})$ is the minister's baseline hazard at t_{ig}. The first two terms in the bracketed expression are individual measures of ministerial performances: $r1_{igt}$ is a dummy variable equal to one after a minister receives a first resignation call (zero otherwise) and $r2_{igt}$ is equal to one after a minister receives a second or higher resignation call (zero otherwise). cr_{gt} is our measure for government performance: the cumulative number of resignation issues at any given point in time for the current government. In some of our models we also include interactions between the individual performance indicators and our government performance measure; this allows the prime minister's response to an individual resignation call to vary with the cumulative number of such calls.

Our first hypothesis is that the prime minister will reward those ministers who perform well with longer tenure relative to those who perform poorly. This hypothesis suggests that a minister's hazard rate is higher when facing a resignation call; as these calls provide new information on the minister's performance, so we expect ψ_1 and ψ_2 to be positive. In estimating two dummy variables, one for a first resignation call and one for later calls, we allow the effect of the first new piece of information to be different from that of information associated with a subsequent resignation call.

Our second hypothesis is that, since the prime minister is often forced to rely on noisy information about individual ministers' performance, she should turn to information on the performance of all ministers, and reward and punish individual ministers according to their performance relative to the government's overall performance. In using all the information that is available to evaluate the performance of her ith minister the prime minister will compare the individual measures of performance against the level of cr_{gt}. Keeping individual performance constant an increase in cr_{gt} should make the minister less vulnerable. It follows that, if relative performance evaluation is an important determinant of ministerial tenure, expected tenure should be decreasing in cr_{gt} and so we expect β to be negative.

It is worth pointing out that when a minister receives, for example, a first resignation call then both $r1_{igt}$ and cr_{gt} increase by one unit. If we consider the logarithm of the relative hazard rates (LRH) of equation (1),

$$\text{LRH} = \text{Log}[\lambda(t_{ig})] + \psi_1 r1_{igt} + \psi_2 r2_{igt} + \beta cr_{gt}, \tag{7.2}$$

the direct marginal effect on the hazard rate due to a change in $r1_{igt}$ from 0 to 1 and from a given cr_{gt} to $cr_{gt} + 1$ is the exponentiated sum of ψ_1 and β. We can test whether the total effect is statistically different from zero by using a Wald test for the null hypothesis $\psi_1 + \beta = 0$ in the LRH model. In the presence of interactions between individual and collective calls for resignations the marginal effect depends on the level of cumulative calls for resignation.[1]

Of course, resignation calls may be correlated with initial traits that characterize the government rather than with the arrival of new information. For example, a government that has been elected by a large margin may face a weak opposition and therefore the actions of its ministers are less likely to be called into question. If, independent of any resignation calls, ministers elected by a large majority are likely to serve longer, any estimate of the effect of individual and collective calls for resignation that does not account for this effect will be biased and inconsistent.

In practice, these issues can be resolved by conditioning on government traits. In our benchmark model we include the following government controls that are fixed at the start of the government spell: majority (percentage share of MPs commanded by the governing party) and government size (number of ministers appointed within the first three weeks of government). We also include dummies for the term currently being served by the prime minister, and allow them to vary with the party in power (by interacting the prime ministerial term dummy with a dummy for government party). Ultimately, we condition on government fixed effects (i.e., the interaction of prime minister times term dummies).

It will also be the case that individual factors are correlated with the arrival rate of resignation calls and with the durability of ministers. For example, cabinet ministers are more likely to be exposed to resignation calls but should also be more qualified for such responsibilities. A negative correlation arises between the innate quality of a minister and the rate at which scandals arrive. This problem can be solved by conditioning on the post a minister is assigned to. In fact, in our benchmark model we can condition on an array of observable ministerial characteristics at the start of the government spell: a public school dummy (equal to one if the minister attended public school – the term used in the UK for private education – and zero otherwise), an

---

[1] The logarithm of the relative hazard rate (LRH) in this case is:

$$\text{LRH} = \text{Log}[\lambda(t_{ig})] + \psi_1 r1_{igt} + \psi_2 r2_{igt} + \beta cr_{gt} + \gamma_1 r1_{igt} cr_{gt} + \gamma_2 r2_{igt} cr_{gt}.$$

Thus, the direct marginal effect on the hazard rate that is due to a change in $r1_{igt}$ from 0 to 1 and from a given cr_{gt} to $cr_{gt} + 1$ is the exponential of the following expression: $[\psi_1 + \beta + \gamma_1(cr_{gt} + 1)]$.

Oxbridge dummy (variable equal to one if the minister attended university at Oxford or Cambridge and zero otherwise), a female dummy, age in years at the start of ministerial spell, a noble dummy (variable equal to one if the minister is an unelected peer and zero otherwise), an experience dummy (variable equal to one if a minister has served under previous governments and zero otherwise), and a past issues dummy (variable equal to one if a minister had resignation calls in a previous government and zero otherwise). We also include three timing varying dummies to control for the level of the post held by the minister.

In summary, since ministerial and government performance could be correlated with systematic features of government and intrinsic traits of individuals, our benchmark proportional hazards model is

$$h_{igt} = \lambda(t_{ig}) \exp\left[\psi_1 r1_{igt} + \psi_2 r2_{igt} + \beta cr_{gt} + X_{ig}\gamma' + B_g\pi'\right], \quad (7.3)$$

where X_{ig} is a vector of individual characteristics, and B a set of government characteristics.[2]

The Cox proportional hazards model makes no restrictions on the shape of the underlying baseline hazard. However, it does not allow the effect of our performance indicators to be affected by the length of time the government has been in existence. This assumption appears strong, as one might expect the prime minister to react differently to resignation calls occurring early in the mandated term. To explore this issue we look at two sub-samples: one includes the first 18 months in government only; the other includes the first 36 months in government.

Finally, we account for the fact that both the number and the effect of resignation calls may vary over different time periods in our sample. There are two reasons why this might be the case. One reason is that understanding of the doctrines of individual and collective ministerial responsibility has changed over time. In Chapter 3 we discussed the generation of those conventions during the nineteenth century, but more subtle changes in the understandings of what they entail might have occurred during the past sixty years. Individual ministerial responsibility was thought to have meant that ministers were held

---

[2] As our data are recorded in days, the continuous time hazard model allows for more efficient use of the information available. In particular it allows us to exploit the difference between cases where ministers resign at different time points within a discrete time period, be it month or year. We report specification tests for the proportional hazards assumptions alongside our estimates.

to account for errors that occurred in their departments, and were expected to shield civil servants from blame when such errors came to light. This was often interpreted to mean that ministers should resign following any great problem within their department even if they were not personally to blame; they would be subject to sacrificial responsibility (Woodhouse, 1994). That myth is exploded when looking at forced exits, as we did in the previous chapter (see also Dowding and Kang, 1998), and well recognized in the academic literature. However, ministers might still be held accountable for departmental failures even without being sacrificed through shorter tenure overall. However, the parliamentary and public expectation that a minister will resign following a call for a resignation is lowered as the myth of sacrificial responsibility is exposed and ministers are less likely to shield those around them. The agency process within the British civil service exposes civil servants to much greater individual scrutiny and blame which has had a knock-on effect on senior civil servants within departments who are much more likely to be named and blamed now than in the past. It follows from these factors that a systematic increase in the number of resignation calls made over time thus corresponds to a difference in the information content of such calls rather than any greater failings among ministers (or indeed their servants). Whilst, on the one hand, the lines of ministerial responsibility have become more blurred, on the other, ministers are more likely to deny publicly any wrongdoing rather than carry the can for those who work under them. A second reason is that media exposure of ministers has varied systematically during our period of analysis. An issue brought to public attention in 1997 might not have been made public had it occurred some decades earlier. This change in media reporting has been documented worldwide (see for example Patterson, 1993; Orren, 1997; Schultz, 1998; Corner and Pels, 2003) where issues once considered not worthy of serious attention now are widely discussed and in a language much less deferential to politicians.

This analysis suggests that the information content of a resignation call may vary over time, and it follows that the prime minister's response to such calls may vary also. To deal with this we split our data set and compare estimates across different time periods. Specifically we look at the period 1945–70 and the period 1970–2007, the latter being the one in which we observe a larger number of resignation calls reported by the media.

Table 7.1. *The impact of individual and government calls for resignation on ministerial tenure. Hazard ratios from Cox models*

Variables	(1)	(2)	(3)	(4)
First individual call for resignation	2.108*** [0.271]	2.588*** [0.353]	2.547*** [0.349]	2.365*** [0.326]
Second or higher individual call for resignation	4.027*** [0.691]	5.121*** [0.938]	5.048*** [0.931]	4.861*** [0.901]
Cumulative government resignation calls	0.989*** [0.004]	0.984*** [0.005]	0.973*** [0.007]	0.956*** [0.008]
Minister controls	No	Yes	Yes	Yes
Government controls	No	No	Yes	No
Prime minister × term fixed effects	No	No	No	Yes
Observations	39,255	39,255	39,255	39,255

Notes: Standard errors in brackets. *significant at 10%; **significant at 5%; ***significant at 1% .

Hazard rate estimates

Using this empirical design allows us to identify the effect of an individual call for resignation and that of an increase in the cumulative number of such calls. In Table 7.1, we present estimates of the hazard rate of ministers, conditional on both individual performance and characteristics as well as the performance and characteristics of the government in which they serve. Column 1 presents results for a model that includes only our performance measures. It shows that the hazard rate for a minister facing his first resignation call is roughly twice that of a minister who has not (yet) faced such a call. The hazard rate of a minister facing a second resignation call is roughly 4 times higher than that of a minister with one resignation call and about 8.5 times higher than that of a minister without resignation calls to his name. A unit increase in the cumulative number of resignation calls reduces the hazard by roughly 1 per cent.

In column 2, we add controls for ministerial traits such as gender, educational background, age and nobility as well as for ministerial attributes which relate to a minister's service in previous governments. Specifically we control for whether a current minister has past experience of government and whether during that time he received a resignation call. Whilst these variables are fixed within a government term we also control for a minister's position in the government rank which may change.[3]

Estimates for this model reveal that the hazard rate for a minister facing his first resignation call is between 2.1 and 2.6 times higher than that of a minister who has not yet faced such a call; a minister facing a second resignation call has a hazard rate 5.1 times that of a minister with one resignation call to his name. In this model, a unit increase in the cumulative number of resignation calls reduces the hazard rate by roughly 1.5 per cent.

In the remaining models estimated we vary the controls for fixed attributes of the government in which a minister serves. Column 3 adds controls for the size of the government majority, government size, which party is in power, a government term and an interaction between these two. Finally, in column 4 we add government fixed effects as well. In all, these variables have almost no effect on the estimates of our individual performance measures on tenure, though the reduction in the hazard rate due to a one-unit increase in our collective performance measure tends to be larger.

In summary, the estimates show that the hazard rate for a minister facing his first resignation call is between 2 and 2.6 times that of a minister with no resignation call to his name. A minister facing a second resignation call has an even steeper increase in his hazard rate. Thus, the effect of the second call is the increase in the hazard rate with respect to one resignation call. Finally, a unit increase in the cumulative number of resignation calls reduces the hazard by between 1 and 4 percentage points, with the largest estimates derived from a model which stratifies the baseline hazard by prime minister. As we explained in the previous section, when calculating the direct marginal effect that is due to a change in $r1_{igt}$ or $r2_{igt}$ from 0 to 1 we must take

---

[3] We might also control for a minister's departmental brief. Since 1945 there have been many reorganizations of government with some departments having contracted whilst others have expanded. Indeed over the sixty years the same or similar job titles have covered very different responsibilities. We coded all departments in nine categories (Home Office, Foreign Affairs, Treasury, Other Economic, Environment, Defence, Education, Agriculture and Other), bundling together jobs with similar responsibilities and importance in government. The inclusion of controls for these departments does not affect our results and so we do not report them.

into account the effect on the cumulative resignation calls of a change in these variables. A straightforward calculation on the full model estimated in column 4 reveals that the hazard ratio for a first individual call is 2.261 with a p-value 0.07, and that a second resignation call increases this hazard rate by 4.6 with a p-value of 0.0001.[4]

Our initial estimates are consistent with predictions based on the theory of performance evaluation when applied to ministerial tenure. The largest direct effect upon a minister's hazard rate is his own performance, particularly if he receives a second call. Consistent with relative performance evaluation, an increase in the cumulative resignations index reduces a minister's hazard rate. Therefore, our data fit what we expect to see from an application of the theory of incentives to cabinet government. Calls for resignation might have a lower informational content than they once did, but more extensive media reporting of issues that once did not receive public attention and wrath (and hence lead to prime ministerial interest) means the increasing calls are not simply more fluff. The growing number of calls is increasing the amount of information that the prime minister considers relevant and to which she reacts.

In Table 7.2, which has a similar structure, we estimate a model which includes an interaction term between our individual and collective performance measures. This allows us to assess whether the effect of an individual resignation call depends upon the number of similar calls that have been made within the same government.

We observe that the likelihood of leaving government upon receiving a resignation call is increasing in the cumulative number of calls. In particular, upon receiving a first resignation call, a minister's hazard rate increases by 2.5 per cent for each previous call made to any minister in the government he serves. We find no evidence of a similar interaction effect when considering second or higher resignation calls. After including the interaction term, we find no direct effect of a first

---

[4] These estimates are based on ministerial features that are observable both to the prime minister and to the political analyst. Other skills may not be so apparent. These effects can create a spurious correlation between the arrival of information and the tenure of ministers. In order to tackle this issue we also factor out fixed unobservable ministerial characteristics by stratifying our estimates by individual. We do not report those estimates here but they show that although the effects of our individual performance measure are very imprecisely estimated, the effect of our collective performance measure is robust.

Table 7.2. *The impact of individual and government calls for resignation on ministerial tenure. Hazard ratios from Cox models*

Variables	(1)	(2)	(3)	(4)
First individual call for	1.487**	1.723***	1.735***	1.609**
resignation	[0.300]	[0.359]	[0.363]	[0.340]
Second or higher	7.261***	7.738***	7.952***	7.671***
individual call for	[2.123]	[2.348]	[2.424]	[2.362]
resignation				
Cumulative	0.988**	0.982***	0.972***	0.955***
government	[0.005]	[0.005]	[0.007]	[0.008]
resignation calls				
First individual call X	1.025**	1.030***	1.028***	1.028***
cumulative	[0.010]	[0.011]	[0.011]	[0.011]
government calls				
Second individual call	0.972**	0.980	0.978	0.978
X cumulative	[0.013]	[0.014]	[0.014]	[0.014]
government calls				
Minister controls	No	Yes	Yes	Yes
Government controls	No	No	Yes	No
Prime minister × term	No	No	No	Yes
fixed effects				
Observations	39,255	39,255	39,255	39,255

Notes: Standard errors in brackets. *significant at 10%; **significant at 5%; ***significant at 1%.

resignation call. As in the previous table, the hazard rate of a minister increases steeply with a second resignation call and a unit increase in the cumulative number of resignation calls reduces the hazard of a minister.

Our analysis reveals interesting aspects of the interdependence of cabinet careers. Upon receiving a first resignation call a minister's hazard is higher when other ministers of the same government have faced similar calls; thus, a minister must bear some of the brunt of his colleagues' failures. Our findings are consistent with expectations based on the doctrine of collective responsibility, according to which a minister cannot absolve himself from joint responsibility for government policy. Whilst political scientists and legal scholars have long analysed this convention (Jennings, 1959; Mackintosh, 1977; Woodhouse,

1994, 2003; Gay and Powell, 2004), to our knowledge ours are the first measurable estimates of its effect.

Our results show that, when controlling for observable traits of ministers and the governments they serve, there are clear and discernable effects of our individual and collective performance measures on ministerial hazard rates. However, to estimate the total effect of a resignation call on a minister's hazard rate we need to consider the interaction between these variables. These calculations are presented in Table 7.3 which provides a substantive account of the total effect of a resignation call by calculating the effects of an individual resignation call at various values of the cumulative resignation calls. We include the p-value for the test that these effects are statistically different than zero. The first column shows the total effect of a first resignation call and reveals that the hazard ratio increases sharply as more ministerial colleagues face similar calls for their resignation. The hazard ratio for a minister receiving his first resignation call when serving a government where there have been twenty-five such resignation calls is roughly twice that of a minister in a government where his is the first such call. From column 2 we observe that, although a second resignation call has a large effect on the hazard rate of an individual minister this effect is fairly constant.

In the first two columns of Table 7.4 we explore whether the impact of resignation calls differs if they occur during the first 18 months of government or during the first 36 months of government. In Table 7.4, for brevity, we only present models with the full set of controls as in column 4 of Table 7.2. In column 1, we look at the first 18 months only and in column 2 at the first 36 months. The effect of a second resignation call has a larger effect when both calls occur within the first 18 months of government. In both cases the direct effect of government performance decreases the hazard, but the magnitude of this effect appears to be stronger in the first 18 months of government.

In columns 3 and 4 of Table 7.4 we look at whether the effect of resignation calls differ over time: column 3 of this table estimates the model for the period 1945 to 1970 (including the Wilson 1966–70 government); column 4 estimates the model for the subsequent period. Results tend to be qualitatively similar with a few exceptions: ministers facing their first call were at less risk in the earlier period; ministers facing more than one resignation call appear to have a higher hazard rate in the latter period; the cumulative effect of resignation calls had

Table 7.3. *The total impact of an individual call for resignation on ministerial tenure at different levels of cumulative government resignation calls. Hazard ratios*

Government resignation calls	1st individual call	2nd individual call
1	1.579	7.268
	[0.0260]	[0.0001]
2	1.623	7.261
	[0.0142]	[0.0001]
3	1.668	7.254
	[0.0071]	[0.0001]
4	1.715	7.246
	[0.0032]	[0.0001]
5	1.763	7.239
	[0.0013]	[0.0001]
10	2.023	7.197
	[0.0001]	[0.0001]
15	2.321	7.149
	[0.0001]	[0.0001]
20	2.664	7.094
	[0.0001]	[0.0001]
25	3.057	7.032
	[0.0001]	[0.0001]
30	3.508	6.961
	[0.0001]	[0.0003]
Model includes:		
Individual and cumulative resignation calls interaction	Yes	Yes
Minister controls	Yes	Yes
Prime minister × term fixed effects	Yes	Yes

Note: p-values for the Wald tests in brackets.

a stronger effect between 1945 and 1970. On this evidence we would conclude that higher exposure to the media has not drastically changed the way the prime minister reacts to resignation calls.

Conclusions

Ministers do not resign as often as they used to following calls for resignation. This had led many to believe that ministerial accountability

Table 7.4. *The impact of individual and government calls for resignation, and their interaction, on ministerial tenure by number of months in office and two eras (1945–1970, 1970–1997). Hazard ratios from Cox models*

Variables	(1)	(2)	(3)	(4)
First individual call for resignation	1.308 [0.508]	1.298 [0.312]	1.235 [0.467]	1.752* [0.507]
Second or higher individual call for resignation	13.791*** [9.983]	7.958*** [2.781]	4.346** [2.785]	10.435*** [4.071]
Cumulative government resignation calls	0.879*** [0.031]	0.943*** [0.012]	0.784*** [0.027]	0.965*** [0.010]
First individual call X cumulative government calls	1.090** [0.048]	1.042*** [0.015]	1.066* [0.038]	1.022* [0.012]
Second individual call X Cumulative government calls	0.945 [0.076]	0.973 [0.020]	1.015 [0.055]	0.970* [0.015]
Minister controls	No	Yes	Yes	Yes
Government controls	No	No	Yes	No
Prime minister × term fixed effects	No	No	No	Yes
Observations	16,591	32,068	10,010	29,245

Notes: Standard errors in brackets. *significant at 10%; **significant at 5%; ***significant at 1%. Column 1 is estimated up to the first 18 months of government only and column 2 is estimated up to to 36 months in office. Column 3 is estimated with those governments in office between 1945 and 1970 (including Wilson 1966–70), and Column 4 is estimated with those in government from 1970 to 2007 (starting with Heath 1970–74).

has been reduced. It is true that sacrificial responsibility for errors is not as great as it once was. This fact in itself might lead to greater calls for resignations on the grounds that calls might only have been made when people thought the minister truly should consider his position, whereas now, since they do not expect resignations, they might make such calls even when they do not consider the issue to be so serious. However, as the number of calls for resignation has increased so has the number of actual resignations. This shows that whilst the pertinent informational content of calls may have reduced, the prime minister still considers that the pertinent information received remains valid when considering whether ministers should resign.

In fact, even though sacrificial responsibility has reduced, with a minister being now less likely to forcibly exit following a resignation call, ministerial accountability might still exist as calls for resignation lead to lower tenure. We have shown this lower tenure occurs with calls for resignation even though ministers are not always forced to exit at the time of the calls. Thus individual ministerial responsibility is stronger than many commentators allow. Collective responsibility is the responsibility of all the cabinet for the actions of each of its members. We show that the hazard for all cabinet ministers increases in resignation calls for any one minister, demonstrating the collective nature of responsibility. Furthermore our results indicate support for the hypothesis that a minister's performance is evaluated relative to that of his fellow ministers. How one is judged is based not only upon how well one does, but also upon how well every other minister does as the government faces the same stream of events. Our findings add to previous empirical analysis of how the prime minister manages her cabinet (Indridason and Kam, 2005, 2008; Dewan and Dowding, 2005; Huber and Martinez-Gallardo, 2004), and we are further able to present strong evidence of relative performance effects upon ministerial tenure.

8 | Conclusion

We have provided an in-depth and detailed investigation into the length of tenure of British ministers. We have examined some of the elements of the job of a British minister and provided some discussion of what British prime ministers look for in their cabinets. We have collected extensive data on the hiring and firing of ministers in the period 1945 to 2007. That data, gathered over several years, records the length of ministerial spells, the background characteristics of those who served in government, and measures of their performance. This is the first book-length study of such micro-level data on British political careers and contributes to a new and engaging literature that looks at issues of accountability in parliamentary democracy in a more extensive and quantitative manner than previously. In analysing that data we have tried to account for the length of tenure of ministers, and provide some new insights into the nature of ministerial accountability.

When looking at the departure of ministers we have done so in two different ways. We examined descriptively the forced departure of ministers either due to disagreements within cabinet, or due to some scandal or other issue. We coded these forced exits into a series of categories which can be considered the proximate reasons for their resignation. The proximate reason is the story behind the removal. In order to get a handle on the proximate reasons for removal we also needed to code for resignation issues that did not lead to a forced exit. This aspect of a minister's tenure is intimately connected with what, certainly in the public but also in commentators' minds, is regarded as retributive accountability: ministers shouldering the blame for their mistakes or leaving a government they cannot support on an important aspect of policy. However, we argue that this is not the entirety of retributive accountability, since ministers who have been criticized but do not resign might still face retributive accountability by having a shorter tenure than ministers not so criticized. We argue that such criticisms provide an important source of information to the prime minister and so act as a performance measure for ministers.

In addition to such performance measures we have information on the background characteristics of ministers. In our more general analyses we are interested in the ultimate causes of the length of ministerial tenure. A scandal or other issue might be the proximate reason why a given minister resigns at a given time, but other factors together with performance provide ultimate reasons for length of tenure.[1] In analysing data on all ministers who serve in British government we found that background characteristics, fixed at the time of entry, have a significant impact on how long ministers survive in office. In short, knowing a minister's age, gender, and experience at the time when they enter office is useful if we want to predict how long they will stay there. As we have seen, establishing these relations is not straightforward since we need to separate the effect of the individual characteristics of ministers from those of the governments in which they serve. However using a variety of statistical techniques we have been able to show the robustness of our finding that individual characteristics determine how long ministers serve in government. This is one of the main findings of our work. It speaks directly to the nature of representation in parliamentary democracies: the fact that people who have a university degree from Oxbridge are not only more likely to serve in government, but also last in office longer than those without such a degree offers an interesting perspective on political equality in the United Kingdom. However, it is possible that this effect is due to a set of skills that correlate with both an Oxbridge degree and serving longer in office. Our analysis, which controls for performance of ministers, suggests that this is not the case. That is, the background characteristics of ministers are important determinants, in their own right, of ministerial tenure.

Moving beyond the background characteristics of those who serve, our model provides new insights into the nature of accountability in British government. A key element of the British constitution is that the powers held by the Crown to hire and fire ministers are exercised by a prime minister who can ask for the resignation of a minister, or refuse to accept a resignation offered. Our data provide some insight

---

[1] See Mayr (1961) for the proximate–ultimate explanation distinction in evolutionary biology.

into the exercise of prime ministerial power. We briefly described the events that faced governments under different premiers, and examined the styles of different prime ministers as perceived by the cabinet and commentators around them. By looking at the tenure of ministers under different prime ministerial regimes we have been able to support, and sometimes to lay to rest, common historical perceptions about how different prime ministers have managed their cabinets, and show that some perceptions are based upon specific periods within their tenure.

An important element of our investigation has been in illustrating not only the effect of different prime ministers, but also, more generally, how the prime minister as a strategic actor responds to the emergence of new information about her ministers that was not available at the time of their appointment. To get at this question we coded data on political scandals and other issues related to resignation calls that might provide some insight into how the prime minister responds to new information. This data collection exercise and its description have provided new insights into critical events in British history: the type of scandals, and their regularity, that affect British ministers via the impact they have on ministerial tenure. Among the issues that lead to calls for resignation are scandals which, as we show, have increased over time. In part we think this occurs because of the changing nature of society and media commentary upon it. We also show that prime ministers have responded to those greater numbers of calls with a greater number of forced exits at roughly the same (or slightly lower) ratio of calls to actual forced exits. This demonstrates that these calls do seem to provide information that prime ministers need to respond to.

As we have shown, the observed correlations between these indicators and ministerial tenure are illustrative of the strategic tensions that determine ministerial tenure. Ministers who experience more than one resignation call have significantly shorter tenure, even when controlling for background characteristics that may be related to their ability to perform their governmental tasks. This demonstrates that retributive accountability cannot be a matter entirely of forced exits. It suggests that individual ministerial accountability is stronger than many commentators, who concentrate entirely upon forced exits, would have us believe.

Perhaps more surprising are our findings that a minister's tenure is conditioned not only on his own personal performance but also on the collective performance of the government in which he serves. Ministers are far more likely to survive in office when the cumulative number of resignation calls, aggregated across the government, is high. As we have shown, these findings are consistent with a principal–agent analysis in which the prime minister makes efficient use of all new information which comes her way. In particular, our data are consistent with the expectation that the prime minister uses overall government performance as a benchmark against which to evaluate the performance of her ministers and justify their retention or dismissal. This also demonstrates that individual accountability is intimately connected to collective responsibility, in the sense that risks that each minister faces are shared to some extent across the governmental team. Here, where the risks are shared, accountability of the government as a whole should be expected through the electoral system, in the manner that we laid out following the principal–agent analysis of Kaare Strom. Individual ministers have to pay the price of failure to keep the parliamentary party happy, but only if there are others good enough to replace them. If they are part of a collective that is failing, then it is the party as a whole that must pay the price. Thus we have demonstrated the true working of individual and collective ministerial responsibility within British government in the post-1945 period as viewed through the lens of principal–agent analysis.

A clear advantage of our single-country analysis is that we can control for the fixed aspects of British institutions and political life that may affect the length that politicians serve in office. In concluding then we should consider the external validity of our findings. In particular, although we have found clear evidence of these relationships in the data from the UK, our single-country analysis does not account for the type of institutional variation that would allow us to test whether these effects vary across institutional environments. For example, with the exception of a brief period of minority government under James Callaghan in the late 1970s, all governments we analyse are single-party majority governments.

There are important institutional variations that govern the hiring and firing of ministers (Dowding and Dumont, 2009a) across parliamentary regimes which affect the strategic considerations of prime ministers especially where they operate with multi-party governing majorities or minority governments. Thus an important difference between the prime ministers we analyse and those elsewhere is that the British prime ministers operate under different constraints to those found in parliamentary democracies elsewhere. However there are similarities also: British prime ministers must maintain the support of key factions within their party or risk putting their own position in jeopardy. Furthermore, we assume that ministers in all systems generally want to retain their posts as ministers and hence criticism can act as a performance indicator. However, this factor is much greater in a single-party government than in coalition governments where a prime minister might be happy to allow an incompetent from a rival party within the coalition to retain his position, if his public incompetence damages the rival party more than his own. Furthermore, often prime ministers in coalition governments cannot choose to fire ministers without the danger of bringing down the government. In that sense the lines of accountability that we witness in theory and in practice are much clearer in the British case than in multi-party coalitions.

Moreover, a key variable we can exploit in the British case is significant variation in the size of the governing majority, a variable that captures key constraints on British, as well as other, prime ministers. The difference of course is that in Britain, with few notable exceptions, including the current administration, the size of the governing majority is determined solely by the legislative weight of the largest party.

It is important to note, moreover, that although the British prime minister has discretion over hiring and firing not afforded to all prime ministers, she is not unique in this regard. Indeed our results suggest that we might expect to find further evidence for the principal–agent model described here in countries where single-party government is the norm, or alternatively where governing coalitions are clearly dominated by a single party. Moreover, we might also expect these relations to be observed in countries where, as in the UK, governments and ministers do not face a formal vote of investiture.

Do our lessons travel beyond such cases? We should not rule this out. All prime ministers in parliamentary democracies have some power to hire and fire ministers albeit under differing constraints. Moreover the mechanism that underpins our analysis is that the prime minister uses the threat of firing her ministers to induce better performance. All prime ministers, whether leaders of single-party majorities or otherwise, are affected by the negative publicity that surrounds their government when ministerial performance falls short and is called into question. In short, all prime ministers have some incentive to remove poorly performing ministers.

In the last resort, however, the extent to which the relations we have uncovered in the British data hold in other parliamentary democracies, or are masked by factors such as the need to maintain coalition governments, remains an empirical topic for investigation. At least our estimates serve as a comparative benchmark for such analysis. We hope that our work will stimulate further research into the career profiles of parliamentarians in Britain and elsewhere that will further our understanding of the issues of accountability and performance raised here.

References

Akerlof, G. (1970): 'The Market for "Lemons": Quality Uncertainty and the Market Mechanism', *Quarterly Journal of Economics*, 84(3), 488–500.

Alderman, R. K. and N. Carter (1991): 'A Very Tory Coup: The Ousting of Mrs Thatcher', *Parliamentary Affairs*, 44, 125–39.

Alt, J. E. (1975): 'Continuity, Turnover, and Experience in the British Cabinet, 1868–1970', in *Cabinet Studies: A Reader*, ed. by V. Herman and J. E. Alt. Macmillan, Houndmills.

Arrow, K. (1963): 'Uncertainty and the Welfare Economics of Medical Care', *American Economic Review*, 55(5), 941–73.

Avon, L. (1960): *The Memoirs of Anthony Eden*. Faber, London.

Baker, G. P., R. Gibbons and K. J. Murphy (1994): 'Subjective Performance Measures in Optimal Incentive Contracts', *Quarterly Journal of Economics*, 109(4), 1, 125–56.

Barker, Anthony (1998): 'Political Responsibility for the UK Prison Service: Ministers Escape Again', *Public Administration*, 76, 1–23.

Barro, R. J. (1973): 'The Control of Politicians: An Economic Model', *Public Choice*, 14, 19–42.

Bennedetto, G. and S. Hix (2007): 'The Rejected, the Dejected and the Ejected: Explaining Government Rebels in the 2001–2005 British House of Commons', *Comparative Political Studies*, 40(7), 755–81.

Besley, T. (2006): *Principled Agents? The Political Economy of Good Government*. Oxford University Press.

Besley, T. and S. Coate (1995): 'Does Electoral Accountability Affect Economic Policy Choices? Evidence from Gubernatorial Term Limits', *Quarterly Journal of Economics*, 110, 769–98.

Best, H. and M. Cotta (2000): *Parliamentary Representatives in Europe 1848–2000: Legislative Recruitment and Careers in Eleven European Countries*. Oxford University Press.

Black, D. (1958): *The Theory of Committees and Elections*. Cambridge University Press.

Blackstone, T. and W. Plowden (1988): *Inside the Think Tank*. Heinemann, London.

Blick, A. (2004): *People Who Live in the Dark*. Politicos, London.

Blick, A. and G. Jones (2010): *Premiership: The Development, Nature and Power of the Office of the British Prime Minister*. Imprint Academic, Exeter.

Blondel, J. (1985): *Government and Ministers in the Contemporary World*. Sage, London.

Boyle, L. (1980): 'Address to the Royal Institute of Public Administration', *Public Administration*, 58, 1–12.

Brock, M. and E. Brock (eds.) (1982): *Letters to Venetia Stanley*. Oxford University Press.

Burch, M. and I. Holiday (1996): *The British Cabinet System*. Prentice-Hall, Hemel Hempstead.

Butler, D., A. Adonis and T. Travers (1994): *Failure in British Government: The Politics of the Poll Tax*. Oxford University Press.

Butler, D. and G. Butler (2000): *Twentieth-Century British Political Facts 1900–2000*. Macmillan, Basingstoke.

Butler, D. and G. Butler (2006): *British Political Facts since 1979*. Palgrave Macmillan, Houndmills, Basingstoke.

Butler, D. and G. Butler (2011): *British Political Facts*. Palgrave Macmillan, Basingstoke.

Caselli, F. and M. Morelli (2004): 'Bad Politicians', *Journal of Public Economics*, 88(3/4), 759–82.

Chester, D. N. (1989): 'The Crichel Down Case', in *Ministerial Responsibility*, ed. by G. Marshall. Oxford University Press.

Childs, D. (1992): *Britain since 1945: A Political History*. Routledge, London.

Cmd, 7617 (1949): *Report of the Tribunal Appointed to Inquire into Allegations Reflecting on the Official Conduct of Ministers of the Crown and Other Public Servants*.

Cook, R. (2003): *The Point of Departure: Diaries from the Front Bench*. Simon and Schuster, London.

Corner, J. and D. Pels (2003): *Media and the Restyling of Politics*. Sage, London.

Cox, D. R. (1972): 'Regression Models and Life Tables', *Journal of the Royal Statistical Society*, 5(34), 187–220.

Cox, G. (1994): 'The Development of Collective Responsibility in the United Kingdom', *Parliamentary History*, 13(1), 32–47.

Cox, G. W. (1987): *The Efficient Secret*. Cambridge University Press.

Crosby, T. L. (1997): *The Two Mr Gladstones: A Study in Psychology and History*. Yale University Press, New Haven.

Currie, E. (2002): *Diaries 1987–1992*. Little Brown, London.

Dal Bo, E., P. Dal Bo and J. Snyder (2009): 'Political Dynasties', *Review of Economic Studies*, 76, 115–42.

Deacon, D. (2004): 'Politicians, Privacy and Media Intrusion in Britain', *Parliamentary Affairs*, 57(1), 9–23.

Delafons, J. (1982): 'Working in Whitehall: Changes in Public Administration 1952–1982', *Public Administration*, 60, 253–72.

Dewan, T. and K. Dowding (2005): 'The Corrective Effect of Ministerial Resignations on Government Popularity', *American Journal of Political Science*, 49(1), 46–56.

Dewan, T. and D. P. Myatt (2007): 'Leading the Party: Coordination, Direction, and Communication', *American Political Science Review*, 1,001(4), 827–45.

Diermeier, D., M. Keane and A. Merlo (2005): 'A Political Economy Model of Congressional Careers', *American Economic Review*, 95(1), 347–73.

Dogan, M. and P. Campbell (1957): 'Le Personnel Ministeriel en France et en Grande-Bretagne', *Reviue Française de Science Politique*, pp. 313–45.

Doig, A. (1989): 'The Resignation of Edwina Currie: A Word Too Far', *Parliamentary Affairs*, 42, 317–29.

Doig, A. (1993): 'The Double Whammy: The Resignation of David Mellor, MP', *Parliamentary Affairs*, 46, 167–78.

Doig, A. (1996): 'From Lynskey to Nolan: The Corruption of British Politics and Public Service?' *Journal of Law and Society*, 23(1), 36–56.

Doig, A. (1998): ' "Cash for Questions": Parliament's Response to the Office that Dare Not Speak its Name', *Parliamentary Affairs*, 51(1), 36–50.

Dowding, K. (1995): *The Civil Service*. Routledge, London.

Dowding, K. (2008): 'Perceptions of Leadership', in *Public Leadership: Perspectives and Practice*, ed. by P. 't Hart and J. Uhr, pp. 93–100. ANU epress, Canberra.

Dowding, K. and P. Dumont (eds.) (2009a): *The Selection of Ministers in Europe: Hiring and Firing*. Routledge, London.

Dowding, K. and P. Dumont (2009b): 'Structural and Strategic Factors Affecting the Hiring and Firing of Ministers', in *The Selection of Ministers in Europe: Hiring and Firing*, ed. by K. Dowding and P. Dumont, pp. 1–20. Routledge, London.

Dowding, K. and W.-T. Kang (1998): 'Ministerial Resignations 1945–97', *Public Administration*, 76(3), 411–29.

Dowding, K. and E. McLeay (2011): 'The Firing Line: Forming and Controlling Cabinets in New Zealand and the United Kingdom', in *How Power Changes Hands: Transition and Succession in Government*, ed. by P. 't Hart and J. Uhr. Routledge, London.

Downs, A. (1957): *An Economic Theory of Democracy*. Harper and Row, New York.

Dumont, P., L. De Winter and R. Dandoy (2001): 'Demissions gouvernmentales et performances electorales des majorities sortantes (1946–1999)', *Courrier hebdomadaire du CRISP*, n. 1,722, 51pp.

Dunleavy, P. (1995): 'Estimating the Distribution of Positional Influence in Cabinet Committees under Major', in *Prime Minister, Cabinet and Core Executive*, ed. by R. A. W. Rhodes and P. Dunleavy, pp. 198–231. Macmillan, Houndmills.

Dunleavy, P. and R. A. W. Rhodes (1990): 'Core Executive Studies in Britain', *Public Administration*, 68, 3–28.

Dunleavy, P., S. Weir and G. Subrahmanyam (1995): 'Public Response and Constitutional Significance', *Parliamentary Affairs*, 48(4), 602–16.

Eggers, A. C. and J. Hainmueller (2009): 'MPs for Sale? Returns to Office in Postwar British Politics', *American Political Science Review*, 1,003(4), 513–33.

Ellis, D. L. (1980): 'Collective Ministerial Responsibility and Collective Solidarity', *Public Law*, 2(5), 367–96.

Fearon, J. D. (1999): 'Electoral Accountability and Control of Politicians: Selecting Good Types versus Sanctioning Poor Performance', in *Democracy, Accountability, and Representation*, ed. by A. Przeworski, S. C. Stokes and B. Manin, pp. 55–97. Cambridge University Press.

Ferejohn, J. (1986): 'Incumbant Performance and Electoral Control', *Public Choice*, 50, 5–25.

Finer, S. E. (1956): 'The Individual Responsibility of Ministers', *Public Administration*, 34, 377–96.

Foley, M. (1993): *The Rise of the British Presidency*. Manchester University Press.

Foley, M. (2000): *The British Presidency: Tony Blair and the Politics of British Leadership*. Manchester University Press.

Fry, G. (1993): *Reforming the Civil Service: The Fulton Committee on the British Home Civil Service 1966–68*. Edinburgh University Press.

Fulton, L. (1968): *Report of the Committee on the Civil Service 1966–68 Cmd 3638*. HMSO (Fulton Report), London.

Gagliarducci, S. and T. Nannicini (2009): 'Do Better Paid Politicians Perform Better? Disentangling Incentives from Selection', unpublished manuscript, Tor Vegata and Bocconi universities.

Gagliarducci, S. and M. D. Paserman (2008): *Gender Differences in Cooperative Environments: Evidence from the Duration in Office of Italian Mayors*. NBER Working Paper 14893.

Gallagher, B., M. Laver and P. Mair (2006): *Representative Government in Modern Europe: Institution, Parties and Government*. McGraw Hill, New York, 4th edn.

Ganz, G. (1980): 'Parliamentary Accountability of the Crown Agents', *Public Law*, 2(5), 456–80.

Gastor, R. (1988): 'Sex, Spies and Scandal: The Profumo Affair and British Politics', in *The Politics of Scandal: Power and Process in Liberal Democracies*, ed. by A. S. Markovits and M. Silverstein, pp. 62–88. Holmes and Meier, New York.

Gay, O. and T. Powell (2004): *The Collective Responsibility of Ministers*. House of Commons Working Paper, London.

Gibbons, R. (2005): 'Incentives Between Firms and Within', *Management Science*, 51(1), 2–17.

Grey, E. (1969): 'Parliamentary Government 1858', in *The Nineteenth-century Constitution: Documents and Commentary*, ed. by H. J. Hanham. Cambridge University Press.

Groseclose, T. and K. Krehbiel (1994): 'Golden Parachutes, Rubber Checks, and Strategic Retirements from the 102nd House', *American Journal of Political Science*, 38(1), 75–99.

Gross, J. (1963): 'The Lynskey Tribunal', in *Age of Austerity*, ed. by M. Sissons and P. French, pp. 255–75. Oxford University Press.

Hamilton, A., J. Madison and J. Jay (1787–8/1982): *The Federalist Papers*. Bantam Books, New York.

Hammond, S. A. (2001): 'Review of the Circumstances Surrounding an Application for Naturalization by Mr. S. P. Hinduja in 1998', No. 0287 2000–01, 9 March, HMSO. www.official-documents.gov.uk/document/hc0001/hc02/0287/0287.9sp.

Hardie, F. (1970): *The Political Influence of the British Monarchy, 1868–1952*. Batsford, London.

Harding, Luke, David Leigh and David Pallister (1999): *The Liar: The Fall of Jonathan Aitken*. London: Fourth Estate.

Headey, B. (1974a): *British Cabinet Ministers*. Allen and Unwin, London.

Headey, B. (1974b): 'The Role Skills of Cabinet Ministers: A Cross-National Review', *Political Studies*, 22(1), 66–85.

Heasman, D. J. (1962): 'The Prime Minister and the Cabinet', *Parliamentary Affairs*, 15(4), 461–84.

Heffernan, R. (2003): 'Prime Ministerial Predominance? Core Executive Politics in the UK', *British Journal of Politics and International Relations*, 5(3), 347–72.

Hennessy, P. (1986a): 'The Westland Affair', *Journal of Law and Society*, 13, 423–32.

Hennessy, P. (1986b): *Cabinet*. Basil Blackwell, Oxford.

Hennessy, P. (2001): *The Prime Minister: The Office and Its Holders Since 1945*. Penguin, London.

Hennessy, P. (2005): 'Rulers and Servants of the State: The Blair Style of Government 1997–2004', *Parliamentary Affairs*, 58(1), 6–16.

Herman, V. (1975): 'Comparative Perspectives on Ministerial Stability in Britain', in *Cabinet Studies: A Reader*, ed. by V. Herman, and J. E. Alt, pp. 55–76. Macmillan, London.

Heseltine, M. (2000): *Life in the Jungle: My Autobiography*. Methuen, London.

Holmstrom, B. (1979): 'Moral Hazard and Observability', *Bell Journal of Economics and Management Science*, 10, 74–91.

Holmstrom, B. (1982): 'Moral Hazard in Teams', *Bell Journal of Economics and Management Science*, 13, pp. 324–40.

Holmstrom, Bengt and Paul Milgrom (1991): 'Multitask Principal–Agent Analyses: Incentive Contracts, Asset Ownership, and Job Design', *Journal of Law, Economics and Organization*, 7, 24–52.

Huber, J. D. and C. Martinez-Gallardo (2004): 'Cabinet Instability and the Accumulation of Experience: The French Fourth and Fifth Republics in Comparative Perspective', *British Journal of Political Science*, 34(1), 27–48.

Hume, D. (1742/1978): *A Treatise of Human Nature*. Oxford University Press.

Indridason, I. H. and C. Kam (2005): 'The Timing of Cabinet Reshuffles in Five Parliamentary Systems', *Journal of Legislative Studies*, 30(3), 327–63.

Indridason, I. H. and C. Kam (2008): 'Cabinet Shuffles and Ministerial Drift', *British Journal of Political Science*, 38(4), 621–56.

Jenkins, R. (1975): *On Being a Minister*. St Martin's Press, New York.

Jennings, I. (1959): *Cabinet Government*. Cambridge University Press, 3rd edn.

Jones, B., A. Gray, D. Kavanagh, M. Moran, P. Norton and A. Seldon (1994): *Politics UK*. Harvester Wheatsheaf, New York, 2nd edn.

Jones, G. (1995): 'The Downfall of Margaret Thatcher', in *Prime Minister, Cabinet and Core Executive*, ed. by R. A. W. Rhodes and P. Dunleavy, pp. 87–107. Macmillan, London.

Jordan, G. (1983): 'Individual Ministerial Responsibility: Absolute or Obsolete?' in *The Scottish Yearbook*, ed. by D. McCrone. Edinburgh University Press.

Jordan, G. (1991): 'The Professional Persuaders', in *The Commercial Lobbyists*, ed. by G. Jordan. Aberdeen University Press.

Jordan, G. (1994): *The British Administrative System: Principles versus Practice*. Routledge, London.

Jordan, G. and J. Richardson (1987): *British Politics and the Policy Process*. Unwin Hyman, London.

Judge, D. (2005): *Political Institutions in the United Kingdom*. Oxford University Press.

Kaufman, G. (1997): *How to Be a Minister*. Faber and Faber, London.

Keman, H. (1991): 'Ministers and Ministries', in *The Profession of Minister in Western Europe*, ed. by J. Blondel and J.-L. Thiebault, pp. 99–118. Macmillan, Houndmills.

Key, V. O. (1956): *American State Politics: An Introduction*. Alfred A. Knopf, New York.

King, A. (1981): 'The Rise of the Career Politician in the UK', *British Journal of Political Science*, 11(2), 249–85.

King, A. (1994): 'Ministerial Autonomy in Britain', in *Cabinet Ministers and Parliamentary Government*, ed. by M. Laver and K. Shepsle, pp. 203–25. Cambridge University Press.

King, A. (ed.) (1985): *The British Prime Minister*. Macmillan, Houndmills.

King, G., J. E. Alt, N. E. Burns and M. Laver (1990): 'A Unified Model of Cabinet Dissolution in Parliamentary Democracies', *American Journal of Political Science*, 34(3), 846–71.

King, S. (2003): *Regulating the Behaviour of Ministers, Special Advisers and Civil Servants*. Constitution Unit, University College, London.

Kuhn, R. (2002): 'The First Blair Government and Political Journalism', in *Political Journalism: New Challenges, New Practices*, ed. by R. Kuhn and E. Neveu. Routledge, London.

Lamont, Norman (1993): 'Norman Lamont's Resignation Speech'. Available online at www.answers.com.

Lee, J. M., G. W. Jones and J. Burnham (1998): *At the Centre of Whitehall*. Macmillan, Basingstoke.

Leonard, D. (2005): *A Century of Premiers: Salisbury to Blair*. Palgrave Macmillan, Basingstoke.

Mackintosh, J. P. (1977): *The British Cabinet*. Stevens and Sons, London, 3rd edn.

Macmillan, H. (1969): *Tides of Fortune 1945–1955*. Macmillan, London.

Madgwick, P. (1991): *British Government: The Central Executive Territory*. Phillip Allen, New York.

Major, J. (1999): *The Autobiography*. HarperCollins, London.

Mandelson, P. (2010): *The Third Man: Life at the Heart of New Labour*. HarperCollins, London.

Marshall, G. (1989): 'Individual Responsibility: Some Post-War Examples', in *Ministerial Responsibility*, ed. by G. Marshall, pp. 127–33. Oxford University Press.

Matthew, H. C. G. (1997): *Gladstone 1809–1898*. Clarendon Press, Oxford.

Mattozzi, Andrea and Antonio Merlo (2008): 'Political Careers or Career Politicians', *Journal of Public Economics*, 92(3–4), 597–608.

Mayr, E. (1961): 'Cause and Effect in Biology', *Science*, 131, 1,501–6.

McCubbins, M., R. Noll and B. Weingast (1987): 'Administrative Procedures as Instruments of Political Control', *Journal of Law, Economics and Organization*, 3, 177–243.

McCubbins, M., R. Noll and B. Weingast (1989): 'Structure and Process; Politics and Policy: Administrative Arrangements and the Political Control of Agencies', *Virginia Law Review*, 75, 382–431.

McCubbins, M. and T. Schwartz (1984): 'Congressional Oversight Overlooked: Police Patrols Versus Fire Alarms', *American Journal of Political Science*, 28, 165–79.

McLean, I., A. Spirling and M. Russell (2003): 'None of the Above: The UK House of Commons Votes on Reforming the House of Lords, 2003', *Political Quarterly*, 74, 298–310.

McLeay, E. (1995): *The Cabinet and Political Power in New Zealand.* Auckland University Press.

McLeay, E. (2006): ' "Buckle, Board, Team or Network": Understanding Cabinet', *New Zealand Journal of Public and International Law*, 4(1), 37–54.

Merlo, A. M., V. Galasso, G. Landi and A. Mattozzi (2010): 'The Labour Market of Italian Politicians', in *The Ruling Class: Management and Politics in Modern Italy*, ed. by T. Boeri, A. M. Merlo and A. Prat. Oxford University Press.

Michels, R. (1915/1958): *Political Parties: A Sociological Study of the Oligarchical Tendencies of Modern Democracy.* Free Press, Glencoe.

Milne, R. S. (1950): 'The Junior Minister', *Journal of Politics*, 12(3), 437–50.

Mosca, G. (1896/1939): *The Ruling Class.* McGraw-Hill, New York.

Nicholson, I. F. (1986): *The Mystery of Crichel Down.* Oxford University Press.

North, D. C. and B. R. Weingast (1989): 'Constitutions and Commitment: The Evolution of Institutions Governing Public Choice in Seventeenth-Century England', *Journal of Economic History*, 49(4), 803–32.

Oliver, D. and R. Austin (1987): 'Political and Constitutional Aspects of the Westland Affair', *Parliamentary Affairs*, 40, 20–40.

Orren, G. (1997): 'Falls from Grace: The Public's Loss of Faith in Government', in *Why People Don't Trust Government*, ed. by J. Nye, P. Zelikov and D. King, pp. 77–108. Harvard University Press, Cambridge, MA.

Page, E. C. (2001): *Governing by Numbers: Delegated Legislation and Everyday Policy Making.* Hart, Oxford.

Palmer, G. (2006): 'The Cabinet, the Prime Minister and the Constitition', *New Zealand Journal of Public and International Law*, 4(1), 1–40.

Palmer, G. and M. Palmer (2004): *Bridled Power: New Zealand's Constitution and Government*. Oxford University Press, Auckland, 4th edn.

Pareto, V. (1935): *The Mind and Society*. Cape, London.

Parris, M. (1995): *Great Parliamentary Scandals*. Robson, London.

Patterson, T. E. (1993): *Out of Order*. Vintage, New York.

Paxman, J. (2002): *The Political Animal*. Penguin, Harmondsworth.

Plumb, J. H. (1960): *Sir Robert Walpole: The King's Minister*. Cresset Press, London.

Pyper, R. (1983): 'The FO Resignations: Individual Responsibility Revived?' *Teaching Politics*, 12, 200–10.

Rentoul, J. (2001): *Tony Blair: Prime Minister*. Little Brown, London.

Rhodes, R. A. (1997): *Understanding Governance: Policy Networks, Governance, Reflexivity and Accountability*. Buckingham University Press, Buckingham.

Rhodes, R. A. W. and P. Dunleavy (eds.) (1995): *Prime Minister, Cabinet and Core Executive*. St Martins Press, New York.

Richards, D. and M. J. Smith (2002): *Governance and Public Policy in the UK*. Oxford University Press.

Riker, W. H. (1982): *Liberalism Against Populism: A Confrontation Between the Theory of Democracy and the Theory of Social Choice*. W. H. Freeman and Co., San Francisco.

Robinson, M. R. (1953): 'The Lynskey Tribunal: The British Method of Dealing with Political Corruption', *Political Science Quarterly*, 68(1), 109–24.

Roodhouse, M. (2002): 'The 1948 Belcher Affair and Lynskey Tribunal', *Twentieth Century British History*, 13, 384–411.

Rose, R. (1971): 'The Making of Cabinet Ministers', *British Journal of Political Science*, 1, 394–414.

Rose, R. (1987): *Ministers and Ministries: A Functional Analysis*. Clarendon Press, Oxford.

Schultz, J. (1998): *Reviving the Fourth Estate: Democracy, Accountability and the Media*. Cambridge University Press, Melbourne.

Scott, S. R. (1996): 'Ministerial Accountability', *Public Law*, Autumn, 410–26.

Seldon, A. (2005): *Blair*. Free Press, London.

Shell, D. (2000): 'Labour and the House of Lords: A Case Study in Constitutional Reform', *Parliamentary Affairs*, 53, 290–310.

Short, C. (2004): *Deception? New Labour, Iraq and the Mirrors of Power*. Simon and Schuster, London.

Smith, M. J. (1994): 'The Core Executive and the Resignation of Mrs Thatcher', *Public Administration*, 72, 341–63.

Smith, M. J. (1999): *The Core Executive in Britain*. Macmillan, Basingstoke.

Strom, K. (2000): 'Delegation and Accountability in Parliamentary Democracies', *European Journal of Political Research*, 37(3), 261–89.

Strom, K. (2003): 'Parliamentary Democracy and Delegation', in *Delegation and Accountability in Parliamentary Democracies*, ed. by K. Strom, W. C. Muller and T. Bergman. Oxford University Press.

Sutherland, S. L. (1991): 'Responsible Government and Ministerial Responsibility: Every Reform Is Its Own Problem', *Canadian Journal of Political Science*, 24(1), 91–120.

Theakston, K. (1987): *Junior Ministers in British Government*. Basil Blackwell, Oxford.

Theakston, K. (1999): *Leadership in Whitehall*. Macmillan, Basingstoke.

Thomas, G. P. (1998): *Prime Minister and Cabinet Today*. Manchester University Press.

Tiernan, A. (2007): *Power Without Responsibility: Ministerial Staffers in Australian Government from Whitlam to Howard*. University of New South Wales Press, Sydney.

Tocqueville, A. de (1835): *Democracy in America vol. 1*. Vintage Books, New York.

Turpin, C. (1993): 'Ministerial Responsibility: Myth or Reality', in *The Changing Constitution*, ed. by J. Jowell and D. Oliver. Oxford University Press.

Walter, D. (1984): *The Oxford Union: Playground of Power*. McDonald, London.

Walters, R. (2003): 'House of Lords', in *The British Constitution in the Twentieth Century*, ed. by V. Bogdanor. Oxford University Press.

Weber, M. (1978): *Economy and Society*, Vols. 1 and 2 edited by G. Roth and C. Wittich. University of California Press, Berkeley, CA.

Weller, P. (1999): 'Disentangling Concepts of Ministerial Responsibility', *Australian Journal of Public Administration*, 58(1), 62–4.

Weller, P. (2004): 'Parliamentary Accountability in Australia', *Parliamentary Affairs*, 57(3), 630–45.

Weller, P. (2007): *Cabinet Government in Australia, 1901–2006*. University of New South Wales Press, Sydney.

Wheare, K. C. (1975): 'Crichel Down Revisited', *Political Studies*, 26, 390–408.

Wheen, F. (1990): *The Soul of Indiscretion: Tom Driberg: Poet, Philanderer, Legislator and Outlaw*. Chatto and Windus, London.

Wigg, L. (1972): *George Wigg*. Macmillan, London.

Williams, P. M. (1964): *Crisis and Compromise: Politics in the French Fourth Republic*. Archone Books, Hamden.

Woodhouse, D. (1994): *Ministers and Parliament: Accountability in Theory and Practice*. Oxford University Press.

Woodhouse, D. (1998): 'The Parliamentary Commissioner for Standards: Lessons from the "Cash for Questions" Inquiry', *Parliamentary Affairs*, 51(1), 51–61.

Woodhouse, D. (2002): 'The Reconstruction of Constitutional Accountability', *Public Law*, pp. 73–90.

Woodhouse, D. (2003): 'Ministerial Responsibility in the Twentieth Century', in *The Constitution in the Twentieth Century*, ed. by V. Bogdanor, pp. 281–332. Oxford University Press.

Index

Adonis, Andrew 37
adverse selection 7–8, 10, 11, 12, 14
Afghanistan 49
age (ministers') 55, 59, 65, 67, 68,
    150, 174
    hazard rates 79
agency model (elections) 8–12, 13, 14
    empirical evidence 12
    parliamentary democracy,
        application in 15–20, 21
Aitken, Jonathan 143–4, 149
Al-Fayed, Mohammed 143, 144
Anne, Queen 22
Asquith, H. H. 131
assistant whips 33
Atkins, Humphrey 136
Attlee administration 5, 28, 47, 49, 52,
    53, 64, 92, 103, 112, 115
    Attlee's cabinet style 90, 98
    forced exits 119, 121, 141
    main issues 89–90
Australia 97, 122
Ayas, Mr 144

Balogh, Professor Thomas (later Lord)
    98
Bank of England 107, 141
Barber, Anthony 100
Bauwens, Mona 140
Belcher, John 141
Benn, Tony 42
Bevin, Ernest 90
Bill of Rights (1689) 22
Black Wednesday (16 September 1992)
    105
Blair administration 5, 25, 26, 29, 37,
    39, 41, 47, 48, 49, 50, 52, 53,
    61–4, 73
    Blair's cabinet style 108–9

forced exits 121, 125, 127, 128,
    131, 132, 140, 147, 149
    main issues 107–8
Blunkett, David 118, 141, 143, 144,
    147, 149
Bofors Scandal (India 1980s) 118
Boothby, Robert 131
Bray, Jeremy 147, 148
Brayley, Lord 141, 142–3
British Aerospace 146
British Constitution 24
British Empire 49, 89
British government, structure of 21–53
    constitutional requirements 21–6
    see also cabinet; House of
        Commons; House of Lords;
        ministers
British Guiana 94
Brittan, Leon 144, 145–6
Broadcasting Act (1990) 139
Brown, George 41, 98
Brown, Gordon 5, 25, 41, 107, 108,
    109
Butler, R. A. 24, 25, 92, 94–5, 96
Byers, Stephen 137–8

cabinet 26–30
    collective responsibility 2, 21, 29,
        32, 33, 42, 44–6, 117, 118, 119,
        121, 132, 133, 137, 148, 163,
        168, 172, 176
    'core of the core executive' 27
    establishment and power 22
    incentives, system of 17–19, 21
    parliamentary democracy, and
        13–14
    reshuffles 38–9, 43, 44, 81, 88, 95,
        99, 109, 122, 123–4
    shadow cabinet 30

see also committee system (cabinet);
ministers; prime minister's
relationship with cabinet
Cabinet Office 26, 36, 52, 95, 145
Cabinet Secretariat 52
Cabinet Secretary 143, 144
Caithness, Earl of 147
Callaghan, James (Heath
administration) 142
Callaghan administration 25, 26, 97,
98, 176
Callaghan's cabinet style 102
forced exits 125
main issues 101–2
Campbell, Alastair 119
Canning Town Glass investigation
(1974) 142
Captain of the Honourable Corps of
Gentlemen-at-Arms 33
Captain of the Queen's Bodyguard of
the Yeoman of the Guard 33
career politicians 15, 16, 35, 54, 152
Carlisle, Mark 104
Carrington, Lord 23, 102, 136
'cash for questions' affair (1990s)
143
Central Policy Review Staff 52
Chancellor of the Duchy of Lancaster
31, 49, 145
Chancellor of the Exchequer 31, 49,
91, 95, 102, 104–5, 118, 136,
140, 145
characteristics (ministers') 61–5, 150,
151, 173
separating the effect of 76–8,
174
Chief Secretary to the Treasury 31, 48,
49, 105, 144
Chief Whip 24, 30, 32, 37, 48, 50, 91,
100, 131, 138
Churchill administration 24, 26, 72,
90, 99, 108, 110, 132
Churchill's cabinet style 91–2
main issues 90–1
citizen-candidate model (elections)
10–11
civil service 30, 34, 47, 98, 104, 107,
164
reform 97, 103
Civil Service Yearbook 53

Civil War (1642–51) 22
Clarke, Kenneth 106
Clegg, Nick 25
committee system (cabinet) 26, 31, 32,
33, 104, 108, 143, 145
Select Committee on Estimates 36
Select Committee on Public
Administration 47
communism 89, 90
Conservative Central Office 117
Conservative Party 24, 37, 41, 96,
100, 104, 105, 106, 108, 115,
129, 138, 140, 145
Cook, Robin 131, 132
corruption *see* scandals
Cousins, Frank 36, 37
Crichel Down affair (1954) 82, 135–6
Criminal Justice Bill 139
Cripps, Stafford 90
Cruikshank, Harry 92
Currie, Edwina 140, 144, 146
Cyprus 94

Daily Mirror 94
Daily Telegraph 121
Dalton, Hugh 90, 118, 144–5
Davies, Ron 140–1
de Gaulle, Charles 94, 97
de Sancha, Antonia 139
deputy prime minister 25, 29, 50
DNA Bioscience 143
Douglas-Home administration 23, 24,
25, 100, 106, 133
Douglas-Home's cabinet style 96–7
main issues 96
Driberg, Tom 131
Dugdale, Sir Thomas 135–6
durability (ministers') 44, 67, 68, 79,
81, 82, 84, 85, 86, 99, 119, 120,
122, 163
duration (ministers') *see* longevity of
service (ministers')
Duration Models *see* hazard rates
(ministers')

Economist, The 146
Eden administration 24, 25, 92, 95,
97, 128, 132, 137
Eden's cabinet style 93
main issues 92–3

education (ministers') 64, 65–6, 78,
    79, 82, 156
  longevity of service, effect on 55, 70,
    72, 83–4, 174
EEC *see* European Economic
    Community (EEC)
Egypt 92–3, 99
  see also Suez Canal crisis
elections
  1945, in 90
  1950, in 90
  1959, in 94
  1966, in 97
  1970, in 97
  1974 (February), in 24
  1974 (October), in 24, 100
  1979, in 102
  1983, in 102, 123
  1992, in 105
  2001, in 108
  2005, in 108
elite theory 56–7
Elizabeth II, Queen 23, 24, 26, 33, 96,
    105
EU *see* European Union (EU)
European Community 137
European Economic Community
    (EEC) 97, 99, 101
European Exchange Rate Mechanism
    106
European Union (EU) 27, 29, 34, 41,
    49, 94, 103, 105–6
executive *see* cabinet
experience (ministers') 3, 55, 59, 61,
    65–8, 74–6, 86, 98, 150, 153,
    156, 166, 174
  hazard rates 68, 69, 70, 79–81, 85
  longevity of service, effect on 70,
    74–5, 85, 150

factions 40–1, 45, 67, 81, 95, 98, 103,
    133, 177
Fairbairn, Nicholas 138–9, 144,
    145
Falconer, Charlie 108
Falklands War 82, 102, 103,
    136
'fire alarm' procedures 17
First Division Association
    108

First World War 52
Fletcher-Cooke, Charles 144, 145
forced exits (ministers') 4–5, 33, 34,
    37–8, 43–4, 87, 107, 117–49,
    151, 152, 153, 154, 164
  conclusions 148–9
  introduction 117–19
  prime ministers, differences between
    127–32
  proximate causes 132–48, 173;
    departmental error 135–6; 'other
    controversies' 121, 144, 147–8;
    performance 136–8, 140; personal
    error 135, 137, 138, 140, 144–7,
    149; personality clash 133, 137;
    policy disagreement 132–5, 137,
    148, 173; scandal *see* scandals
  resignation issues 43, 44, 117,
    119–27, 132–48, 161, 173
  resignations and non-resignations
    119–27, 148
  'sacrificial' responsibility 43, 44,
    135, 136, 164, 171–2
  unforced exits 44
Foreign Office 34, 47, 48, 49, 95, 100,
    136
Foreign Secretary 23, 25, 37, 49, 90,
    92, 95, 102, 105, 147
Formosa (Taiwan) 119
Fourth Republic (France) 86
France 92–3
Fraser, Tom 137
Fulton Report (1968) 97

Galbraith, Tom 144, 145
gender (ministers') 55, 56, 59, 61–4,
    73–4, 79, 150, 156, 174
George VI, King 25
German Socialist Party 56
Gibson, George 141
Godfather, The 41
Great Reform Act (1832) 22
Great Train Robbery (1963) 96
Gresham's Law 7
Guardian 144

Hailsham, Lord 25, 96
Hamilton, Neil 141, 143, 144,
    149
Harvey, Ian 131

hazard rates (ministers') 68–72, 74–5, 120, 157, 161, 172
  determinants 78–83
  estimates 165–70
Heath administration 24, 26, 29, 49, 53, 70, 95, 96, 97, 103, 104, 142
  Heath's cabinet style 100
  main issues 99–100
hereditary peers (ministers) 23, 38, 56, 64, 65, 66, 82, 96, 107, 163
  hazard rates 82
  Life Peerages Act (1958) 23
  Peerage Act (1963) 96
Heseltine, Michael 25, 104, 105, 106, 132, 145–6
Hinduja, Srichand 118
Hitler, Adolf 147
Home Office 34, 47, 95, 118, 142, 145, 166
Home Secretary 34, 49, 51, 118, 135, 136, 142, 155
House of Commons 22–3, 30, 31, 33, 35, 37, 44, 70, 85, 94, 95, 106, 108, 118, 121, 138, 141, 143, 144, 146, 147
House of Lords 22–3, 30, 31, 32, 33, 82, 85, 97, 108, 148
House of Lords Act (1999) 23, 107
Howard, Michael 41
Howe, Geoffrey 102
Hughes, Beverley 144, 147
hydrogen bomb test 94

incentives 46, 54, 151, 154, 155, 178
  cabinet as system of 17–19, 21, 167
  misalignment of incentives 152–3
  principal–agent relations 3, 6, 7–10, 12, 14, 15
Independent Television News (ITN) 146
Industrial Relations Act (1971) 99
informational asymmetry 9, 16–17, 19, 153–4, 175
IRA 106
Iraq War 49, 107, 132
Irvine, Derry 108
Israel 89, 92–3, 99

Jellicoe, Lord 131
John Bull magazine 95
Joint Parliamentary Secretary to the Ministry of Technology 148
Joint Under Secretary of State 145
junior ministers 3, 30, 32, 33, 34, 36, 38, 42, 52, 61, 65, 66, 81, 82, 85, 95, 97, 120, 125, 132, 136

Kaldor, Professor Nicholas (later Lord) 98
Kaufman, Gerald 98
Keeler, Christine 131, 138
Kilmuir, David 95
Korean War 91, 119

Labour Party 24, 25, 29, 37, 50, 97, 98, 101, 102–3, 107, 108, 129, 143
  National Executive Committee (NEC) 98
Lambton, Lord 131
Lamont, Norman 106, 107, 133, 140
Lawson, Nigel 105
Liberal Party 13, 24, 25, 100, 103
Life Peerages Act (1958) 23
Lilley, Peter 41
Lloyd, Selwyn 95
lobby groups 9, 118, 144
Local Government Act (1972) 99
longevity of service (ministers') 1, 54, 55, 59–61, 64, 65–76, 80–1, 83–6, 87, 150, 173
  conclusions 83–6
  political effects 76
  see also age (ministers'); characteristics (ministers'); education (ministers'); experience (ministers'); forced exits (ministers'); hazard rates (ministers'); performance and tenure (ministers'); who serves as ministers; women (ministers)
Lord President of the Council 31
Lord Privy Seal 31, 49
Lords in Waiting 33
Lords of the Treasury 33
loyalty 40, 82, 85, 90, 91, 98, 105, 108, 111, 118, 136

Luce, Richard 136
Lynskey tribunal (1948) 141

Maastricht Treaty (1992) 106
MacLeod, Iain 95, 96, 100,
    133
Macmillan, Lady Dorothy 131
Macmillan administration 24, 25, 52,
    61, 90, 91, 106, 112, 115, 133
    Macmillan's cabinet style 94–6
    main issues 93–4
Magna Carta (1215) 22
Major administration 25, 41, 53, 61,
    72, 108, 110, 112–15, 137
    forced exits 14, 127, 128, 129, 133,
    139, 140, 144, 147
    main issues 105–6
    Major's cabinet style 106–7
Malaya 94
Mandelson, Peter 118–19, 141, 143,
    144, 147, 149
Mates, Michael 144, 147
Maudling, Reginald 95, 96, 141–2
media 4, 5, 9, 35, 82, 87, 96, 106, 108,
    118, 119, 120, 121, 127, 164
    forced exits and 130–1, 133, 135,
    138, 139–40, 144, 145, 146, 147,
    148–9, 175
Mellor, David 106, 138, 139–40,
    147
Metropolitan Police 142
Millennium Dome 118
miners' strike
    1974, in 99, 100
    1984–5, in 103
Minister of State for Citizenship and
    Counter Terrorism 147
Minister of State for Europe 48, 49
Minister of State for Higher Education
    31, 37
Minister of State for the Home Office
    47
Ministerial and Other Salaries Act
    (1975) 31
Ministerial Code of Conduct 143
ministers 30–46
    categories 30–3
    Code of Conduct 143
    different prime ministers, survival
    functions under 109–15, 149, 175

full cabinet ministers 31, 36, 38, 42,
    48, 61, 66, 132
ministers of cabinet rank 31–2, 36,
    42, 52
motivation 15–16, 17, 18
pay 11, 12, 18
public service 16, 18
role 30, 33–6, 42, 91
shadow ministers 37
types 34–5
see also age (ministers'); cabinet;
    characteristics (ministers');
    education (ministers'); experience
    (ministers'); forced exits
    (ministers'); gender (ministers');
    hereditary peers (ministers); junior
    ministers; longevity of service
    (ministers'); performance and
    tenure (ministers'); prime
    minister's relationship with
    ministers; resignation, calls for;
    responsibility (ministers');
    scandals; who serves as ministers
ministers of state 30, 31–2, 33, 36, 48,
    61
Monckton, Walter 93
moral hazard 8, 9, 10, 12, 13, 14
Morris, Estelle 138
Morrison, Herbert 90

Nadir, Asil 147
National Farmers' Union 146
National Health Service 90
New Statesman 142
New Zealand 97, 122
Nigeria 97
1922 Committee 146
no confidence vote 26, 59,
    152
North Sea oil 101
Northern Ireland 97, 99, 100
    Downing Street Declaration (1993)
    106
    Good Friday Agreement (1998)
    108
    Stormont Government (Northern
    Ireland) 49
Northern Ireland Act (1998) 49
Nott, John 118, 136
nuclear weapons 89, 92, 94, 97

O'Brien, Mike 118
O'Donnell, Gus 143
Oxford Union 70

Palestine 89
Palestine Liberation Organization
140
Parliament Act (1949) 23
parliamentary democracy 2, 6, 7,
13–14, 56, 87, 173
agency model, application of 15–20,
21
executive, and 13–14
power relations in 56–61; elite
theory 56–7; political dynasties
57–9
parliamentary private secretaries
(PPSs) 29, 32, 33, 37, 42, 95
parliamentary secretaries *see* junior
ministers
Parliamentary Secretary to the Board
of Trade 141
Parliamentary Secretary to the
Treasury 32
parliamentary undersecretaries of state
see junior ministers
Paymaster General 31, 93
Peel, Robert 13, 45
Peerage Act (1963) 96
peers of the realm *see* hereditary peers
(ministers)
People, The 139–40
performance and tenure (ministers') 1,
150–72, 173, 174, 175
assumptions 150–4; imperfect
information 9, 16–17, 19,
153–4, 175; ministerial motives
152; misalignment of incentives
152–3
conclusions 170–2
descriptive analysis 157–60
empirical strategy 160–5
forced exits 136–8, 140
introduction 150–2
performance indicators, resignation
calls as 1, 151, 154–7, 174
see also hazard rates (ministers')
PMO *see* Prime Minister's Office
(PMO)
'police patrol' procedures 17

poll tax (Community Charge) 103,
105, 107, 137, 147
Portillo, Michael 41
Poulson, John 141–42
Powell, Enoch 96, 133
power relations in government
56–61
elite theory 56–7
political dynasties 57–9
PPSs *see* Parliamentary Private
Secretaries (PPSs)
Prescott, John 25, 29, 50
press *see* media
Press Complaints Commission 139
prime minister
delegation 14, 16, 39
imperfect information 9, 16–17, 19,
153–4, 175
Question Time 95
role 14, 17, 22, 42, 52, 86, 151
Royal Prerogative 46–7
see also prime ministerial style;
prime minister's relationship with
cabinet; prime minister's
relationship with ministers
prime ministerial style 89–116, 151,
175
*see also under individual prime
ministers*
Prime Minister's Office (PMO) 53,
131
prime minister's relationship with
cabinet 14, 15–20, 87–116
survival functions under different
prime ministers 109–15, 149, 175
see also prime ministerial style
prime minister's relationship with
ministers 14, 15–20
appointment and dismissal 17, 18,
19, 37, 42, 46, 67, 87, 173, 174,
176–8
choosing ministers 17, 18, 19,
37–42
departmental changes 46–53
principal–agent model 39, 42, 151,
154, 177
see also forced exits (ministers');
performance and tenure
(ministers'); prime ministerial
style

principal–agent relations
  adverse selection 7–8, 10, 11, 12, 14
  citizen-candidate model 10–11
  incentive 3, 6, 7–10, 12, 14, 15
  introduction 6–7
  moral hazard 8, 9, 10, 12, 13, 14
  parliamentary democracy 15–20, 21
  principal–agent view 7–8
  see also agency model (elections); cabinet
principal–agent view (elections) 7–8
privatization 103, 106
Privy Council 22
Profumo affair (1963) 96, 131, 138, 144
public office 6, 7, 16, 56
public sector strike (1979) 102
public service (ministers') 16, 18

Question Time (parliament) 95

rank, hazard rates in relation to 81–2, 84
Redwood, John 106
reform 23
  civil service 97, 103
  Great Reform Act (1832) 22
  House of Lords Act (1999) 23, 107
Register of Members' Interests 143
resignation, calls for
  performance indicators, as 1, 151, 154–7, 174
  see also forced exits (ministers')
responsibility (ministers') 5, 19, 42–6
  collective *see* cabinet
  individual 2, 21, 29, 38, 42–4, 117, 122, 132, 133, 148, 163–4, 172, 176; 'sacrificial' responsibility 43–4, 135, 136, 164, 171–2
Rhodesia 97, 99, 102
Ridley, Nicholas 144, 146–7
Ritz Hotel (Paris) 143, 144
Robinson, Geoffrey 141, 143
Royal Prerogative 46–7

Sainsbury, Lord 141, 143
Salisbury, Lord (1830–1903) 23, 45

Salisbury, Lord (1916–2003) 24, 95
scandals 1, 4, 17, 19, 33, 38, 40, 43, 106, 117, 123, 127, 147, 149, 157, 162, 173, 174, 175
  financial 40, 106, 118, 121, 127, 132, 138, 140, 141–4, 149
  security 96, 103, 131
  sexual 40, 106, 121, 129–31, 140–1, 148
  spy 103, 145
  see also Profumo affair (1963)
Scargill, Arthur 103
Scotland, Patricia (Baroness Scotland of Asthal) 47
Second World War 5, 25, 52
secretaries of state 31, 51, 117, 136, 142
Secretary of State for Defence 51, 118, 136
Secretary of State for Education 104, 138
Secretary of State for National Heritage 138
Secretary of State for Trade and Industry 96, 145, 146
Security Council (UN) 92
Selective Employment Tax (1967) 97
Serious Fraud Squad 147
shadow cabinet 30
shadow ministers 37
Shore, Peter 98
Short, Clare 132
Six Point Group 119
Smith, John 107
Smith, Tim 141, 143, 144, 149
social choice theory 6
Social Democrats (party) 103
Solicitor General (England and Wales) 146
Solicitor General for Scotland 138
South Africa 97, 99
Spectator 146
Speed, Keith 117–18, 136
Stanley, Sydney 141
Stanley, Venetia 131
Stewart, Allan 144, 147
Stoddart, David (Baron Stoddart of Swindon) 47
Suez Canal crisis (1956) 92–3, 94–5
Summerskill, Edith 119

Sunday Times 142, 144
Symons, Liz 108

tenure *see* longevity of service
(ministers'); performance and
tenure (ministers')
terrorism 89, 100
11 September 2001 attacks (USA)
47, 107
Thatcher administration 25, 27, 39,
41, 53, 61, 100, 105, 106, 108,
111, 115, 139, 147
forced exits 118, 122, 123–4, 125,
128, 136, 137, 138, 145–6
main issues 102–3
Thatcher's cabinet style 103–5
Times, The 120, 131, 142, 145, 146
Tory Party 13
see also Conservative Party
trade unions 37, 99, 103, 120
see also miners' strike
Trades Union Congress 97
Treasury 35, 41, 42, 47, 49, 98, 100,
102, 105, 107, 108, 166
'star chamber' 104–5

Ulster Unionist Party (Northern
Ireland political party) 24
Under Secretary of State for Defence
142
Under Secretary of State for Defence
for the Army 142
Under Secretary of State for Defence
for the Navy 117
Under Secretary of State for Northern
Ireland 147
Under Secretary of State for Scotland
145
unions *see* trade unions

United States 93, 99, 107
congressional careers 54, 57–9
Homeland Security Department 47
terrorist attacks (2001) 47, 107

Vassall spy case (1962) 145
Victoria, Queen 22

Walker, Patrick Gordon 37, 147–48
Westland affair (1986) 132,
145–6
Whigs (political party) 13
whips 3, 29, 30, 32–3, 37, 42, 61, 65,
66, 81, 107, 120, 132
see also assistant whips; Chief Whip
Whitehall *see* British government,
structure of
Whitelaw, William 104
Whitty, Larry 108
who serves as ministers 54, 55–65
conclusions 83–6
introduction 54–5
political effects 76
power relations in government
56–61; elite theory 56–7; political
dynasties 57–9
see also characteristics (ministers');
longevity of service (ministers')
Wigg, George 98
Williams, Marcia 98, 132
Wilson administration 24, 25, 36, 37,
41–2, 102, 108, 111, 112
forced exits 123, 125, 127, 128,
136, 142, 148
main issues 97, 100–1
Wilson's cabinet style 97–9, 101
women (ministers) 55, 56, 59, 61–4,
73–4, 79, 150, 156, 174
hazard rates 79, 83–4